Living in Christian Community

Arthur G. Gish

HERALD PRESS
Scottdale, Pennsylvania
Waterloo, Ontario

Library of Congress Cataloging in Publication Data

Gish, Arthur G
   Living in Christian Community.

   Bibliography: p.
   Includes index.
   1. Christian communities. 2. Church
renewal. 3. Christian life—Church of the
Brethren authors. 4. Church. I. Title.
BV4405.G57   262   79-11848
ISBN 0-8361-1887-1

The paper used in this publication is recycled and
meets the minimum requirements of American
National Standard for Information Sciences—
Permanence of Paper for Printed Library Materials,
ANSI Z39.48-1984.

LIVING IN CHRISTIAN COMMUNITY
Copyright © 1979 by Herald Press. This edition published
   by New Covenant Fellowship, 13206 Dutch Creek
   Road, Athens, OH 45701. All rights reserved.
Library of Congress Catalog Card Number: 79-11848
International Standard Book Number: 0-8361-1887-1
Printed in the United States of America
Design: Alice B. Shetler

94 93 92 15 14 13 12 11 10 9 8 7 6 5 4 3 2

To
Joel Chalmer Gish

ACKNOWLEDGMENTS

Parts of Chapter 3 were published in *The Other Side,* XII (September-October, 1976) in the article "Your Family Can Blossom in Christian Community," pp. 58 ff.

Parts of Chapter 5 were published in *The Other Side,* IX (March-April, 1973) in the article "Love as Church Discipline," pp. 12 ff.

Parts of Chapter 10 were published in *Call the Witnesses,* ed. Paul M. Robinson (Elgin, Ill.: The Brethren Press, 1974), in the chapter "Called to a Covenant Community," pp. 113-123.

Unless otherwise indicated, all biblical quotations are from the Revised Standard Version of the Bible, copyrighted 1946, 1952, © 1971, 1973.

Quotations marked NEB are from *The New English Bible.* © The Delegates of the Oxford University Press and The Syndics of the Cambridge University Press 1961, 1970. Reprinted by permission.

A loving thank you to the Hutterian Society of Brothers for permission to quote from their Plough Press books.

TABLE OF CONTENTS

INTRODUCTION

When Art and I began to talk about the need for Christian community in our lives, it was mainly theoretical for us. Yet we felt moved in that direction and we began seeking. It was only after living and sharing more closely with other Christians that the concepts took flesh. We began to see and understand more than with our minds what community meant—but also with our hearts and innermost beings.

Not only did the church become alive to me, but I also found myself challenged to examine and deepen my own faith and commitment to God. I began to experience much more the daily leading of the living Christ in my personal life and in the corporate life of the Christian fellowship. The Scriptures began to speak more directly and authoritatively to me.

I began to see that so much of the gospel does not really make sense taken in fragments, as concepts, or "Christian principles." It must be understood and experienced in a loving, sharing, deeply committed community of believers who daily lay down their lives for each other. Apart from such a fellowship, so much of what Jesus calls us to seems impractical and impossible to live out. It has been exciting and encouraging in our pilgrimage to discover groups of Christians who, in spite of their human weakness and imperfections, have been living out their faith together with real depth and power.

In an age when individualism, independence, and fear of authority are so prevalent, many may assume that in community living one would be stifled or put down. As a woman I have been told by movements in our society that I need to discover and develop my gifts and to be "my own person." I know that as a Christian I need to break away from traditional patterns and expectations which have no part in God's kingdom. And I understand that the kingdom provides for genuine liberation and complete fulfillment. I go against God's plan if I block His work in my life or take part in oppressing any of God's children. But I can no longer accept a way of seeking liberation and fulfillment which focuses first on myself and *my* fulfillment. The most liberating thing is to submit all I have and am to God and His church and to seek how I am to be used. When committed and trusting brothers and sisters in the church really seek to help me grow and use my gifts, I have no need to fight for my rights or be worried about them taking advantage of me.

We need to discover and admit that what God wants for our lives is far greater than what we could even imagine, or plan, or humanly try to develop. Other Christians can help us discover what God's will is and what barriers need to be removed to follow it. And that is the most liberating and joyful way to live. We can discover that by becoming weak and defenseless we can be made strong, that by losing our life we can gain abundant life.

Many people wonder whether my needs and our family's needs are considered important in community. My experience has been that our needs are taken even more seriously in a loving, sharing fellowship—not only material needs, but our deeper spiritual and emotional needs as well. But to have our own needs met should not be our first concern and should never be the basis for joining Christian community.

It is possible to find a meaningful and full life with a

deep Christian fellowship, but not an easy life, or one without struggle and failures. The more deeply we open our lives to other people in service, the more demands it makes on us. A fulfilled life is not a condition for us to achieve, but something which is given by God—something which comes naturally when we are filled with God's Spirit and with such love that we cannot help but want to give up all we have to serve each other and the world. We will continually fail if we seek first to build up ourselves or our group of people. We can only be faithful with a singleness of focus—God's kingdom first.

Peggy Faw Gish

AUTHOR'S PREFACE

One of the characteristics of our age is loneliness, lack of relatedness, isolation, and alienation—the feeling that no one understands or even cares. It seems that there are no people to listen and even if they did, they would not understand. Not only that, we are afraid that if they did know us they would not like us. We are hesitant to share our deepest feelings even with our own families.

A curious fact of our age is that we have lost both privacy and community. Our lives are crowded with activities, but remain empty. Our clubs, recreation, friends, and television programs cannot fill the spiritual void which remains in our lives. In spite of many organizational commitments we are lonely and hungry for deeper relationships. Even the institutional church with all its programs, religion, and group dynamics often does not provide meaningful community. We are a lonely crowd.

One of the deepest longings of people and certainly one of the dominant themes of current thinking is the search for meaningful relationships. While people in the middle ages were concerned with death, and those in the Reformation with sin, the preoccupation in the twentieth century is with alienation and lostness. One of the tragedies of our time is that while there is such a deep longing for community, few people are aware of this as a living possibility.

Yet a rich heritage of community exists that most of us know little about. Rather than a utopian dream of idealists, community living has been a common experience throughout history. Through most of history a strong sense of community prevailed and has been the pervasive form of social organization for most of the world. Both primitive tribalism and the medieval village were forms of community living. But recent Western civilization has led to a disintegration of primary relationships and a turn toward formal, impersonal relationships.

No, community is not something new. Neither is communal living. The Essenes at the time of Jesus were a communal group. Communal living was practiced by the early church. Roman Catholic monasteries and orders have lived communally for many centuries. The Beguines and Beghards were a significant communal group during the Middle Ages.[1] Since the Reformation the Hutterians, the Moravians, the Shakers, the Amana Colony, and many more have lived in community.

Today Christian intentional communities are springing up all over the world, in addition to many other kinds of communities.

Although communal living is an important part of this book, the heart of our concern is what it means to be the church. No, the concern goes still deeper. The basis of the book really is the question of what it means to be a Christian, what it means to live out our lives in complete commitment of everything to Jesus and His kingdom and live a life of love to our sisters and brothers. It is the question of allowing our lives to be opened to God's love and realizing that that love cannot be separated from giving love to one's neighbors and receiving love from them in return. So the ultimate question behind our study is what it really means to live in the fullness of God's love, to give our lives completely to follow Jesus, and to seek first the justice of His kingdom. Christian community must be the *result* of this deeper commitment, not the focus of our commitment.

The perspective from which we will approach these questions comes out of the believers' church,[2] free church, Anabaptist tradition of Christianity, sometimes also called the gathered church, the radical church, or sectarian (Troeltsch) Christianity. Beginning with the radical life and witness of the early Christians, and in every century since then, various groups of people who desired to follow Jesus in all their relationships have found themselves in conflict with the religious establishments of their day. The Fransiscans, Waldensees, *Unitas Fratrum,* Collegiants, Anabaptists, and Quakers are a few examples. This vision with its roots in the Gospels and the vision kept alive by the monasteries, radical Catholics and medieval sectarians, has found new expression in radical groups since the Reformation and has lately been the focus of new interest.

This tradition is best understood not as a branch of mainline Christianity (Orthodox, Protestant, or Roman Catholic), but as having different roots and a basically different understanding of what the faith is all about. As Franklin Littell, the church historian, put it,

> The free churches are not simply marginal or corrective to mainline protestantism ... the free churches represent a fundamentally different view of church history, theology, ethics and Christian living.[3]

In the literature about this significant stream of Christian faith, often there has not been enough emphasis on the importance of the gathered Christian community and a proper understanding of discipleship. Personally I have come to realize that this vision is incomplete without full Christian community, a body of people who have given up everything to follow Jesus, commiting our whole lives to our brothers and sisters who also want to follow Jesus. This community is a fellowship of deep love and sharing, which includes support, discernment, discipline, and a corporate witness to the world.

This book is a description of what the church ought to be, an attempt to deal with the concrete issues of what it really means to be a Christian community, the body of Christ. It is intended to be a doctrine of the church, a radical ecclesiology. Although there is no one correct form that the church must take, it does need to be a community. It seems to me that groups like the early Hutterians have taken the gospel to its full and logical conclusion: a full community of love and sharing. I have come to see a clear connection between the breakdown of community in the early church and the loss of the gifts of the Holy Spirit which had been so powerful in the beginning. I have little hope for any significant and sustained renewal of the church today without the development of Christian community.

Much has been written about the believers' church and intentional communities by sociologists, church historians, and theologians. This book proclaims this vision as I have experienced it. Thus in a sense it is a manifesto. Its purpose is more to flesh out the vision than to carefully argue each point. Therefore the reader will sometimes find assertions with no supportive arguments. You, the reader, will need to decide the validity of everything that is said as you wrestle with the same questions. What is presented here is a whole. Each chapter presupposes the others and is not intended to stand alone.

To some, what is written here may sound idealistic. That has been a common criticism of radical Christianity. For me it is a living reality that I have seen, touched, and tasted. God really does give people the strength to live out the new life that is offered to us. Although still very human and imperfect, genuine community is possible for all who will open their lives totally to God's love.

Another reason for not seeing this as idealistic is that, not only down through history, but also today, many communities are actually trying to live by the Sermon on the Mount, are living in peace and unity, and are demonstrating for the rest of the world the reality of God's kingdom.[4] Ever since Ernst Troeltsch this vision has been granted a degree of respect. However, while seeing some validity in it, most have not seen such an approach to Christianity as a live, compelling, and practical option. In this book we will consider seriously what it would mean to see Christian community as an option for our lives.

I want to thank all who helped in the preparation of this manuscript, all the many people who read and criticized it, all those who helped point me in this direction: the Christian communities such as the Hutterian Society of Brothers (Bruderhof) and the Shalom Covenant Communities who showed me something that words could never convey. A special thanks to all those in the Philadelphia Fellowship who were of so much help to me, and to New Covenant Fellowship which has provided the community for which I have longed for many years. My thanks also to the Church of the Brethren, a group that once embodied the vision presented here and nurtured me in it.

I want to thank my parents who stressed to me the importance of complete Christian commitment. When I was a boy and decided to make a Christian commitment, my parents asked if there was anyone to whom I needed to confess anything or any relationships that needed reconciliation, and then they drove me around to the people with whom I needed to talk. That said something very important to me about discipleship and Christian community.

Finally, life together with my wife, Peggy, and our children has been a beginning of Christian community. I thank God for all they have meant to me.

Art Gish

Chapter 1

THE CHURCH AS COMMUNITY

> What life have you if you have not life together?
> There is no life that is not in community,
> and no community not lived in praise of God.
> Even the anchorite who meditates alone . . .
> prays for the Church, the Body of Christ.[1]
> —T. S. Eliot

We will begin our search by looking at the biblical basis for our understanding of the church and will consider how community has been God's intention for us from the beginning. Paul Minear has suggested that there are four major themes which include most of the biblical images of the church.[2] These are the people of God, the new humanity, the fellowship of believers, and the body of Christ. These themes will serve as an outline for our thinking in this chapter.

The People of God

From the very beginning God created us for fellowship, both in relation with others and with God. It has been suggested that in Genesis 1:26, 27 the phrase "Let *us* make man in *our* image" indicates that the fellowship in the Godhead created the man-woman community to reflect God's concern for fellowship and communion. The human "we" identity is to be a reflection of the divine "we." Man by himself was inadequate. He needed woman for community. The man-woman relationship is the beginning of a wider community that God would bring into being.

The harmony of the garden was broken by the human will for autonomy from God. Then came alienation from God, nature, and each other. When their eyes were opened Adam and Eve hid from God and each other. We all know the rest of that tragic story: war, strife, alienation. However, God was not content with this and has ever since been calling us to redemption. The whole purpose of God's redeeming work in history has been to restore unity and fellowship.

The Bible is the story of how God in the past has been acting in history and calling people together in community to be His people. Throughout history God repeatedly has worked through a people. God called Abraham to leave all behind and journey to a new land with the promise of becoming a new people. Abraham left the community of Ur for a more intentional community. God called Moses to lead a group of slaves out of Egypt and transformed them into a people. God took a group of frightened and disillusioned disciples of Jesus and through the resurrection and the power of Pentecost transformed them into a new community. At Pentecost a group of people realized that God had acted in a special way in their midst to give them a new covenant and to form them into a new body which was the beginning of a new people God was gathering. Because of what God had done in Christ, old dividing walls of hostility were broken down so that they were "no longer strangers and sojourners, but . . . fellow citizens with the saints and members of the household of God" (Eph. 2:11-22). Because of this they could proclaim,

But you are a chosen race, a royal priesthood, a holy nation, God's own people, that you may declare the wonderful deeds of him who called you out of darkness into his marvelous light. Once you were no people but now you are God's people; once you had not received mercy but now you have received mercy. 1 Peter 2:9, 10.

The early Christians understood that this was not the first time God had acted to gather a people. They saw themselves in continuity with the history of Israel. Although there was a difference between the new and the old covenants, the early Christians saw themselves as the true Israel, as part of the people God had been gathering from the beginning. They were the new Israel.[3] They knew that Jesus was again doing what God had done through Abraham, Moses, Joshua, and the prophets. He was gathering a people who would live by God's will.

The main purpose of God's revelation of Himself has always been to create a people with whom He could have fellowship. He even sent His Son to gather His people. God's acts and revelation in history result in creating a people for Himself. God calls a people to share in the life He offers. "I will be your God, and you shall be my people" (Lev. 26:12). The most visible sign of God's grace is the calling together of a people.

God's message of salvation involves becoming a part of the new community of God's people. Although personal relation to God is vital, according to biblical thought God is more concerned with creating a people than with private religious experience. This is true of both Old and New Testaments. Even in the new covenant passages in Jeremiah 31:31-34, although stress is put on the heart, this is seen in connection with peoplehood. Reconciliation is not only with God, but with our neighbor as well. Of the more than ninety different images of the church used in the New Testament most are corporate images—images such as the ark, branches on the vine, a household, fish and net, and the body. The Bible uses many more plural pronouns than singular ones. Salvation is not only what God is doing in my life but even more what God is doing in *our* midst. God wills to have a people, not just individual believers.

The prophetic call is for a people to embody God's will

for the whole world. This is at the heart of the Christian faith.
This call may not be reduced to social concern, philosophical
abstractions, or personal salvation. The people of God is not
an abstract idea, but God's primary way of working out His
purposes in history. The focus of God's action in the world is
in His people, a gathered community called out of the world
by God to minister to the world. It is there that God is creating the new humanity.

The New Humanity
     The New Testament sees in the coming of Jesus the
inauguration of a new era, the beginning of the kingdom of
God. A new age has begun. There is a new creation (2 Cor.
5:17). The good news of the gospel is that the promise of salvation and a new creation can become a reality among us. In
Ephesians 2 Paul describes the new life in Christ, how we
have been made alive together with Christ and become a new
humanity. Because of this Paul could write,

> Put off your old nature which belongs to your former manner
> of life . . . and be renewed in the spirit of your minds, and put
> on the new nature, created after the likeness of God in true
> righteousness and holiness. Ephesians 4:22-24.

There is now a new creation, a new humanity, a redeemed
community. The kingdom of justice, love, mercy, joy, peace,
and reconciliation is already being realized.
     The Christian community is composed of those who
recognize that a new age of salvation has dawned upon us
and, because of that, have been reconciled with God and each
other. They are those who have accepted the new life which is
offered to us. The church is to be the community of this new
age. She lives in the realm of redemption (Col. 1:13). She is
the visible sign of God's saving work in the world, a beach-
head that serves as the beginning of a new life that God wants
to spread throughout the whole world. The church is where

God's victory over the powers of evil begins to become visible
and take on flesh.

The Christian community is the first fruit of the
kingdom (Rom. 8:23; Jas. 1:18; Rev. 14:4), the forerunner of
a new age which is coming into being. A rich biblical symbol,
the first fruit that ripens is a sign that there will be a crop; it is
a foretaste of the harvest. The Christian community as an
expression of the realm of redemption is a preview of what
God wants to do for all humanity. A redeemed humanity is a
sign to the world of the coming of Christ's kingdom, a mirror
on earth of what is happening in heaven.

What is this kingdom and how can the world know
anything about it? The answer is that as Christians are
gathered together, their common life should demonstrate for
the world what the kingdom and redemption are all about.
The world will see the signs of redemption before their eyes.
The Christian community is an essential aspect of salvation.
As John Howard Yoder puts it,

> The church is then not simply the *bearer* of the message of rec-
> onciliation, in the way a newspaper or a telephone company
> can bear any message with which it is entrusted. Nor is the
> church simply the *result* of a message, as an alumni association
> is the product of a school or the crowd in the theater is the
> product of the reputation of the film. That men are called
> together to a new social wholeness is itself the work of God
> which gives meaning to history. . . . [4]

The church is more than the result of the gospel message, it is
part of that message. We cannot even talk about salvation or
redemption without talking about the embodiment of that
salvation in community. The church is not an extra piece of
baggage, but the means of transportation.

The church is not primarily an institution or hierarchy,
an instrument for proclaiming the Word, or an encouragement for personal piety, but rather an expression of the in-
breaking of the kingdom of God in which the fullness of

Christian discipleship is expressed and lived.

Although the church is to be an expression of the kingdom, it is not the kingdom, for when they are considered one and the same the result is either institutionalism or an exclusive elitism ending in legalism. There is more to come. The church is only the beginning.

Concern for the coming kingdom of God in the biblical sense means not speculation, periodization, or a focus on the future that disregards the present, but rather an emphasis on being ready by beginning to live in that kingdom now. The Christian community is meant to be an anticipation of and the beginning of the final consummation of God's salvation. We live together with the constant expectation of Christ's return and the completion of His kingdom. That is the focus of our passion. We become part of the church primarily not for fellowship and support, but more to be a part of the new kingdom which we see becoming a reality. We are a community which is discerning how, in the midst of the issues being raised by the world, we can point to new possibilities and give shape to them. The Christian community is a people free to move toward the future. We anticipate and demonstrate today what the kingdom will be tomorrow. This is not an escape from the world, but a creative and powerful way of relating to it. It is both the sign of love and peace, and the means of reaching it.

God's salvation involves bringing people together in a new community. The church is an essential part of God's plan of salvation, the womb in which God brings His children into being. We do not enter the kingdom alone, but with our brothers and sisters. Part of our sinfulness (alienation) consists of turning in upon ourselves which cuts us off from both our neighbor and God. This rejection of fellowship is a denial of grace. If sin is alienation from God and each other, salvation is fellowship with God and each other. Since salvation is reconciliation where sin has divided and alienated, salvation implies fellowship both with God and with brothers and sisters. Salvation comes mediated through a fellowship of believers.

The Fellowship of Believers
    The church should not merely have fellowship as one of her concerns, rather the church is to be the embodiment of fellowship. Rather than a place where the bishop presides, or a place where the Word is properly preached and the "sacraments" rightly administered, the church is a covenant community which has been called into being. Without a community of people committed both to the gospel *and* to each other there is no church.
    To be brought together in faith and love with others is not of secondary importance. It is an integral part of the good news. Those who have experienced new life in Christ find themselves in fellowship with other Christians. We are bound together because of our joyous response to the gospel. The decision to follow Jesus is a decision to become part of the fellowship of His followers. It is more than a private relation to Jesus. As Christians we are no longer independent individuals before God, but now individuals-in-community before God.[5]
    The Book of Acts makes it quite clear that the primary work of the Holy Spirit is the creation of the new community composed of Spirit-filled individuals. As C. Norman Kraus points out, for the early Christians

> It was not a matter of an inner experience of "receiving Jesus into their hearts" and then urging them to find a church (voluntary society) of their choice for fellowship. It was not a matter of an inner experience of justification or even conversion that made them members of the spiritual or invisible body of Christ to be followed up by baptism and "joining church."[6]

Rather their experience of God's Spirit molded them into a

new community. The gift of grace is more than forgiveness, for it involves the gift of a new life in Christ's body.

The Spirit and Word of God, when freely accepted, result in fellowship. Perhaps one reason for our lack of community may be that we have substituted something else for the gospel. Lewis Benson could have mentioned many other substitutes when he wrote,

> The gospel has fellowship-forming power, but, as long as we rely on group dynamics to make up for the lack of fellowship in the institutional church, we are postponing the day when the real *koinonia* of the Spirit will become a reality through the power of the gospel.[7]

An important biblical expression of this fellowship is covenant, a relationship of mutual love and commitment between God and His people. It is God's unconditional pledge of love to us and our promising with others to follow God's will completely. Covenant includes a bond of love and communion, a circle surrounding all partners. This is something more than the "social contract" of Rousseau and Locke, an association of independent individuals. It is to be bound together by God into a new people. This bond should not be thought of as a restriction, but a relationship of love and intimacy. Covenant can be seen as a guard against legalism, for covenant is a relationship rather than a set of rules.

The best analogy for God's covenant is marriage. In fact, in the Old Testament, Israel is called the bride of Jehovah, and the New Testament church is called the bride of Christ. Christian marriage is not primarily a commitment to monogamy, but a commitment to a relationship so deep and permanent that by its nature makes anything but monogamy impossible. The Christian covenant, like marriage, is a commitment to relationship and involves participation in the community of God's people.

A covenant is a relationship which is established permanently and can never be broken. That is one reason the covenants made in marriage and baptism are so serious. They can be violated, but never broken. Even when Israel violated the covenant, God's covenant with His people remained. None of the Old Testament prophets in all their proclamations of judgment and destruction suggested that there would be no more people or covenant. This is an act of grace. Because God will not break His covenant, we know that God is not capricious and can be trusted. God remains faithful to us even when we are unfaithful.

Covenants do carry with them expectations and boundaries. Since the initiative for covenant comes from God, it is God who states the terms of the covenant, not we. This means that no covenant community can ever become an end in herself, for her existence is always related to the source and the demands of the covenant. Covenant implies fidelity. Exodus 19:5, 6 is a good example:

> ... if you will obey my voice and keep my covenant, you shall be my own possession among all peoples ... and you shall be to me a kingdom of priests and a holy nation.

With Abraham, Isaac, and Jacob, in the event of the Exodus, and at Sinai, God made a covenant with Israel which bound them to God and to each other. That covenant was fulfilled in Jesus Christ who brought a new covenant promised by Jeremiah (Jer. 31:31-34; Heb. 8:6-13). The Christian fellowship is the community of the new covenant as Israel was the community of the old covenant. We are invited to participate in the new covenant established by Christ. Once we were strangers to the covenant and far off, but now have been brought into covenant relationship by God's action in Christ (Eph. 2:12, 13).

The covenant God makes with us is not only a continuation of the new covenant in Christ, but also has an element of newness and immediacy. The new covenant is just as new and fresh today as it was for the early Christians, for it is instituted by and rooted in the same living Christ.

God's covenant is universal. God's covenant with Abraham was meant to be a blessing to all nations. Covenant community does not mean "because I love you, you are my brother/sister." This is human eros. Rather, it means, "because you are my brother/sister, I love you."

This covenant is not as aspect of the natural, created order, but is a special gift given by God. Our relation to God and to each other is not a natural coming together, but is the result of God's initiative and our response. In this covenant relationship love is rooted in our relation to God rather than human emotion, attraction, or similarity of class, personality, or background. Communities built on human relationships are narrow, exclusive, and shallow. Community based on God's gift is open to all who will receive it.

The covenant community is by definition a close-knit, loving fellowship with a common commitment to God and to each other. It is a brotherhood and sisterhood. The "household of God" is a family in which all are brothers and sisters.

The church is a *fellowship* of brothers and sisters. The Greek word for fellowship is *koinonia,* which means to share with someone in something, to participate and share in what others also share, to hold in common. It means fellowship and partnership, a common participation in Christ. The New Testament uses this same word to describe our relationship with God and with our brothers and sisters. It is the fellowship with other believers which necessarily comes from fellowship with Christ (1 Cor. 1:9). *Koinonia* is more than a feeling of togetherness or sociability, though it will be accompanied by such feelings. It is not transient or superficial, but a deep covenantal relationship.

If the church is *koinonia* she will be a community in

which people are so closely knit together that they are called
the body of Christ.

The Body of Christ

The Christian community is more than a voluntary
association of individual Christians. She is a body, a living
unity. She has an organic and corporate character. We are
not Christians by ourselves, but members one of another and
knit together in one body (Rom. 12; 1 Cor. 12; Eph. 4). To be
"in Christ" means to be part of His body.

This imagery should not be misunderstood. We are not
literally or ontologically the resurrected body of Jesus. That
would make Christ and the Christian community identical,
and would deny transcendence. This metaphor is to be understood in a participatory and representative way. Through the
Christian community Jesus continues His saving action in the
world. To be His body means solidarity with Christ.

To say that the church is the body of Christ (1 Cor.
12:12) is not to say that body is a good symbol for community, but that the very nature of Jesus Christ is body: historical, concrete, and incarnated. This reflects the biblical
understanding of body which refers not merely to flesh and
bones, but to one's total personhood and character. The
point is that Christ is a body. We *are* a body because we
belong to Jesus and derive our existence from Him. Because
of who Jesus is we are members of one another. From *Him*
we are "knit together" (Col. 2:19; Eph. 4:16). "We are
members of *his* body" (Eph. 5:30). Nothing, except Christ
Himself, can hold us together. The body image is never used
in the New Testament for humanity as a whole, but only for
the Christian community.

The image of the body reminds us that Jesus is the head
of the church. To confess Jesus as Lord is therefore to affirm
that we are part of *His* body.

The relation of the church to Christ is an organic relationship. One part does not stand over against the whole, but is part of the whole. "I am the vine, you are the branches" (Jn. 15:5). We are not a pile of dead wood, but a beautiful living plant, grafted into the true vine, and bearing fruit. We are in Christ not as a bird is in a cage, but as a branch is in a tree. We are part of His body.

The biblical church is not an abstract idea, but something concrete which we are to be living now. We are the body of Christ because we are now the physical form of Christ's existence, the present historical expression of Christ's life and ministry. The church is the extension of the incarnation. The body is not dissolved after the benediction on Sunday morning, but is expressed in the total life of the members. We are always the body of Christ.

The Visible Community

The images of the people of God, the new humanity, the fellowship of believers, and the body of Christ point to a visible, historical community of people who live in obedience to God. The biblical message calls us out of our isolation as individuals into community.

In light of this blessing of community which is offered to us, and all the biblical emphasis in this direction, it is curious that a tendency in Protestant thinking from the Reformation period to the present has been to maintain that the true church is invisible.[8] Many Protestants today do not even have a doctrine of the church. For them salvation is individual and, at most, there can be a gathering of individual Christians for praise and edification, but little sense of the visible, corporate body of Christ.

Protestantism has been weak in the whole area of its vision of the church. The Reformation was more concerned with reform of worship and doctrine than the nature of the church. Many popular revival preachers openly suggest that new converts go to any existing church which suits their fancy. The implication seems to be that there are not many differences between groups, or that these differences are not important. The emphasis in the Bible is on a visible community of faith. There is no mention of an invisible church in the New Testament nor any suggestion that the true church is the invisible collection of individual, pure Christians around the world. Although the church certainly has a spiritual foundation and nature, this is expressed in her social character and cannot be separated from it. Rather than "an external support of faith" (Calvin), the church is a necessary consequence of faith. [9]

In the New Testament, the church existed as a congregation in Jerusalem, in Corinth, in Antioch, and in each place had a form and identity distinct from the surrounding society. When Paul thought of the church it was the church in so-and-so's house (Col. 4:15; Rom. 16:3-5). Although they were quite imperfect, Paul saw these communities as being the church.

The doctrine of the invisible church has been called ecclesiastical docetism, for it seems to deny that the divine aspect of the church can be expressed through her humanity. The true church is very much a human community. Grace does not negate nature, but transforms it and works through it. The body of Christ, the people of God, must be visible. Our faith must take on social form. The two cannot be separated. The Word must become flesh today as it did in Jesus. We participate in the universal church through deep involvement in a local church community. In the gathering of the local community we participate in the life of the entire church of all times and all places. Not only is the local congregation visible, but the universal church is also visible to the world.

The question we must wrestle with is, What should be the shape of a people today who would together live out their Christian faith as a New Testament community?

Chapter 2

THE FAITHFUL COMMUNITY

If any man would come after me, let him deny himself and take up his cross and follow me. For whoever would save his life will lose it; and whoever loses his life for my sake and the gospel's will save it.—Jesus, Mark 8:34, 35.

No Other Foundation

For community to exist there must be a common unity, a common center, focus, and direction. Community can center around most anything imaginable. That center can be a particular ideology, a common cause, or a person. It may be one's race, hatred of a common enemy, or a noble dedication to a humanitarian cause. Community can be either good or bad, depending upon the center.

As Christians, we find our center in Jesus. He is the basis, the cohesive force, the guide, and the goal of Christian community. He is Lord, President, and Chairman. He draws us to Himself. We follow Him. He is our rock, our salvation. Paul was right when he said, "No other foundation can any one lay than that which is laid, which is Jesus Christ" (1 Cor. 3:11). Not only is Christian community based on Jesus Christ, but Christians also affirm that there can be no authentic, no lasting community apart from Jesus Christ. Many associations and interest groups have a kind of unity based on some principle or common interest. But to be united in this way is far different than being united in Christ. People can agree on principle and yet have no personal commitment to each other. They can even hate each other. Or they may share together as deeply as the human spirit is able, but still not realize the unity that God can give. There is a difference between *esprit de corps* and being led by the Holy Spirit.

In Christian community we are a people who " . . . all who received him, who believed in his name . . . were born, not of blood nor of the will of the flesh nor of the will of man, but of God" (Jn. 1:12, 13). Jesus said the same thing when He told us, "I am the vine, you are the branches. He who abides in me, and I in him, he it is that bears much fruit, for apart from me you can do nothing" (Jn. 15:5). Christian community is rooted in Jesus Christ and has her life in Him.

Our assertion that true community is impossible without Christ does not deny the presence of Christ in some groups that do not recognize the reality they experience by that name. In no way should Christians reject fellowship with groups that are not explicitly Christian, but we do long for them to recognize more clearly the One who lives and moves among them.

The example of Christian communities will inspire many imitations of her life. While these imitations may fall far short of the kingdom, as do Christian communities, we can rejoice if our example helps the world move at least one step away from total chaos and destruction. While the imitations may never be seen as the church, we rejoice wherever they exist. They, in their feeble way, also point to the kingdom and the need for a deeper infilling of the Spirit.

Community can be duplicated and a fine spirit can exist, but human community is built on sand and will not last. For example, groups can achieve a kind of unity and a good spirit by building a new building, but after the building program is over that feeling is soon lost.

True community is not something that can be created by human effort or by an act of the will as believed by many utopian thinkers. In fact, the harder we work at it and try to build community the less likely it is that we will have community. Community cannot be forced, as many have learned after making such a valiant effort. So many carefully planned communities with the backing of plenty of talent and energy have ended in miserable failure.

The focus of our lives must never be community, for Christian community can exist only as the result of something much deeper, a decision to live in God's kingdom. Christian love exists only as God's gift to us. We cannot create it. It is not an ideal that we strive for, but a divine reality which is given to us as we open our lives to God and each other. We seek community not because that is good, but because of a reality which is already burning in our hearts.

The Christian community exists only as it is called into being by God and is an expression of His grace. Unless God gathers us, we are not a true community. Therefore the life of the community can never be adequately described in sociological or psychological terms. Our life is totally dependent on God's creative and sustaining work among us. God's people exist only because God has chosen them, guides, sustains, and judges them.

> It was not because you were more in number than any other people that the Lord set his love upon you and chose you, for you were the fewest of all peoples; but it is because the Lord loves you. Deuteronomy 7:7, 8.

Community can exist only as a continuing gift of the Spirit. The Spirit is always a gift, never a possession. When the Spirit is gone, the community either disintegrates or holds herself together with an authoritarian structure. Laws are developed when the Spirit and vision are lost. Community can never be perpetuated institutionally, but must continually be reborn. She lives by constant repentance and sustaining power of God.

To say that community is a gift is to apply the doctrines of grace and justification to the life of the church. The institutional church so often seems to believe that she must or can perpetuate the church, and that without all the works of clergy, buildings, investments, and organization the church would disappear. A kind of rational doctrinal orthodoxy may be defended and guaranteed by institutions, but faith and love cannot. They are gifts.

It has been said that the believers' church is always only one generation from becoming extinct since each generation must rediscover the vision anew. Maybe it would be more accurate to say that we are only one day from extinction. Community is always in a precarious state, for she is in constant danger of being perverted, of having her virtues twisted into demonic vices. Her goodness can so easily be spoiled by pride and self-righteousness.

When a meaningful community is born there is always the danger of continuing the form after the Spirit is gone, sometimes without even realizing that the Spirit has departed. There is always the danger that by the second and third generations expressions of faithfulness become formalized and external. Then legalistically obeying the rules is considered a sign of faithfulness.

While one of the chief problems plaguing mainstream churches is acculturation and accommodation, a constant danger for the believers' church and Christian community is moralism and legalism. This is a problem we all need to face. It needs to be recognized and guarded against. Legalism is a sign of lack of faith in God. It is a human attempt to preserve faith and community, not believing that God can do it. When the faith has already been lost, legalism will not be able to revive it. The need then is for a deep spiritual rebirth.

Community, like love, is a gift, but involves a lot of hard work. I did not create the love my wife and I share. It is a gift to us from God, but we must continually struggle and work at the things that would divide us. In a sense the term "intentional community" is a contradiction in terms, for we cannot will ourselves into a relationship of community. But in another sense community comes into existence wherever people together hear and obey the call of the living Christ. We can either run away from the call or allow ourselves to be in a position where community can be given to us.

Community is a gift. It is not based on mutual admiration, emotional attraction, or common personalities, but is a result of being drawn together by God. In community we are often drawn together with the kind of people we would not have chosen to be close with. There is a difference between community and a clique. Community can be open and free only as we see it as a gift rather than a human creation.

To say that Christian community is rooted in Jesus Christ is more than an intellectual affirmation. It is the recognition that Jesus is alive and has come to lead and guide His people. We follow not an idea of Christ, a set of doctrines, nor even the teachings of Jesus, but the living Christ who confronts us and calls us to follow Him. We are not following the dead founder of the Christian religion, but a living Lord. The authoritativeness of the Christian faith is in the personal nature of the call. Will we, or will we not follow the One who calls us? If He is not living and present, there is no urgency. Our discipleship is related to the One who calls us.

Christian community is a living testimony to the reality and power of the resurrection. Our faith in the resurrection is more than an affirmation of an event in the past, but also a living reality in our life together. Our life is based on the presence of the living Christ who leads us into community and creates a common bond among believers. We are gathered together by Christ and dependent upon Him for our existence. Without His presence, the church, like a chicken with its head cut off, engages in much frantic, purposeless action, but her life is short and accomplishes nothing.

Community is not an experiment, but a free response to what God is doing among us. Community must involve real commitment to share and forgive. An experiment will not last long unless it is transformed into something else.

If not led by the Holy Spirit, the community will disintegrate. Conflict over little things can tear a community apart. Little differences can be blown into insurmountable problems. But to the extent that we allow God to take over and surrender ourselves to His leadership, this can be overcome. If we are truly led by the Spirit and really come to love each other, neither the little things nor even the big things can draw us apart.

We must not become romantic about community, for community is a most dangerous way to live. The potential for tyranny and manipulation is almost unlimited when the community is controlled by an evil spirit. Paul warns us to have no *koinonia* with *(synkoinoneite)* evil (Eph. 5:11). An anti-community which is an expression of evil can also exist. Unless community is led by the Holy Spirit of God it should be avoided.

If there is nothing beyond herself, the community soon becomes ingrown, but worse than that, she makes herself ultimate and absolute, and thus idolatrous. She becomes the final authority by which to judge everything.

It is especially easy for the church to become a victim of her own ideology, because her claims are so absolute. She begins to justify anything in the name of God. "God is on our side." Our goals become mistaken for the will of God. We need to be aware that communities, like individuals, tend to act in their own narrow self-interest. Any community needs a source of meaning and direction beyond herself, an order-creating power by which she is sustained.

What is called for here can be called transcendence, essential for any healthy community, for without it relationships cannot have depth. Brotherhood and sisterhood are impossible without transcendence, for without a parent (a common source of meaning beyond ourselves), there can be no brothers or sisters.

What else can give us this unity and love? Common experience alone has little power to unite people. The traumatic and universal experience of birth and the common experience of death have not brought unity to the world. Experience can bring a sort of unity, but unless strong measures are taken to ensure that no different experiences are allowed, the unity based on experience soon erodes. When members of a school class gather together for a reunion there is a mood of nostalgia and reminiscence, but not a deep sense of unity of vision and purpose.

Neither can a common religious experience itself hold people together. The intense feeling generated by religious revivals is usually short-lived. A commitment much deeper than this is necessary. A community cannot be held together simply by a common history, but only by the living Lord in her midst who is the Founder, Sustainer, and Purpose in all she does.

The rejection of alienation, depersonalization, and the stifling institutions of the sick society is not an adequate basis for lasting community. It is not enough to want to get away from the rotten mess of society. Commitment to the idea that community is the best way to live will not carry us through. Even human love is not enough. Human love can destroy community because it is based on desire and tries to force community. Only the love of God can create true community.

Christian community is not based on the mistaken idea that cooperation, harmony, and peace rather than competition, conflict, and domination are the natural states of human existence. It is not based on a back-to-nature and back-to-the-land movement, seeking life untainted by the developed world. Rather, Christian community is based on the new life we have received in Christ. It is based not on idealism, but on what God is doing in our midst. Community is an expression of our commitment to follow Jesus.

An intellectual or even theological commitment to community is no guarantee that there will be community. Theoretical concepts about community are not enough. Often people with only a strong intellectual commitment are unwilling to be very open or close to others. They keep their defenses intact.

In 1 Corinthians 1-3 Paul showed his understanding that the world's wisdom does not lead to salvation or community. Rather it is destructive for Christian community. The Corinthian church was split because various leaders thought they knew the whole truth. Human wisdom is divisive. It causes members of the community to strive for fulfillment of their own wills rather than for the leading of God's Spirit. Paul's only hope for the church was for her to be centered in Christ, led and taught by the Holy Spirit (1 Cor. 2:12, 13). Community cannot survive on human wisdom alone.

Since Christian community exists only by the creative and sustaining power of God it is important that our lives always be focused on the One who is our Lord. Without Him, we would not continue in community. Jesus Christ is Lord of the church.

Following Jesus

We accept the lordship of Jesus only insofar as we follow Him in our lives, to the extent that our lives are transformed by His power and His Word becomes operative in our daily lives. Changed hearts *will* result in changed lives. Faith is authentic only to the extent that it is lived. Intellectual affirmation is not enough. Menno Simons wrote, "Whosoever boasts that he is a Christian, the same must walk as Christ walked."[1]

Faith without discipleship is a religion without Christ, a dead system without a living Lord. We cannot believe

without obeying, just as we cannot obey without believing.
Faith and obedience cannot be separated, for without works
there is no faith (Jas. 2:14-26). Dietrich Bonhoeffer has called
this empty religion "cheap grace."

> Cheap grace is the preaching of forgiveness without requiring
> repentance, baptism without church discipline, communion
> without confession, absolution without personal confession.
> Cheap grace is grace without discipleship, grace without the
> cross, grace without Jesus Christ, living and incarnate.[2]

A belief in the visible church implies there can be no distinction between ethics and faith, life and doctrine, justification
and sanctification. Christian teaching and living cannot be
separated. The message of Jesus must either be lived or rejected. As Jesus put it, "Not every one who says to me, 'Lord,
Lord,' shall enter the kingdom of heaven, but he who does
the will of my Father" (Mt. 7:21).

Simple, childlike obedience does not mean all issues are
simple, but wherever they are clear we simply obey without
rationalizing or seeking to evade what we know is right. The
question is never how far on the fringe can we be and still be a
Christian, but how close and how fully can we follow Him.
We do not merely give God a place in our life, but center our
whole life in Christ. God wants not a religion tacked on to the
fringes of our lives to give support and strength to the
activities we choose, but for us to put God in the center and
allow all our activities to revolve around Him.

Nothing in all the world is as important as following our
Lord. Nothing else may stand in our way. We may set no
conditions for our discipleship. The man who wanted first to
say good-bye to his family was not ready to follow (Lk. 9:61).
A partial commitment is no commitment at all. "No one who
puts his hand to the plow and looks back is fit for the
kingdom of God" (Lk. 9:62).

Obedience to Christ is a life of joy. It is done not out of necessity, force, selfishness, or seeking reward, but out of love, freedom, and willingness to serve. Rather than a servile obedience, Christian discipleship is a loving relationship. Simple obedience is the opposite of legalism. Legalism is the development of our little petty rules and demands into which we expect everything to fit. The yoke we choose for ourselves is many times more heavy than Christ's yoke.

The Christian way is not submission to a static legal code, but rather a living relationship with the One who leads us. It is a conversation in which God's Word to us must be answered. If we do not answer, there is no conversation. The depth of the conversation depends on our willingness to listen and respond.

Rather than being doctrine-centered or sacrament-centered, we also have the option of a faith which is life-centered. How we live is the important question. The radical Christian vision down through history has seen the essence of faith as following Jesus. Faith means to trust and follow, not merely to believe a proposition. Although sound doctrine is important, we can intellectually believe all the correct doctrines and still be the worst scoundrels on earth. Likewise, having had an emotional conversion experience or involvement in a sacramental life is not enough. The important question is whether we are willing to follow Jesus, to live the life He calls us to.

Rather than a denial of grace, this is an affirmation that grace is real and will be demonstrated in our lives. Paul not only talked about justification and grace, but also about new life in Christ. The only appropriate response to God's love is grateful obedience. We are faithful because God has been faithful to us. Faith and discipleship are the result of grace. We live the ethic of the Sermon on the Mount not through willpower or determination, but through the grace of the One who gives us the will and power to do it.

This is done in the faith that God does not ask us to do anything for which the strength will not also be given to carry it through. In no way does discipleship mean works righteousness, but rather a total dependence on God's grace, and actually believing in the constant reality of that grace.

The work of Christ is related to more than justification by faith. He also functions as Teacher, Prophet, and Leader. Many theologians have given lip service to the idea of Christ being not only Priest (atonement) and King (incarnation), but also Prophet (discipleship), but they have seldom spelled out any functional meaning to this office. Jesus as Prophet and Leader has too often been only a formal concept. What Christ does in this office has not been taken seriously. Few seminaries offer courses in discipleship.

How different this is from the early church which took discipleship so seriously that she remembered that Stephen died while proclaiming Moses' prophecy of Christ being a Prophet. If Jesus is a living Prophet and Teacher, then we must begin to view Him differently than mainline theology does. Orthodox theology has given little attention to words of Jesus like, "Sit at my feet and listen to my word," "Learn of me," "Hear my voice," "Be my disciple."

The essence of discipleship is found in the nature of Christ's lordship. By "worshiping" Jesus, some people feel they do not need to take seriously what He said. Some see the primary meaning of His life and death in terms of substitutionary atonement and so are able to reduce justification by faith to cheap grace. The emphasis then is on something that happened in the past rather than on the new life in Christ now. Even if we see Jesus primarily as a Revealer of truth and ideals, with a little rationalizing on our part, our daily lives can be lived quite apart from those ideals. But if Jesus came as Lord and Leader, then we either follow Him or reject Him.

Discipleship is not an abstraction. When closely tied to the life, death, and teachings of Jesus it becomes quite specific and concrete. Discipleship involves a concern for both the words and life of Jesus, not just one of these. This concern will result in a fairly literal acceptance of Jesus' teachings, especially of the Sermon on the Mount, leading to rejection of violence and coercion, wealth and conspicuous consumption, social injustice, swearing of oaths, divorce and adultery, *and* to a concern for prayer and personal piety.

Radical Christian discipleship is more than the discipleship expounded by Thomas a Kempis in his important book, *The Imitation of Christ,* which sees discipleship as an inner spiritual discipline. Almost completely missing in this book is any critique of the larger social order or any call to a new community. By avoiding conflict with the world and the struggles of Christian community, the meaning of discipleship is significantly reduced and the cross means little more than an inner self-purification.

We need not only an inner piety, but also the cross and crown of thorns, an outer obedience which is the true sign of inner commitment. Rather than being satisfied with a private relationship with Christ, discipleship commits us to the prophetic work of proclaiming the coming of the kingdom, bearing the cross in opposition to the evil world, and engaging in battle with the structures of evil. Salvation cannot be reduced to an inner feeling and discipleship to a state of mind. True spirituality is not a retreat from the world, but a new way of living in the world. Prayer is to be not only a period set aside, but an integral part of all we do.

The Christian faith has been divided into a personal and a social gospel. What we need is the whole gospel. But to restore the whole gospel will mean more than simply adding the two together, for both were distorted in the process of being divided. One cannot add pounds and inches. What is needed is a new encounter with biblical faith and its Founder who can lead us into a new understanding of both personal and social transformation within a new community.

It is important that the demands of discipleship be understood as applying to all believers. While monasticism was able to keep alive the vision of costly discipleship, it also became a justification for the institutional church to lower her standards for the general membership and let everyone choose the level of discipleship most comfortable to them. A mistake of monasticism was the failure to proclaim the demands of Christ as binding on all believers. Maybe all Christians should be seen as members of a religious order which could be called worldly monasticism. Discipleship is not a special call for some, but a way of life for every believer.

The call to follow Jesus comes not only to us as persons, but also corporately to the whole community of believers. Jesus is gathering people into a new social order which will be obedient to His voice.

Discipleship can be a corporate experience of a whole community of faith engaged together in following Jesus. Discipleship is best done with others who are also disciples. Our personal obedience is expressed in a corporate obedience.

Surrender of Self

Christian community is a result of surrendering our lives to God's kingdom. Our commitment to our brothers and sisters is an expression of our commitment to God and His will for our lives. Membership in Christian community involves a serious claim of God upon our lives. In Christian community this claim is recognized and accepted. Christian community is not like a service club which competes with other groups for the loyalty of its members. Commitment must be total. To participate in the kingdom of God we must give up all loyalties and commitments that in any way conflict with or hinder our commitment to God.

Christian community is more than an association of independent individuals, for membership involves the very heart of a person's being in all its dimensions. One is not truly in community unless all is committed and shared. Community always includes a price. It means giving up something else, being here rather than there, giving up other options. But the sacrifices are nothing in light of what is received. In fact, the more we give up and the higher the cost for us, the more valuable and significant community will be for us. Those who give little also receive little. The degree of success of intentional communities is directly related to the strength of commitment in those communities.

Commitment in Christian community is the degree to which a person has given up self-interest for the good of the larger community, the amount of personal investment and sense of belonging in the community, and the degree to which one's whole future is seen as linked with that of the community. This sociological definition[3] is not enough for Christian community, however.

Christian commitment in community is not based on the extent to which we see the community fulfilling our own needs or the extent to which the interest of the total community matches our self-interest, but rather the extent to which we have given up self in order to live the new life to which God has called us. Unless we are prepared to die for each other we are not ready to love and live for each other.

Community has many benefits, but they come at the cost of death of the old person in each of us. Just as we must give up self to know Christ (Phil. 3:7-11), so we must die to ourselves to enter God's kingdom. The old self must die for the new to be born, for us to become the new people we are called to be.

Without this surrender, community is impossible. Each of us brings with us our own agenda from the past, our own ways of fixing meals, our different patterns of living. To the extent that each of us insists on our own way and clings to our pet ideas, community is impossible.

Not only is this self-surrender necessary in community,

but it actually is an important part of the Christian gospel. We are asked to give up everything for the sake of the kingdom. Jesus put it right on the line: "So therefore, whoever of you does not renounce all that he has cannot be my disciple" (Lk. 14:33). That means everything. All that you have. Even your ego. "Circumcise therefore the foreskin of your heart, and be no longer stubborn" (Deut. 10:16). Unless we are willing to die, we are not prepared to live.

One of the main hindrances to doing God's will is our unwillingness to give up self, our constant desire to have our own way. Even most people who do good want to keep control of their own lives and instruct God on how He can help them in doing more good. All too often we pray to God primarily to give us strength to do what we want to do.

God will do little in our lives unless we surrender our wills to Him and allow God's will to become our will. Then we can say with Paul, "It is no longer I who live, but Christ who lives in me" (Gal. 2:20). As we offer ourselves wholly to the Lord our will becomes identified with that of Christ. Then we can pray, "Lord, do what You want with my life." As long as we hold back something for ourselves we cannot receive the power, victory, and freedom that God would give us. It is those who have nothing to lose who are most free to be faithful.

God keeps asking more of us than we are able to give. And after it seems like we have given every last bit of our selves and our energy, God still asks more of us. But every time it happens, God gives us new strength we never expected.

Our lives are demanded of us not only when we face persecution, but just as much in good times. When things are going well we are also called to surrender all to God and our brothers and sisters. The Christian calling is a cross on which all our desires, ambitions, and possessions are put to death. Holding on to the smallest thing and being unwilling to surrender it is as bad as the pride of the richest of the rich. This is not just a surrender of our outer nature so that the "pure inner nature" may shine through, but a surrender of everything, including our innermost selves.

The German word for this is *Gelassenheit*. *Gelassenheit* is what is left after you have turned over everything to God and are not holding back anything for yourself. It means surrender, yeildedness, let-go-ness, defenselessness, resignation, vulnerability, serenity, and peace. It is the meekness of those who have been broken by the Spirit.

Christian surrender is quite different from a selfish desire for personal salvation and inner peace. This is not a self-centered commitment, but a decision to submit our total lives to the claims of Christ's kingdom. It means to give up one's own selfish concerns in order to reach out to God and our neighbor, to sell everything we have to acquire the pearl of great price, to buy the field with the hidden treasure. It is for the sake of the one thing worth having, namely life with God in His kingdom.

A big difference exists, however, between genuine self-surrender and an unhealthy passivity or giving in to the community. Deep humility does not mean self-depreciation or lack of self-worth. *Gelassenheit* does not mean being a washrag, having no integrity, not being a genuine person. It is much different from a relationship of dependency. We are not speaking of the passive and individualistic surrender of the mystics, but an active giving and living in the kingdom of God.

Actually we need to learn more about what it means to be assertive. Often we feel the need to apologize when someone steps on our feet. Because of anxiety, fear, and lack of self-worth we are often either passive and withdraw or we strike out in an aggressive way. Violence, anger, and stubbornness are usually signs of weakness rather than strength. On the other hand, when we feel good about ourselves and others, and know that we are loved and accepted by God, then we need not make any apologies for who we are. Then we will neither feel the need to repress our feelings nor to hurt anyone else, but will be able to respond freely and honestly to God and others, being neither passive nor rebellious.

To surrender everything to God is a deep act of self-affirmation, for it is a recognition that God does love and care for us. How different this is from egoism, with all its deceit and fear. What freedom it is to no longer need to be at the center, to be right, or to prove our worth. What freedom not to need to pretend to be all powerful, all wise, and above most human limitations. All of us have tried to create our own little world with ourselves in the center. The history of our lives is the story of our attempts to manipulate everything according to our own wills and dreams. Sometimes we are willing to fit God somewhere into our plans, but often there is little room for God.

The reality we create, however, seldom corresponds with the real world, or with God's desire for us and the world. The result is frustration, alienation, fear, distrust, anxiety, and bitterness. We have set out on a path that cannot lead to life. We are defeated from the start. And no wonder, for we were never meant to be in the center of the world. Only God is big enough for that. Our place as mature adults is to be gathered together in a circle around God, at peace with others, self, and God's creation.

Here is the basis for living in Christian community. Only as our rebellious, conceited self-wills are broken by the Spirit can we participate authentically in community. Only then are we ready for what God wants to give to us. When King Ussiah died, Isaiah's hopes were shattered, but it was then that God spoke to him (Is. 6:1). The more we are broken by the Spirit, the more open and sensitive we can be to God's will and to our brothers and sisters.[4]

We cannot of ourselves give up our self-will, for that also

requires self-will. But we can allow God to take it away. The point is not to try to be humble, but to be humbled by our relationship with God. To the extent we are broken, we are no longer obsessed with ourselves and are available for God to use us.

One of the reasons faith and community are so difficult for us is that we hold back and refuse to surrender so much. It may be secret sins, an unwillingness to do what we know needs to be done, our pride, our ambition, or maybe our intellectualism. The greatest obstacle to community is refusal to surrender our wills. How hard it is to give up our own opinions, our stubbornness, our conceit, our cleverness! How difficult it is to pray, "Not my will, but Thine be done." It is possible to give away all our possessions and still hold on to our will. The struggle with self will is a daily struggle, confronting us again and again with decisions regarding whether we will live in love.

Maybe our fear of commitment to God and each other is based on our fear of death. We are afraid that radical commitment may be costly to us. Fearful of being rejected or shown that we are wrong, we hold back and cling to our little present securities. The Bible reminds us, however, that the experience of the resurrection comes after the cross. The gospel is about liberation, but liberation includes death. It comes after the cross and involves becoming a slave. We are asked to be crucified with Christ (Gal. 2:20). This means forsaking self-interest, giving up all attachments to the world. The symbol of baptism as spelled out by both Jesus and Paul points to the need for us to die to sin and self (Rom. 6:3-11). "Those who belong to Christ Jesus have crucified the flesh with its passions and desires" (Gal. 5:24).

Jesus said, "Except the grain of wheat falls into the ground and dies, it cannot bear fruit" (Jn. 12:24). The truth of this was stated well by Andreas Ehrenpreis, an early Hutterite leader, when he wrote,

Seed had to die for the unity of the loaf. Only in this way could
it bear fruit. In the same way each individual must give himself
up, must die to himself, if he wants to follow Christ on His way.
Then the grain must be crushed and milled if it is to be turned
into bread. Our self-will undergoes the same for community. It
must be broken if one is to belong to the community of the Supper and to the service of communal work. Furthermore: The
grains had to be brought together into one flour and one loaf.
Not one of them could preserve itself as it was or keep what it
had. No grain could remain for itself. Every grain had given itself and its whole strength into the bread. In the same way the
grapes must be pressed for the wine. Every grape gives all its
strength and all its juice into the uniform wine. In it no grape
can keep anything for itself. Only in this way does wine come
into being. Grapes or grain that remain whole are only fit for
the pigs or the muck heap. They have nothing to do with bread
and wine. If they kept back strength and body for themselves
they lost everything. And they remained lost. In this we have
the most powerful picture of community. That is how Christ
presented it to those who were with him at the Supper. But to
continue: This whole loaf is broken as Christ let his body be
broken. That means for us that the stubbornness of self-will is
broken and that we must be ready in community to suffer and
die.[5]

It needs to be understood that the death of the old self is
not something to be lamented, but is the occasion of great
joy. It does not mean we are destroyed, but transformed into
something new and better. It means a discovery of our real
selves. It is not so much the end of the old as the beginning of
a new life. The gospel concerns overcoming death. Instead of
living in death, we die that we might find life.

Our selfish will sees any kind of discipleship, community, or discipline as a loss of individuality and personal
freedom instead of regarding it as a living relationship which
gives us the freedom and power to be who God wants us to
be, unencumbered by all the enslaving powers of self and the
world. Many Christians have experienced that when the ego
is no longer dominant the personality is able to bloom and

develop. Suppression of our nature and feelings is vastly different from submission and surrender of them. It means to let go of them. Surrender is a liberation from bondage to ourselves. We become free only as God heals our twisted nature and makes His will truly our own. Through the power of God we are liberated from the oppressive domination of the powers and structures of evil.

Just as the biblical understanding of communion with God does not mean absorption of the human into the divine, which is often claimed by mysticism, so the person is not absorbed, but fulfilled, by the community. Although communion with God implies faithful obedience and community implies surrender of self-will, the distinction between God and His people, between the community and the person, always remains. Paul wrote, "Now you are the body of Christ and *individually* members of it" (1 Cor. 12:27, italics added). The community being an organism does not lessen the value or individuality of each member. For a finger to be a part of the body increases the importance of the finger. In community the qualities and gifts of each person are developed and supported. The good of the whole is not separate from the good of each part. Neither is the good of any member separate from the good of the whole.

It is in impersonal, individualistic society that individuality is so often lost and denied. True freedom and individuality are found not in autonomy, unrelatedness, and independence, nor in struggling against others, but in relation to God and our brothers and sisters. Without community there is no true freedom, nor is there any true community without freedom.

What we are talking about is something different than anything found in the world. It is not individualistic, yet neither is it a totalitarianism in which the uniqueness and importance of each person is sacrificed for the sake of unity. Rather it is a whole new world in which each unique individual freely lays down his/her life in service and love to each other.

Western capitalist culture puts great value on heroic individuals, people who stand alone and follow their dream, bending the future to their own wills, not matter what the consequences. The great people are seen as masters of their own destinies. When anything of significance happens, it is viewed as the result of the actions of some brave individual, without recognizing the involvement of the other people, social forces, and God. This vision carries not only the implication that we should stand alone, but even worse, that people really cannot get together, cooperate, and follow a dream that transcends the individual ego. There is the implication that only a few isolated individuals can be faithful, can break out of bondage, and live a new reality.

A basic Western assumption since the Renaissance is that the individual is a separate unit. Only secondarily do we have relationships with others, and these are seen as restrictive of our personal freedom. Life is seen as a jungle in which everyone must fight for survival. We work not with others but against them, everyone struggling against nature and competing with others to climb the ladder of success. Individualism is a defiance of our bond with others and God. Often it results in a directionless wandering usually mistaken for a pilgrimage. It means that we become our own authority, cutting ourselves off from others and the meaning of our existence. Even the claim of an individual to follow only Jesus may be a prideful denial of Jesus speaking through another.

Of course, living in community means a restriction on my freedom in terms of not being able to have my own way, to act in unloving ways, to escape responsibility. But it can increase my freedom to be the person God wants me to be. Over and over this deeper freedom is experienced by those living in Christian community.

The Bible calls us to live in mutual submission to one

another. This is true not only of the direct command of Ephesians 5:21, but is implied in all the passages on servanthood and the commands to put the needs of others ahead of our own. Submission to God without submission to others is empty. The basis for our submission is Jesus' submission to God's will. He was completely submitted to God's will. Judy Alexander challenges our fuzzy thinking on the area of authority.

> So why is submission important? Part of the reason may be found in the submission directives where the phrase is added: "As to the Lord" (Eph. 5:22; 6:5; 1 Pet. 2:13). Often the Bible assumes that our human relationships reflect our relationship to God. "If a man says I love God and hates his brother, he is a liar" (1 Jn. 4:20). Perhaps the purpose of everyone having some role of submission is to teach us, in a situation we can understand, to subject ourselves to Him. Is it possible for a man to say, "I submit myself to God's authority," when he is unwilling to submit to any human authority?[6]

We submit our lives to one another as an expression of our submission to God. This mutual submission is the basis for true freedom. My wife and I find that the more we are in submission to one another the more freely our relationship can develop. It is difficult to live with anyone who is not submissive, especially in marriage and in community.

In most of our world the individual counts for little except as a means for some end. People feel insignificant, powerless, and trapped. But in a relationship of mutual submission to one another each individual person is considered worth more than the whole world. How could it be otherwise if we have committed our whole lives to God and to each other?

Although dying to self can be a painful process, the important part is not the giving up, but the great joy and liberation that we experience in being freed from the oppressive slavery of selfishness, pride, and bondage to self-will. The new life in Christ is a life of joy. In comparison with the joy and love which God wants to share with us, all of our selfish pleasures are dirt and filth. The truth is, however, that while the humble person can experience God so powerfully that one's heart will want to shout for joy, the possibility of this experience is cut off for the proud.

The call to discipleship is a call to liberation. It is a call to reject all other loyalties and to cast away every burden. The more completely we follow the one Lord, the easier and lighter the burden becomes. Jesus said, "Take my yoke upon you, and learn from me, for I am gentle and lowly in heart, and you will find rest for your souls. For my yoke is easy, and my burden is light" (Mt. 11:29, 30). Indeed our lives can become unburdened and free.

We find liberation as we surrender all to follow Jesus. It comes as a gift as we put ourselves aside, when we lay down our own problems and are able to reach out to another person in need, emptying ourselves of our own self-centeredness. Liberation is found not in ourselves as the teachers of Zen and popular psychology would tell us, but comes from beyond ourselves as we reach out to others.

How different this is from the cult of self-actualization and self-realization which is primarily concerned with self-fulfillment and is centered on self. Personal growth, self-realization, individual fulfillment cannot be goals in themselves for Christians. These can be attained only to the extent that we stop seeking them. We discover God not so much as we discover our real selves, but rather as we discover God we also discover our real selves. Jesus was right, unless you lose your life, you will never find it (Mt. 16:25). There is a great difference between seeking self-fulfillment and being a servant, living a life of love. Lasting community cannot be based on self-fulfillment, for selfishness must first be given up. In community we no longer make demands for ourselves, but joyously praise God for all that has been given.

It is important that we come to terms with our own selfishness. Unless we do that, our communities will be little more than reflections of the old society we hoped to overcome. It is not enough to reject the selfishness and materialism of the larger capitalist society. The cause of the human condition is not only the corrupt environment in which we live, but also the condition of our inner selves which needs to be transformed.

The life of the community must be a manifestation of the new life in Christ which has become real in the experience of each member of the community. We cannot simply come together in community and carry the cancer of the old society with us. Community is possible only to the extent that we leave our old selves behind and are cleansed. To become a member of the new community we need to be converted and reborn.

Commitment and surrender are demanded not only of each individual Christian, but also of the total Christian community. Renunciation of individual ego is no guarantee that a collective pride and egoism will not take its place. We can become proud that we are so faithful and humble. The selfishness of "mine" and "thine" can be exchanged for the selfishness of "ours" and "theirs." The faithful church is a community which is completely broken and submissive to God's Spirit. The church must be willing to die, yes, go out of existence. Any church that is concerned with her own preservation has already lost the faith.

The Christian faith involves the call to leave everything to follow Jesus together with our brothers and sisters.

Chapter 3

THE SHARING COMMUNITY

By this all men will know that you are my disciples, if you have love for one another.—Jesus in John 13:35.

The Meaning of Love

One of the distinctive marks of Jesus' followers is their love for each other. Probably the most visible and amazing aspect of true Christianity is how Christians love and share together. Just as in a happy marriage, although it sometimes may be difficult, there is no question about sharing and drawing close together. Given the love that defines our existence, we can do no other. Sharing is not a law, but an inevitable result of being bound together in love and unity.

Paul's image of the Christian community being a body implies sharing. What the hand does is for the good of the whole body. The feet are not concerned about hoarding up shoes for themselves. In a body, when one hurts all hurt, when one rejoices all rejoice (1 Cor. 12:26). When one member is in prison all consider themselves imprisoned with that person (Heb. 13:3). The church is not to be like a theater to which one goes alone, listens, and then leaves alone without sharing with others, but rather she is a community in which all the members reach out in love to each other in order to serve all their needs. Sometimes it may be true of us, as it was for the little girl who was asked if she ever eats with people who are not her friends. "Yes," she replied, "at church suppers." A group of Baptists were on the right track when in 1611 they wrote in their "Declaration of Faith,"

> That the members off everie Church or Congregation ought to knowe one another, that so they may performe all the duties off love one towards another, both to soule and bodie. Matt. 18:15. 1 Thes. 5:14. 1 Cor. 12:25. And especiallie the Elders ought to knowe the whole flock, whereoff the HOLIE GHOST hath made them overseers. Acts 20:28. 1 Pet. 5:2, 3. And therefore a Church ought not to consist off such a multitude as cannot have particuler knowledge one off another.[1]

Those who criticize community as being a haven for weaklings do not realize how correct they are. Everyone is weak and needs support. That is why we share each other's burdens. The weak and the strong bear with each other. In the midst of any misfortune, problem, or persecution, one never needs to stand alone. When we share, our joys are doubled and our sorrows cut in half. Someone has said, "If a friend gave a feast and did not invite me I would not be offended. If a friend has a sorrow and did not share it with me, I would be most offended."

Some would define community as the people with whom we deeply share our lives. Community life does involve a continual process of sharing and mutual support among all the members. It is a sense of oneness and we-ness, but more than the togetherness experienced in seeing how many people can crowd into a Volkswagen. Feelings of togetherness are not always the work of the Holy Spirit. The basis of our love for each other must be a spiritual rather than a human relationship, for in human relationships we selfishly reach out to other persons and seek to bind them to ourselves. All of us have experienced the restrictions of human relationships. Relationships with only a horizontal dimension have no depth. Interpersonal relations take on depth when seen in the context of our relation to God, when we realize that it is God who brings about the inner meeting of persons.

In the Christian community, sharing includes a dimension not found in encounter groups which ask us to share without an adequate basis for sharing. Because of our relation and commitment to Jesus Christ, the community is drawn together by His living presence. In praying together we experience something much deeper than human relationships. This is something different from the idea that "the more we get together the happier we will be." We know God in our relation with others. They are seen as *thous* rather than *its*.

Our faith is the basis of our sharing together. We see each other as bearers of the good news of the gospel. Our brothers and sisters are signs of God's grace and love to us. Because of God's love we have been given brothers and sisters. Even as they love and accept us, we know that God has accepted us. Because of this we eagerly respond to them, for in each of them we see *both* Christ and the persons they are. We then receive each other as Christ receives us (Rom. 15:7). Here is the basis of Christian fellowship.

When we discuss sharing we touch the deepest aspects of our being. One of our deepest human needs is to share with others. When this is prevented our personalities become twisted. Unless we love, our whole life is poisoned. Love and sharing are essential aspects of what it means to be human, of what God intends for us. When we do not love and share we lose touch not only with others, but with reality and ourselves as well. We can only know and accept ourselves to the extent that we share with others, and at the same time can only share with others as we know and trust ourselves. Cutting ourselves off from community is suicide. Our real selves will be found only in communion with others and with God.

Our salvation cannot be separated from our relationship to others. Our openness to God is expressed in our openness to other people.

> If any one says, "I love God," and hates his brother, he is a liar;
> for he who does not love his brother whom he has seen, cannot
> love God whom he has not seen. 1 John 4:20.

When we close ourselves to the needs of others, we cut ourselves off from God's love. When we are filled with the Holy Spirit of God, a whole new relationship with others is given. "If we walk in the light, as he is in the light, we have fellowship with one another" (1 Jn. 1:7). Since love is at the innermost heart of God's being and nature, the closer we are drawn to God the more deeply we can love each other. As we cut ourselves off from God's grace, we cut ourselves off from our neighbor, and vice versa. The result is an empty and inauthentic life—and exploitative, oppressive relationships with others and with nature. The neighbor and the environment then are manipulated and exploited rather than received as expressions of God's grace.

Rather than community being impractical, it is modern individualism which is breaking down and becoming less and less viable. Rather than a relic from the past, community is becoming increasingly important. The major elements of what it means to be human are nurtured in primary groups, groups in which there is intimacy and close relationships. We cannot survive in a network of secondary relationships without primary relationships to sustain us. We were created for community and cannot be fully human without it.

The more we love and share, the more we learn of the coming of God's kingdom. Our sharing together is a concrete and visible anticipation of the kingdom which is coming and is already present among us. Our life together anticipates and demonstrates what is coming. We share together as joint heirs of the same promise (Eph. 3:6). The extent to which a community shares is an indication of the depth and spiritual health of that community. Where there is little sharing there is also little true love.

The word must become flesh. It cannot remain abstract.

The truth must be incarnated and lived. Love is more than a sentiment or a beautiful idea. What meaning does our love and unity have if not expressed in material ways? We not only intellectually affirm that God is love, but we together live and share that love from day to day. If we look forward to the day when Jesus will be the only King, when competition and striving will end, when the rich will not oppress the poor because there will be no rich, and people will love each other and share all they have, then why not begin to live that way? The kingdom is breaking in upon us now. Why reject it?

The cross is the ultimate symbol of love. We are to give ourselves to each other as Jesus gave Himself for us. On the evening before He was crucified, Jesus told His disciples to "love one another; even as I have loved you" (Jn. 13:34). We are to love each other as God loves us. How does God love us? He gave His life and died for us. We are asked to lay down our lives for each other even as Jesus laid down His life for us (1 Jn. 3:16). Christian surrender is not only a death of our old selves, but also a willingness to die for each other. As of the early Christians, it also should be said of us, "See how ready they are to die for one another."

Now we are asking one of the central questions concerning community. Do we love each other enough to die for each other? To live for each other? Community is serious. Will we love each other so deeply? Will we daily give our lives for each other? Here is the heart of love and relationships. Loneliness, on the other hand, is the result of desiring only to be loved, of not being able to love others.

When one knows all in the community will seek to be faithful unto death, a special bond is experienced. Without that bond, sharing will always be limited. Once we have crossed that barrier there is a new consciousness. This is the deepest fellowship possible. It is the community known by the martyrs. Only those who have committed themselves unto death know what this is about.

Agape love does not demand or seek anything for itself. It desires the good of others ahead of its own good. Its nature is to surrender and abandon its own right, to do away with all possessive desire. It is a love that gives and forgives everything. This is what Paul meant when he wrote, "Let no one seek his own good, but the good of his neighbor" (1 Cor. 10:24). In 1 Corinthians 13 he says it even more beautifully.

True love is unconditional and undiscriminating. There can be no conditions set on our love for each other. Love does carry with it responsibility but even the worst sin by another person does not lessen our love for that person.

The Early Church

It is instructive for us to look at the early Christian communities which formed after the resurrection of Jesus, not that we should imitate them, but that we be guided by the same Spirit as they were. It is a pity that the study of church history has focused more on doctrinal disputes and power struggles than on the rich heritage of community and fellowship that has existed in every century.

When the Holy Spirit had come upon the early Christians, they were liberated from selfishness and greed and began to share all they had with each other. All of their activities and property were restored to their proper place in the kingdom. Sharing was a natural response to the love they knew in Jesus. In his description of the early church, Eberhard Arnold wrote,

> Love that ultimately surrenders all and everything was so much the hallmark by which Christians were recognized that the decline of this love was considered tantamount to the loss of the Spirit of Christ. Urged by this love, many sold themselves into slavery or went to debtors' prison for the sake of others. Nothing was too costly for the Christians when the common interest of the surrendered brotherhood was at stake, so that they developed an incredible activity in the works of love.[2]

Paul's request that the Corinthian community send aid
to Jerusalem was not only an act of charity, but also an act of
faith reflecting the nature of the gospel. The needs of all the
Christians were taken care of, including materials needs,
healing, support, and worship. Common meals were a daily
occurrence. Deacons were chosen to wait on tables and to
look after people's needs. This love extended beyond the
Christian community, for the early Christians were expected
to look for the poorest people, going street by street, seeking
them out. Caring for the poor was a major concern. The rela-
tively small Christian community in Rome in the year 250
helped support 1,500 needy people.[3]

One of the unique elements of early Christianity was that
they not only gave gifts to the poor, but in their communities
they organized a system of mutual aid and worked to abolish
poverty in their midst. In contrast to Roman custom, giving
was done in relation to need rather than status or position.
Neither was sharing done to prove how liberal and gracious
one was, but out of genuine concern and compassion for
those in need. It was self-denying rather than self-seeking.[4]

The contrast between the attitude of the Christians with
that of the Greco-Roman world goes back to the Old Testament where God's people were commanded by God to accept
the rights of the poor (Deut. 15:1-11). Compassion and mercy
were expected of all God's people. God asks us to reach out
to those who are unworthy. Even in Plato, one of the more
enlightened representatives of the Greco-Roman world, there
was little concern for the poor and those who could not
provide for themselves. The whole of Greek and Roman
philosophy never did move beyond egoism, for even liberal
sharing was primarily for the good feeling and prestige it
brings to the giver.[5]

The early Christians were living the new life in Christ, a
new reality they shared with each other. Paul Minear writes
that this

... flowed from the Master's life into all the interstices of human relations. All Christians, for instance, shared in life-giving grace (1 Pet. 3:7; Phil. 1:7). In the fullest sense they participated as joint heirs in the single promise (Heb. 11:9; Eph. 3:6) and in the joy that God's love brought into their hearts (Phil. 2:17, 18; 1 Cor. 1:6). Mutuality was expressed at the depths of intercessory prayer (2 Cor. 1:11) and of intercessory action. Consolation, strength, and nourishment from a single source permeated their life together (Rom. 1:12; Eph. 4:16). If some of them were rulers, then, by the logic of the new age, all must be rulers with them (1 Cor. 4:8). To the degree that one imiated Christ, others should also share in imitating him (Phil. 3:17).[6]

Sharing Ourselves

The witness of the early church is an example for us. If we follow the same Spirit which filled the early Christians we will be led in the same direction as they were. Our commitment to God cannot be only inner and spiritual, but must be expressed in a visible way to the brothers and sisters. Rather than any law or burden, this is a wonderful privilege for us.

An important aspect of sharing in community involves interpersonal relations. It is indeed ironic that often it is in the church where we are least open and honest with each other, unable to share and deal with the concerns that touch people most deeply. Part of the meaning of fellowship is to know and be known by others. Within this fellowship we should be able to share from the depths of our souls. There should be no need for pretending. Before God all our attempts at self-protection are worthless anyway. We cannot fool God and it is questionable whether we will fool others either. If we feel accepted we do not need to live behind a wall of secrecy, fearing that others may discover who we are and not like us.

Jesus called the devil a liar and the father of lies (Jn. 8:44). The demonic is a distortion of reality. When the demonic enters into our relationships with others we are cut off and set against each other. The alternative is to share ourselves with each other in openness and truth. Anything less than honesty and truth destroys fellowship. Daily we need to seek this openness.

In community we can take off the masks and give up defense mechanisms as they are no longer needed. In community we can overcome the gap between our public face and private face, the difference between the way we act at home and the way we act with others. We can feel free to share both who we are and what we have, our strengths and weaknesses, assets and needs. We can completely give ourselves to each other.

Being open with each other is not easy, of course, and we need to seek God's help in this. It is easier to share our possessions than ourselves. We have been conditioned against being honest with others. Sharing means being open to change, being willing to die to the old. We have many fears of being hurt. We need to be especially sensitive to this fear in others and through lots of love and acceptance help them to trust. Sometimes people will use their intellectual ability to hide this fear. Gently we will inform them that we are interested in them, and not only their intellectual theories.

Sharing does involve risk, for as we lower our defenses we become vulnerable to being hurt through being exploited or betrayed. Sharing can be destructive if not based on love. It is nothing to be played with. In community there are many opportunities and possibilities for oppressing others. The human spirit can be crushed to a pulp and the person made unable to respond in any free way. The more sharing we do and the closer we become, the more potential there is for interpersonal conflict, and so the more we need to rely on the guidance of the Holy Spirit and to be forgiving toward each other.

The Bible does not call us primarily to trust each other, but to trust God. People are not always trustworthy. But we can trust God who will enable us to love people even when we cannot trust them or they cannot trust themselves. Because of this faith we can make ourselves vulnerable. If our faith in God is secure, we can act in a trusting way to those who are untrustworthy just as God loves us even though we are often untrustworthy.

Although it may be difficult, we do have a deep desire to share and be honest. We want community, not polite compliments and formalities. We want to be able to say something ridiculous without being ridiculed. Through faith in God and a loving community we can take the risk of being open and honest.

This openness with each other will include sharing our deepest longings, hopes, and dreams. Not only do we need to share them, but also the community needs to hear them. One of the ways a community moves forward is by responding to these longings.

Negative feelings also need to be shared rather than bottled up within us. When discouraged, it is so easy for us to become accusers of the community before God. When we feel alienated, it is easy for us to complain to God, but this is usually an expression of pride and self-righteousness. Certainly we will pray for the community, but that needs to be done with love, understanding that we are in need of the same grace and power as the rest of the community.

A significant part of sharing is listening to others. How we hurt each other when we do not take time to listen to each other! So few people are interested or concerned enough about others to take the time to just listen without interrupting or intruding with one's own experience and feelings, although there is a place for that too. As we listen, we become aware of the hurts and needs in the community and are more able to respond in a helpful way.

Sharing involves not only giving, but also receiving. Sharing is a two-way experience. Unless sharing is mutual, it leads to paternalism and dependence. Real fellowship is impossible without both giving and receiving, ministering and being ministered unto, for that is how the body is built up. Too often because of our pride we want to be self-sufficient and even put a stigma on receiving aid from others. We would never stoop so low as to ask for or admit that we need help from others. This is pride. Only being willing to give and serve may be a way of keeping others at a distance. In pretending that we are the source of all good gifts, we attempt to make ourselves God. God has given us needs and what a joyous blessing it is to have them met.

Another aspect of sharing is to build each other up, encourage each other, and give praise where praise is due. It is easy to criticize and say what is wrong, but it takes a special effort to tell people what is right and how much we appreciate them. Conscious effort needs to be put into sharing our positive feelings toward each other. We should pray for each other and the community every day. Supporting each other also includes teaching. The Greek word *oidodomē* is translated both as building and edification. To edify means to build up. Love is the most edifying of all.

Community of Goods

Since our commitment to God's kingdom and to each other is not only spiritual but includes all things, it is inconceivable that the love and unity that exists in the community will not be expressed in material ways. The sharing of who we are is incomplete if we do not also share what we have. If we truly love each other, how can we want to hold anything back from our brothers and sisters? When we turn everything over to God, we want to share it with others. Andreas Ehrenpreis, the early Hutterite leader, put it very starkly: "Where the love of Christ is not able to accomplish as much towards one's neighbor as to have fellowship with him also in temporal needs, there the blood of Christ cannot cleanse from sin."[7]

Community at the deepest levels is possible only to the extent we let go of our material possessions, when there is nothing left to hold us back. This has been found to be true by communities in every century. The early Christians were given this depth of community and had everything in common. Acts describes this aspect of their community:

And all who believed were together and had all things in common; and they sold their possessions and goods and distributed them to all, as any had need. Acts 2:44, 45.

Now the company of those who believed were of one heart and soul, and no one said that any of the things which he possessed was his own, but they had everything in common. And with great power the apostles gave their testimony to the resurrection of the Lord Jesus, and great grace was upon them all. There was not a needy person among them, for as many as were possessors of lands or houses sold them, and brought the proceeds of what was sold and laid it at the apostles' feet; and distribution was made to each as any had need. Acts 4:32-35.

Rather than being based on some economic theory, this came as an immediate result of the infilling of the Holy Spirit. It was because they were of one heart and soul that they met constantly, prayed together, ate their meals together, and shared all their possessions. The sharing of goods was an acknowledgment of the oneness and unity they knew in Jesus and was expressed in the common table as they shared together in the Lord's Supper. The basis for economic sharing is the *koinonia* we have in Christ. Without this *koinonia*, all our sharing is empty and forced. First must come this unity and power of the Holy Spirit. Eberhard Arnold describes the moving of the Holy Spirit in the early church in this way:

Communal life with its white-hot love began. In its heat property was melted away to the very foundations. The icy substructures of age-old glaciers melt before God's Sun. The only way to abolish private property and personal assets is through the radiant power of the life-creating Spirit. All ownership feeds on stifling self-interest. When deadly selfishness is killed by love, and only then, ownership comes to an end. Yet it was so in the early church: under the influence of the Spirit of community, no one thought his goods were his own. Private property was an impossibility; here the Spirit of love and unity ruled.[8]

Common goods was not a law for the early Christians, but the sense of the Spirit, love, and unity together were so strong that this type of sharing was what they desired. They could not help but share all that they had. Since they were a family, they began the kind of common sharing that exists in a family. Because of their love and unity, the boundaries of private property dissolved. This was expressed in a common treasury. They shared everything not because they had to (Peter made this clear to Ananias), but because they wanted to. And in Jerusalem apparently all did.

There is a possible connection between the early Christian communities and the Essene community of Qumran. Jesus was probably aware of the Essenes and possibly deeply influenced by them. Both communities were committed to a present and future kingdom of God, had common goods and communal meals. Living in community was not a new idea at the time of the early church.

The two descriptions of community of goods in Acts are not exceptions, but examples of something common and assumed in the early Christian communities.[9] Community of goods was neither an emergency measure nor an instance of an irrational and immature expression of the excitement of a new faith. Although it may be that not everyone in every place gave everything to the community, it is irrefutable that the early church practiced community of goods on a wide scale and not just in Jerusalem. And this practice apparently continued for a long time. This can be seen from reading the writings of the early church. Writing possibly at the beginning of the second century, the author of the *Didache* was expressing the norm expected of the Christian community in writing these words:

> Do not turn away from those who are in need, but share all things in common with your brother. Do not claim anything as your own, for if you have fellowship in the immortal, how much more in perishable things! *Didache* 4:8.[10]

Justin Martyr, writing around the middle of the second century, was able to claim that

> We who formerly treasured money and possessions more than anything else now hand over everything we have to a treasury for all and share it with everyone who needs it. Justin, First Apology 14.[11]

In the Epistle of Barnabas in the Codex Sinaiticus, written about 120, we find these words:

> Thou shalt communicate in all things with thy neighbor; thou shalt not call things thine own, for if ye are partakers in common of things which are incorruptible, how much more should you be of those things which are corruptible!—Epistle of Barnabas 19:8.[12]

Around the year 200, Tertullian wrote to the pagans and said,

> We do not think of goods as private. While in your case your inherited wealth makes all brotherhood impossible, in our case it is by our inherited wealth that we become brothers. ... We who are in communion in heart and spirit do not hold anything back from the communion of goods. Everything among us is in common, except marriage.[13]

The pagan author, Lucian, wrote, "Christians despise all possessions and share them mutually."[14] Other texts could be quoted. As late as the year 400, John Chrysostom talked about the ideal of a communism of love.

As is well known, the early Christians gradually lost the vision and developed into an institutional, sacramental church. But even there the vision continued and burst through in many ways. In the office of the bishop, the communitarian view was preserved by expecting bishops to give away all their private property when becoming a bishop. The formation of groups of monks even before the Edict of Milan was an attempt to recover the *koinonia* and *vita apostolica* of the primitive community. In the monastaries the communitarian teaching of the early Christians was preserved. This protest against the secularized and fallen church was an attempt to live out the early more radical vision of the church.

Some say community of goods has been tried but failed. Well, what human effort has ever been tried that has not failed? That is life. We do fail. But God does not fail. When we fail God gives us the grace to try again. But to what extent has it failed? We cannot accept the claim that the New Testament proclaims ideals which are not possible. The argument that the "failure" of the Jerusalem community proves the impracticality of community life is a poor one. Groups like the Hutterites have been living this way for hundreds of years. The monastic movements were hardly failures. The Jerusalem community was burdened by a famine and by hosting many Jewish Christians on pilgrimage to Jerusalem. Possibly they failed to make adequate plans because of their expectation of Jesus' imminent return. And Jerusalem was completely destroyed. But all of this in no way detracts from the normative nature of Jesus' teachings and the example of the early Christians. Jesus' command to love enemies and to turn the other cheek have also been called impractical.

By having all things in common, the early Christians consciously attempted to follow what they believed Jesus had taught and intended for them to do. They were deliberately continuing Jesus' communitarian style of life. They believed it was the living Spirit of Jesus who led them to share all possessions, and they saw this as a fulfillment of Jesus' promise that "the Holy Spirit, whom the Father will send in my name, he will teach you all things, and bring to your remembrance all that I have said to you" (Jn. 14:26). The basis for common goods was Jesus, His life, teachings, and living presence among them. As Eberhard Arnold described it,

> Just as Jesus wanted His close friends, His disciples, to be always close to Him, so His Spirit urged the early Christians to be close to one another so that together they could live the life of Jesus, so that they could do the same as He had done for them.[15]

Maybe those who had spent so much time with Jesus and were so filled with the Holy Spirit had a better understanding of Jesus' expectations than we do. But how can we interpret the teachings of Jesus in any other way? Jesus lived in community with His disciples and they had a common purse. Jesus repeatedly told people to sell all that they had. These are not exceptional statements, but fit with the whole of Jesus' teaching. Parables like the pearl of great price point in this direction. Jesus praised the widow who gave everything she had. The clear teaching of Jesus not to lay up for ourselves treasures on earth can never be made compatible with holding on to private property. Jesus called for total devotion to the new kingdom He was bringing. If His other teachings are an example for us, then His views on possessions also should have authority for us.

Paul can also be understood in this light. When the true spirit of sharing did not exist in the Corinthian community, Paul rebuked them for their selfishness and lack of sharing, and told them not to eat more than others at their common meals (1 Cor. 11:17-22). In Romans 12:13 Paul tells the Roman Christians to "practice *koinonia*" in relation to the needs of the saints. The Greek here can be translated, "make all things common." In a simple way, Paul is telling them to do what was being done in Jerusalem. Apparently there was so much sharing in Thessalonika that a problem developed with people not being willing to do their share of the work. So Paul said that those who do not work should not eat. This comment refers to life in the Christian community, not a philosophy of welfare.

In 2 Corinthians 8:13-15 Paul spelled out his views on equality and sharing as clearly as could be done. He asked the Corinthians to send aid to the Jerusalem community to equalize the standard of living between the two communities.

> I do not mean that others should be eased and you burdened, but that as a matter of equality your abundance at the present time should supply their want, so that their abundance may supply your want, that there may be equality. As it is written, "He who gathered much had nothing over, and he who gathered little had no lack."

When the Israelites were on their journey to the promised land and were fed manna by God, they discovered that those who gathered little had no less than the rest. That is always the way it is when we truly live in the Spirit. Paul makes his position even plainer in 2 Corinthians 6:10-13:

> ... as sorrowful, yet always rejoicing; as poor, yet making many rich; as having nothing, and yet possessing everything. Our mouth is open to you, Corinthians; our heart is wide. You are not restricted by us, but you are restricted in your own affections. In return—I speak as to children—widen your hearts also.

Paul apparently saw economic sharing as very important.

It might be true that there is no direct command in the New Testament to have everything in common, but it is impossible to obey many of the commands of Jesus if we hold on to private property. How could we obey the commands to "sell all," "renounce all," or "not lay up treasures on earth"? If we hold on to private property we must either spiritualize these commands or say that Jesus did not really mean what He said.

Possibly community of goods was so common and taken for granted in the early church that usually it is not even mentioned. Actually there could be no direct command to share all, for this kind of sharing cannot be a response to a command, but must be a free expression of love and the work of the Holy Spirit in bringing people together. The early Christians were so filled with the Holy Spirit and the urge to share that they could do no other.

The early Christians held everything in common as an expression of their total surrender of all to God and His kingdom. The total surrender *(Gelassenheit)* that love demands leads us to give up control and possession of anything for ourselves or even for the community. Jesus meant what He said when He told us that "unless you renounce all that you have, you cannot be my disciple." Here is the difficult part. But when all self-will, pride, and self-reliance is given up, then the sharing of possessions is easy.

Sharing our possessions is also an expression of our love for each other. True love holds nothing back. It gives everything. How could we hold anything back from those we love? The life of love is foreign to the desire to possess. It is the very opposite of the spirit of Mammon. Love does not seek its own advantage. It seeks to work for others rather than itself, for the common good rather than self-advancement (Phil. 2:2-4). Common goods is an expression of life in the kingdom of God. It is one of the fruits of the new age which is coming. Those who have been released from the bondage of evil now live in the jubilee (Lev. 25; Lk. 4:19).[16] All debts are canceled and the wealth redistributed. The result of receiving the gospel is the beginning of a new social order having little in common with the old order of selfishness and greed. Creation is returned to its original purpose with material things seen as vehicles of love and sharing. All needs are met and the poor regain their rightful place in the world. For this to happen, however, greed and property rights must be renounced in favor of God's kingdom. No longer may our egos be attached to any possessions. All that we are and have are to be given to God's kingdom.

Some will respond by asking how we can go so far as give up all security of our own for the future. This is a very important question and really raises the central issue of how much we are willing to trust God and how deep a relationship of love and trust we want to have with our brothers and sisters. The more we hold back for ourselves the less able we are to love and trust each other and God. But as we come to love and trust more, we then become able to share more.

Giving up property is a test whether our commitment of everything to Jesus and His body is a practical one with implications for daily living. Unwillingness to give up our hold on property may be a sign that we do not want to give up our control over other areas of our life as well, that we do not want to be totally subject to Christ and His body, or it may mean that we want to keep for ourselves some form of financial security just in case God is unfaithful to His promise to us. If we cannot trust God, then we had better hold on to everything. But if we can trust God, then why hold on to any possessions?

The German word for property *(Eigentum)* makes this especially clear, for literally translated it means "that which is mine." In this sense, Christians cannot have any property, for everything belongs to God. The Mammon spirit and ownership mentality must be totally resisted. The distinction between mine and thine has been the cause of so much alienation, oppression, and war. Peter Walpot, the early Hutterite leader who wrote so powerfully concerning community of goods, warned that

Covetousness is a dangerous and evil disease which blindeth
man's eyes, stoppeth his ears, so that naught is more contempt-
ible and tedious to him than to hear of community and letting
all things go. It withereth the hands so that they are of no use in
serving others. They lose understanding and know not what
they do on earth or why they are on the earth.[17]

Jesus wants us to not be so concerned about financial security, but to trust in God for that as much as for salvation.
Those of us living in community of goods have experienced
that economics can become a secondary aspect of our lives
instead of primary. Deep economic anxiety and insecurity
can be overcome. Money need not be such an important part
of our lives. We can be free to give our whole lives to God's
kingdom and to serving others. Nothing need hold us back.

There is no one correct form community of goods will
take. There are many possible forms, depending on culture,
circumstances, and depth of faith. To say that we will share
everything does not mean we will share our toothbrushes, because our brothers and sisters would not rejoice in that sharing. Our sharing is neither legalistic nor absurd, but a living
expression of our commitment to Jesus and our love for each
other.

If we do not go the common goods route, at the very
least we must agree with the question early Anabaptists put
to new members when they asked

... whether they, if necessity require it, would devote all their
possessions to the service of the brotherhood, and would not
fail any member that is in need, if they were able to render aid.[18]

A Church of the Brethren statement written in Colonial
America states the same requirement for all Christians.

To this extent "mine" and "yours" may be spoken on this
basis, that this is mine and that is yours to administer and keep
until a time of need for the poor and suffering in and outside of
the congregation.[19]

If some things are held individually, it must be clear that they are intended to be shared with all. The wealth of the earth is for the benefit of all people, not the private use of a few. Since everything belongs to God, no one may use what he/she has been given without considering the needs of all our brothers and sisters, both in our community and in the whole world. At the very least we will affirm that everything we have is available to our brothers and sisters whenever they have need of it. But this can so easily be taken as an excuse for not sharing. How much more need must there be in the world before we begin to share our possessions?

Our responsibility to those in need goes far beyond occasional alms-giving. Indeed, the poor have a moral claim on all that we do not need. "If any one has the world's goods and sees his brother in need, yet closes his heart against him, how does God's love abide in him" (1 Jn. 3:17)? The parable of the rich man and Lazarus is concerned not with acquiring property in a dishonest way, but with having property in the midst of need.

The minimum of economic sharing for the Christian is to give up private control, to share all our economic decisions with a community, and to receive the counsel of the brothers and sisters regarding one's stewardship. Our individual judgment in the area of finances is usually poor, something that can be seen in the fact that our lifestyle is determined primarily by income rather than the teachings of Jesus. Our powers of rationalizing and the pressures to conform to Mammon are too great to trust these matters to anyone's private and secret care. They need to be shared. Our financial affairs are very much the concern of the community. We need to give up private control of our lives and possessions, putting them under the lordship of Christ and the discernment of the church.

While common goods theoretically may not be the only way, it is questionable how far we will go or how serious we are unless we practice it. We need to take serious and concrete steps that go far beyond mouthing platitudes and idealistic dreams. It is questionable whether the church will be reborn without the result of community of goods, or to put it better, it is difficult to understand how the Holy Spirit would move among us and bring us into deep unity and *koinonia* without also bringing this blessing. The attraction of private property and all the materialistic influences around us make it essential that our lives demonstrate the power and reality of the new creation also in this area.

If we go this direction it is important that it be more than an arrangement to promote collective selfishness. The Christian way is not to pool all we have and divide it equally, but to share everything with others and receive according to need. If some have more needs than others, they receive more. We should remember that the Mammon spirit can thrive just as well in the context of ours/yours as with mine/thine. Community of goods is not in itself a guarantee of liberation from selfishness and greed.

The Christian idea of common goods has little in common with the idea of subsistence living in which by simple living and sharing one need do as little work as possible so that there can be more time for leisure and pursuing private interests. When able-bodied people share, it must include caring for the sick, the poor, and the disabled. That means there will always be plenty of work for all who are able to work.

It is important for the community to continually give away all that is extra, for sharing can soon lead to huge wealth. Even the community cannot consider herself the owner of anything, but merely a trustee of what God has entrusted to her. We will love others so much that the whole community will want to share everything with others. That is the way the Christian faith is.

The sharing and love we enjoy in community involves not only those in the community, but includes an openness to people outside the community and a readiness to share our love and extend hospitality to anyone. "Do not neglect to show hospitality to strangers, for thereby some have entertained angels unawares" (Heb. 13:2). Among Christians there can never be any beggars or destitute. We of the new covenant can do no less than the hope of the Old Testament that "there will be no poor among you" (Deut. 15:4). We are commanded even to give aid and comfort to our enemies (Rom. 12:20).

Our brothers and sisters are those who do the will of God (Mk. 3:35), but they are also anyone in need, for Christ as our brother is identified with anyone in need of food, clothing, or love (Mt. 25:40). The work of charity is closely connected with our sharing in community. When this declines, so does our hospitality and then at the most we give occasional gifts to charity.

While Christians may reject capitalism and private property, they will never use force in bringing the world to this position. They can only voluntarily demonstrate for others what can be done. Since love cannot be forced, a witness in this area is all the more important. Christians cannot be satisfied with paternalistically treating their workers better, while still holding on to private ownership and keeping themselves in control. We need something much deeper than reforming the idea of private property. We need to be guided by a whole new Spirit, the risen Christ.

Equality

The faith and love which leads us to share all also makes us all equal and enables us to live out the vision of no more distinctions between Jew and Greek, slave and free, male and female, but being all one in Jesus (Gal. 3:28). When the gospel is heard and received, social barriers crumble. Even though all are not equal, all are to be treated equally.

If we love each other and are filled with the Holy Spirit,

how could we desire to have privilege or status above our brother or sister, or how could we want to gain an advantage over others or have more than they? This would be the opposite of love and would demonstrate that the love of God is not in us. That would be an expression of the old nature and old way. The Bible means just what it says when it tells us,

> My brethren, show no partiality as you hold the faith of our Lord Jesus Christ, the Lord of glory. For if a man with gold rings and in fine clothing comes into your assembly, and a poor man in shabby clothing also comes in, and you pay attention to the one who wears the fine clothing and say, "Have a seat here, please," while you say to the poor man, "Stand there," or, "Sit at my feet," have you not made distinctions among yourselves, and become judges with evil thoughts. . . ? If you really fulfil the royal law, according to the scripture, "You shall love your neighbor as yourself," you do well. But if you show partiality, you commit sin. James 2:1-4, 8, 9.

No worldly status or position may be brought into the community, for in God's kingdom we are all brothers and sisters and the whole sinful system of class structure has been overcome. Christians will reject any kind of rank based on profession or property. The early Quakers demonstrated this by refusing to tip their hats to anyone, including the king.

In Christian community no distinctions may exist between clergy and laity, rich and poor, educated and uneducated. There can be no place for titles of rank, distinction or special recognition. In the vision Jesus had for His people the use of titles of distinction are out of place, for they contradict the essence of that fellowship. Actually they stem from the same root as other forms of social injustice. Titles are a symbol of pride, something that has no place in Christian community. Jesus understood this when He told us,

> But you are not to be called rabbi, for you have one teacher, and you are all brethren. And call no man your father on earth,

for you have one Father, who is in heaven. Neither be called
masters, for you have one master, the Christ. Matthew 23:8-10.

When pagan titles like doctor, professor, reverand, or even
Mr./Mrs./Ms. replace the use of first names or simple terms
of brother and sister, something important in the community
has been lost. In community there can only be brothers and
sisters. There may be no barriers in God's family.

It is important that no economic inequality or any division of rich and poor exist in the Christian community. Deep,
ongoing fellowship will never be found between people of
widely different economic standards since there will always
be some condescension on one side and a certain amount of
resentment and feelings of inferiority on the other side.

The inequality and injustice we see in our world can only
be an incentive for us to desire and seek equality and justice
all the more. This is expressed in our lives as they take the
shape suggested by an old Shaker hymn.

> Whoever wants to be the highest
>   must first come down to be the lowest,
> and then ascend to be the highest
>   by keeping down, to be the lowest.[20]

Family and Community

For those not living in an intentional community, many
questions are raised concerning the relation of the nuclear
family to the larger community. Those of us now living in an
intentional community have found our life in community
strengthening our family relationships. For Christian communities such as Reba Place, the Hutterites, and the Hutterian Society of Brothers (Bruderhof), the nuclear family is
not only affirmed and supported, but is seen as one of the
basic elements of the community, a creative part of a larger
body. Rather than in any way deemphasizing the importance
of the family, its importance is elevated and seen as a sacred
trust.

A Christian understanding of family life should begin with an understanding of our whole lives being lived under the lordship of Christ and within the context of the kingdom of God, the order of redemption which is coming to reality among us. Marriage can only be what God means it to be if it is in reality an expression of the new order of Christ's kingdom.

Since the reality of this new kingdom is becoming visible in the body of Christ, the context for Christian marriage is the church. In fact, marriage itself is an image of the church. Unity in marriage is to be an expression of the unity experienced in the church where life together is lived under the rule of the Holy Spirit (Eph. 5:29-32). The mystery of unity, of two becoming one, is very similar to individual believers becoming one body.

Of necessity, this means that commitment to God and the church must come ahead of commitment to our family. This will include submitting our family relationships to the discernment and discipline of the body of Christ. This becomes especially clear if we believe that discernment of God's will is to be done by the body rather than each person individually doing what seems right in one's own eyes. In this case, the discernment of the Christian community will be given more authority than the discernment of a family council.

Can it be any other way? Jesus tells us specifically that our commitment to Him and His body must come before father or mother, husband or wife. It is striking to look at Jesus' statements about family life. Many of them almost seem to be a repudiation of the family. At least there is no hint of wanting to save the old structures of society, no nostalgia of combining motherhood and the flag. Although He was not disobedient, Jesus was more concerned about doing God's will than obeying His parents (Lk. 2:41-51; Jn. 2:4). He considered other people to be His true family. Once when

Jesus' mother and brothers wanted Him to go home He stated that His brothers and sisters, His family, are those who do God's will (Mt. 12:48-50). Jesus realized that all the structures of the fallen world are doomed, and therefore called people to a new order that would replace the old, a new community which would include a new family life. We are to seek first the kingdom of God and then all these other things will find their proper perspective.

For many it may sound harsh and even wrong to put commitment to the church ahead of our family. Perhaps they could put God first, but not the church. This may be because of an inadequate vision of what God wants the body of Christ to be. It is true that in most religious institutions today to put loyalty to the church ahead of one's family would mean depriving the family for the sake of an institution. But when the church is a fellowship of love and concern in which every member has made an unconditional commitment to Jesus and to each other, that might be a different matter. Then it could be trusted that the decisions of the community reflected what God wanted, that the needs of each family would have been taken with utmost seriousness in the discernment process. If special demands are made on a family member, the community will then give appropriate support to the family to help in whatever needs this may create.

Rather than weakening the family, to have commitment to God and the Christian community as the starting point gives a much firmer basis for marriage than the unity of the two people based on human attraction. Where this commitment exists, divorce is almost unheard of. To put our commitment to God and the church before our commitment to the other person gives the marriage both a commitment to an unconditional faithfulness which transcends the family and a practical everyday support for that commitment.

It is within this context that Jesus' radical statements regarding marriage, divorce, and remarriage make sense. With this kind of covenant, divorce and remarriage can never be accepted, for the marriage commitment is for life. It is not just for as long as it works out. Rather, even if one's partner is unfaithful, still we can never give up or close any doors to reconciliation and restoration of the relationship. We are called to the same kind of love that the Book of Hosea shows God's love to be. Although it may be helpful for some couples to be separated, divorce and remarriage are not options for the Christian community.

Without a real unity of faith and purpose marriage is something less than what God desires for it. Thus it is important for Christian couples to have a common commitment both to God and to the same church community before marriage. Commitment to God and the church come first. This makes it impossible for a Christian to marry a non-Christian (1 Cor. 7:39; 2 Cor. 6:14).

Marriage is a most serious and sacred commitment and should not be entered into without the discernment of a body that it is God's will for this couple to be united. A couple emotionally bound together is not suited to make this discernment alone. For those of us who were married without this commitment it means making a new marriage commitment, clearly putting our marriage under the lordship of Christ and the discipline of a church community.

* * *

New forms of family life would emerge if we were to begin with our commitment to God and the church instead of traditional concepts of the family. This would mean many changes in the nuclear family structure, but a strengthening of family life. We might remember that when the family is mentioned in the Bible it means not only daddy, mommy, and two children, but includes grandpa and grandma, aunts, uncles, and cousins. The isolated nuclear family is a modern experiment and a rather poor one.

We have put more responsibilities and pressures on the family than it can bear, and at the same time have withdrawn much of the support the family used to receive from the larger society and the church. With husband's and wives' lives unconnected except for the home, and school activities tearing the children in still other directions, often the family is fighting just to survive. Actually, it is a miracle that not more families are breaking up, considering all the pressures, lack of support, and often absence of faith and commitment.

In Christ's new kingdom, however, the family is integrated into God's larger purposes for us. A Christian family exists in the context of a larger commitment and fellowship, something missing for most families in our world.

Living in community can help the family in many ways. One significant way is to help us work at our relationships within the family. My wife and I have discovered that we are not capable of meeting all of each other's needs. Our brothers and sisters in community are a big help to us in this. It has been said that God sees us as our family sees us. So often we relate quite differently to others than to our family. In an isolated nuclear family, we can get away with all kinds of unloving ways of relating to each other, but marriage problems cannot be easily suppressed or hidden in community. As our lives increasingly are shared with a larger community, such areas of our lives can begin to come under the lordship of Jesus. Since living in community, my brothers and sisters have helped me to begin developing more loving patterns of relating to my family. These new patterns might not be developing if I did not have the help of a community which is so much a part of my life.

The isolated family is especially oppressive for women. Many fathers get away from it all for eight hours each day, leaving their wives trapped at home so oppressed and burdened that they cannot share themselves even with their children as they would like. In community the tasks of housework and child-rearing can be shared. Raising children is a great responsibility which two parents cannot manage adequately by themselves. The children need more adult relationships than just those with their parents, in addition to close relationships with other children. Although still the primary responsibility of the parents, in community the responsibility for children can be shared. The children can be part of a larger community.

The isolated family style of living is destructive both for the family and the church. Grandparents are an example. Presently they often are pushed aside and are unable to have close relationships with their children or grandchildren. This not only is alienating for the grandparents, but also is a great loss for the grandchildren.

This alienation is also destructive for the church, which suffers a great loss when the older people are separated away and cannot pass their faith and perspective on to the grandchildren. We forget that in the Bible it is expected that grandparents will take responsibility for their grandchildren (Deut. 4:9). If we do not listen to the old we lose our contact with the past. An important source of wisdom, tradition, experience, and stability is lost to us. In Christian community the elderly can be an integral part of the daily routines of life.

The elderly today are pushed aside, not necessarily because older people are unwanted, but more often because we have developed a lifestyle which gives little room for them. In our individualistic lifestyle, the old and the sick cannot be cared for in the family without being a great burden. A nursing home seems to be the only other possibility. But in community where the work is shared by all, rather than being a burden on anyone, the older people become a real blessing for everyone. And they can make their contribution. As long as they are able and willing, the elderly can participate fully in the work and life of the community. It is terrible to grow old in an individualistic society.

The same could be said for single people and families with one parent. Community can provide them with a broad network of supportive relationships, lessening the feeling that they simply must marry, and giving them a better basis on which to make decisions regarding marriage. In fact, there is a calling for some to be single and this should be recognized and respected by the whole church community. No one should ever be looked down upon for not being married. One can live a full life without being married. In fact, there is biblical basis for arguing that one can live a fuller life if one is not married. At least there is no need for everyone to be married. That gift is not for all. To be single is also a gift.

In Christian community the old, the young, the single adult, the mother, or the father can find a full family life. In Christian community one has so many more possibilities of being surrounded by babies, children, teenagers, middle-age adults, and older people—all part of a larger family. No one needs to be excluded from a broad family life that is available for everyone.

*   *   *

God's intention of sex being an expression of a covenant between two people who have completely committed themselves to each other for life, and for no other purpose than to serve God, takes on added significance in community. The normal flow of relationships in the community can soon be short-circuited by secret affairs or unfaithfulness. Sex outside of the marriage covenant lacks spiritual foundation and soon leads to jealousy and strife. Sex can be a destructive force in community or its true meaning can be enhanced. Exploiting each other in the name of love and openness has no place in community. It is important to see people as brothers and sisters rather than sex objects.

Exclusiveness in sex is very important. The commitment required in community is related to the exclusive commit-

ment to one person made in marriage. Tertullian said, "All
things are common among us but our wives. We give up our
community where it is practiced alone by others" (Apolog.
39).[21]

In a Christian community adultery will usually be less
likely than in the larger society because the relationships and
trust are deeper and therefore are more serious to break.
Adultery is much more likely in a depersonalized society
where relationships are not considered sacred. In community,
at any sign of unfaithful thoughts or unhealthy relationships
the problem can be lovingly confronted before it becomes so
serious as to be expressed in something like adultery. When
someone is facing temptation the community is there to give
support and counsel. In community it is difficult to keep
much of one's life hidden.

Married people do need relationships with others of the
other sex. In community this is part of the daily life. The
stronger and more exclusive the marriage commitment is, the
freer these relationships can be. There then is no need for suspicion or jealousy. The intimacy of the family, rather than
competing with the larger community, can be a building
block for a wider intimacy.

Although one does not have to be in Christian community to have a Christian family life, it does provide an environment in which the family can be daily nurtured and
strengthened.

Love in Action

In occasional encounters with other Christians, we
experience a deep fellowship and love. But how much more
can this love be known by those who live in *daily* fellowship
with each other. Once we taste community we will want to go
deeper and deeper. We cannot be satisfied with only a little,
but will want to open ourselves to all that God wants to give
to us.

We have a need to share in more ways than in formal meetings. So many of us share little bits of ourselves with many people, but our whole selves with practically no one. Our life is a series of fragments. Community implies relationships of the whole person, not just deep sharing in one way or role. The unity of a group is related to the extent to which all aspects of our lives become part of the sharing and commitment within the community. The more we are being pulled in other directions, the less fully we can give our lives to each other. Our lives need to cross as many times and in as many different ways as possible during the week. Day-to-day contacts are vitally important for deepening and broadening relationships. How else can we be wholly present to each other?

The structures and life of the church have not kept up with the times, for we no longer live in a close-knit rural society in which everyone has known each other for a long time. Then the church could survive with an hour or two of formal meeting a week, for the real community was continued the rest of the week. That is no longer true. Now most members never see each other until the next Sunday when again they briefly meet, but have little significant contact with one another.

In many churches one could be absent from meetings for a whole month and no one would ever contact that person to find out what is wrong. Simply missing one meeting should be a reason for concern, for it may be a sign of sickness in the family, and others could be of assistance. It seems inconceivable to me that in a community of faith every member would not be visited by another member at least once a week, although that is not nearly enough.

As we grow together in community it becomes increasingly clear that how far we live from each other makes a big difference. We do not drop by for two minutes to see those who live a half hour away. The further people live from each other the more difficult community becomes. Unless we see each other often and learn to know each other in many ways, how can we be of help and support in each other's needs? We cannot bear each other's burdens unless we share enough to know what those burdens are.

If we do not live together, it at least helps to live close to each other. Church groups need to take this seriously and should consider encouraging groups of members moving together in the neighborhood of the meetinghouse. This would increase the possibilities for both sharing and mission in the neighborhood. Or several geographical centers could be formed around which sharing could begin. But why not share all of our lives?

Two possibilities of living together are either to live together as a colony or a village and be a new society, or to live as households, a group of people larger than one nuclear family, living together in one house. This second possibility may have been practiced in the early church as suggested by Romans 16:5-16. The Bruderhof is the best example of the former while groups like Reba Place Fellowship have demonstrated extended households within a few blocks of each other as a way of living in community within a large city.

It is important to have as much time and variety of activities to share together as possible. Meetings for worship, discussion, decision making, and study are important, but not enough. Eating together is very important and should be done as often as possible. Playing together helps break down barriers and allows people to know each other in new ways. It is important to have fun together as a community. Sharing the little details of daily living is significant. Working together on projects (anything from preserving food to serving others) brings a feeling of wholeness and completeness.

An ongoing activity in the community will be responding to each other's needs by giving help whenever needed, no matter how trifling. The greater fund of common experiences we have to draw upon, the deeper our life together can be. In community our individual experiences can become corporate.

Work is an important leveler and brings people together in a significant way. It is one of the best and quickest ways of learning to know people. At the very least, groups should engage in occasional work projects such as painting someone's living room. It is especially helpful to engage in physical work together.

As communities become closer, they may find themselves considering finding some kind of common work so that work can also be an expression of community. This has proved to be a great blessing for our community, and others as well. Employment should not be used as an excuse for not going deeper into community or dealing with important issues before the community. Certainly our work should have less claim on our lives than the church. If a community has a common work, then employment need not tear the community in different directions with a segment of life divorced from community.

In a community of work, attitudes of competitiveness, hostility, and pride can be dealt with in a healthy environment. It is especially valuable for a community that wishes to relate in a healing way to people who need a lot of love and care. Working together can be a real asset in ministry. Common work also provides a means of daily participation for all, especially visitors and the elderly. This is especially striking at the Hutterian Society of Brothers where everyone in some way can participate in the total life of the community.

The important question is to what extent we want to give ourselves to a life of love and sharing. Since God created us for love and community there is both the deep longing within all of us for this, and the promise that God will give it to us if we earnestly seek it.

Chapter 4

THE DISCERNING COMMUNITY

Beloved, do not believe every spirit, but test the spirits to see whether they are of God; for many false prophets have gone out into the world. 1 John 4:1.

Seeking God's Will as a Community

While people share in many ways within the institutional church, seldom does that sharing include seeking God's will together in relation to important decisions. We have failed to see decision making and discernment as one of the marks of the church. In fact, in the span of a year's time most churches never gather together once to make a decision on a question of deep spiritual importance. There are activities centered around worship, study, prayer, and action, but not discernment. We let everyone make his/her own decisions.

One of the reasons for the unfaithfulness of the church has been the inability to properly discern God's Spirit from the other spirits. How else could German and American Christians in World War II have each believed that God wanted them to kill the other? The times when Christians have been able to discern the will of God correctly have been sporadic at best.

We need a way of making decisions which is consistent with our understanding of the body of Christ, a way of hearing and obeying together. We are called to be a gathered people who together discover how to distinguish the voice of our Lord from all the other voices around us and how together to live that new quality of life Jesus calls us to. We are asked to test everything (1 Thess. 5:21), to weigh what others say (1 Cor. 14:29).

Since there are many voices and many spirits, it is important that we distinguish properly between the leading of Jesus and the way of the evil one who often comes disguised as "an angel of light." To discern means to separate, divide, distinguish, to sift through all the stimuli, demands, calls, leadings, longings, desires, enticements, needs, and influences, and determine which are of God and which are not. Discerning is proving (testing) "what is the will of God, what is good and acceptable and perfect" (Rom. 12:2).

While it is in community where the Spirit can act most freely and with the most power, it is also true that in collective behavior the spirits of evil have most power. Consider the energy and power released in a mob. A community must constantly be on guard against destructive forces operating and multiplying in the community. Anger and hostility, if not carefully confessed and dealt with, can soon envelope the whole community in an uncontrollable whirlwind. Negative forces may never be ignored but must always be discerned and dealt with.

The most important aspect of discernment is to recognize the presence of the living Christ. The promise of Jesus that "where two or three are gathered in my name, there am I in the midst of them" (Mt. 18:20) is to be understood primarily not as some warm feeling in the congregation, or even awe, but as a promise of guidance in decision making and discernment.

The significance of this promise of the presence of Christ for communal decision making becomes even clearer when we note that it is given in connection with the authority to "bind and loose." Jesus is recorded in the four Gospels as using the word church *(ekklesia)* only two times and both are in connection with "binding and loosing," which involves discernment. As will be noted in the next chapter, binding and loosing is an important aspect of the authority Jesus has given to the church.

The New Testament word for church, the *ekklesia,* implies discernment. Both the Greek word and the Aramaic word Jesus probably used mean a public gathering or assembly to do community business. It means a town meeting.[1] The *ekklesia* is God's people gathered to do God's business, to make decisions in the light of Jesus Christ. The New Testament takes this common word and gives it a new content, making Christ the center of the decision-making body.

Maybe the most important function of the Holy Spirit is to convict, convince, and to lead us into all truth. While the emphasis in Acts 1 and 2 is on the Spirit empowering the disciples to witness, the rest of Acts emphasizes the work of the Holy Spirit in decision making. The Holy Spirit works through group process.

Discernment is one of the most important functions of the Christian community. The church is not merely an assembly for worship, a place where we can get our batteries charged to go out and do our own thing. Even worship includes being judged by the Word, finding direction, and discerning the truth. Without this, worship becomes an empty formality devoid of a sense of the Holy Spirit who will lead us into all truth. Unless our deepest concerns are dealt with, a vital aspect of the faith has been lost. The main purpose of gathering as Christians is to seek God's will together and together to obey it.

The purpose of discussion in the Christian community is to discern God's will for His people. Too often discussion groups in the church discuss issues and share ideas, but never seek to conclude what God's will might be, at least not in any binding way. When we are led by the Spirit, the words of our brothers and sisters are binding on us. One of the tragedies of the church is that so little is said that is binding on anyone. Discussions which go around in circles but never come to any conclusions or actions have limited value. Sharing ideas is important, but it is never an end in itself.

The church should be that community which influences the daily decisions of our lives more than all the other forces in society put together. It is difficult for any of us to withstand the pressures of the world without the help of a body in making our decisions. Rather than let the world make our decisions for us, together we can seek God's will.

* * *

The discernment process is a key to Christian ethics. Distinguishing between right and wrong, good and bad, is the work of God moving through the whole body. Out of this process we can make valid ethical decisions. Ethical decisions are to be made in relation to the Christian community.

Christian faith is not a simple list of do's and don'ts, but involves a continual process of searching by a community which listens, hears, and obeys together. This process should not be confused with situational ethics. While each situation is always taken seriously, the norms do not come from the situation itself, but from the living Christ as discerned by the community. Neither is this principle-centered ethics, for we seek God's will in each situation more than simply applying principles to the situation. Neither is this the absolutist position of no standards, for the community *can* discern how God is leading His people. The key is for a community to be led by the living Lord.

Rather than decision making focusing on the color of the carpet for the sanctuary, the annual budget, or whether to hire another staff person, the focus should be on wrestling through the important concerns facing the body and each member. One reason why church council meetings are so poorly attended and boring is that they usually do not deal with the vital issues of life. The decision-making meetings of the church should be among the most profound worship experiences of the whole church, for it is here that we most deeply seek God's Word for us.

The discernment of the Christian community will be brought to bear on any issue that has importance for the community or for any of the members. It is important that discernment only deal with issues which are actually facing the community. Little time should be spent working through problems thought up by writers of church curriculum materials. We do not seek truth in the abstract, but truth in relation to concrete issues facing members of the community. Neither should a major amount of time be spent going around in circles discussing what the direction of the community should be. It is best to keep the focus on how God's Word relates to the concrete situations now before us. When we bring our important questions and decisions, Bible study and discussion come alive.

It is especially important that controversial issues be dealt with, for often they are the important questions. All too often there have been important issues which we will discuss almost anywhere but in the church. Could that be because we are concerned about these issues but would rather not bring our thinking on them under the lordship of Christ?

The concern that discussion of controversial issues would tear a church apart is a sad commentary on the state of the church, the level of commitment to each other, and the willingness to seek God's will earnestly in all things. When the community has faith and trust the most sensitive issues can be dealt with without fear of destroying either persons or the community. Actually few churches are so fragile that controversy would destroy them. Often this is a convenient excuse for not going through the pain of submitting our ideas to God's judgment through the community.

Controversial issues need to be wrestled with prayerfully by the community rather than pontificated upon from an unapproachable and unquestionable pulpit. What good does it do for a pastor to harangue the members and keep making them feel guilty about what most of them are doing? Better for the church together to wrestle with the problem and come to a decision on it. Then preaching on that issue will have power, for it will represent a position the community is in fact beginning to practice. If the church were a discerning community, pastors would not need to be torn constantly between feeling the need to preach boldly and to hold back. In a community where there is sharing and freedom to question each other, people can openly state what is on their hearts.

Sharing All Important Decisions

In Christian community we are given the privilege of making important decisions in our lives with the help of our brothers and sisters. We begin to have the freedom to share with others the decisions and burdens we have been dealing with individually. Discipleship is not a matter of individually picking and choosing according to personal taste, of doing "our own thing." It involves a body which seeks to come to a faithful response to the living Word of God in every decision of life.

Part of the process of becoming more sensitive to the leading of the Holy Spirit is to share our "leadings" with the community who can help us learn to distinguish between true leadings and our own subjective and often self-centered desires. The community can act as a mirror for us to look more clearly at our "leadings" and see them for what they are. This is done in the faith that the true Spirit of God is revealed in a group in which all submit their own insights to the discernment of the community which has a common covenant and earnestly seeks God's will.

In community our decisions are shared so that together we may come to a faithful decision. Questions like employment, any large expenditure of money, personal problems or leadings are tested and discerned by the community. No one should ever write books or articles without having them thoroughly criticized before publication. Profoundly serious decisions such as marriage cannot possibly be made without the approval and support of the community. It is unthinkable that such serious matters could be individual decisions. Decisions which have a deep effect on the body need to be made in relation to the body and must be subordinate to our commitment to God and the community. Neither job considerations nor any other pressure from the world may dictate the shape of our lives. In Christian community we think as a body rather than merely as individuals.

There are various examples of this in the New Testament. When questions were raised about Peter going against tradition by eating a meal with Cornelius, an uncircumcised man, Peter submitted this to the church which then recognized God's will in what Peter had done (Acts 11:1-18). The church did have the right to challenge Peter. It is also instructive to note that the call for Paul to go on a missionary journey did not come through Paul, but was given to the church during a time of prayer and fasting. The church then sent Paul and Barnabas (Acts 13:1-3).

As individuals we simply cannot be trusted to make decisions on our own. We have such a fantastic ability to rationalize and deceive ourselves. What sin has not at some time or other been rationalized and justified? All of us have the tendency to interpret God's will to suit our own purposes. All too often we consider ourselves the final authority in discerning God's will for ourselves. It is true that "the road to hell is paved with good intentions." Each of us needs help in overcoming the enslaving tendencies of our own egos. As Paul put it, "Wretched man that I am! Who will deliver me from this body of death?" (Rom. 7:24).

The answer to this question is the grace of God which comes to us through the community of believers. We can expect our brothers and sisters to be more honest with us than we can be with ourselves. Corporately in community we expect to be more faithful than as individuals. As R. W. Tucker puts it, "The community is wiser and holier than the sum of its parts."[2] The corporate witness of the community can be more faithful than the lives of her members, for even though a member falls, the witness of the community is maintained by speaking the needed word to that person. Each of us should expect the church to call us to a better life.

To share all important decisions with the community is not to give up personal responsibility or develop an unhealthy dependence on others. When we bring a concern to the community it is not to get their opinion or have them do our thinking for us, but for the community to help us to discern God's will, to help us come to clarity. We need to make many decisions along the way, but never on our own. The Christian community provides not easy answers, but the context for deep personal soul searching and a personal leap of faith.

Community demands a strong sense of personal responsibility. In community all are held responsible for their actions. Away with the irresponsibility of individualism. Responsibility is increased rather than decreased. Responsibility now is in relation to others rather than private. Community does not negate the importance of personal searching, prayer, and commitment, or God's speaking through an individual, but these are always tested by the community.

Maybe a greater temptation in community is to want to give support to whatever a person feels he/she should do. Feelings are always important and to be carefully considered, but feelings are only one part of decision making. Often our feelings are twisted because of egoism, fear, pride, or some other sin. At times our feelings need to be challenged. "Respect for others" may be a sign of unwillingness to deal with important issues, a cheap relativism that refuses to respect others enough to talk with them about important concerns we have. Tolerance may imply that we do not take each other or the truth seriously.

Again it must be said that the Christian way calls for complete surrender. To earnestly seek God's will rather than our own is to give up every selfish desire and be drawn into a new relation of truth and love. This means a total submission of individual will to the leading of the Holy Spirit. Sometimes we may personally desire one choice and yet recognize that a personally less desirable choice would be better for the whole community. Indeed, God may well call us to the opposite of our own desires.

In community we will always seek the common good before our own good. When this gets turned around the discernment process is thwarted and we can do little more than go in circles. "We" must be more important than "I." This also means seeking the good of the whole body of Christ and the whole world above the good of our own community.

The Responsibility of the Whole Community

Discernment is a process involving the whole community. God does not speak primarily through the preacher but through the congregation. We keep in touch with God partly by relating with others who are in touch with God. Theologizing is always a process of group discernment. It is more than an individual activity. The Bible is to be interpreted not individually on the basis of personal experience, but by a community which takes personal experience into account.

Although there are different gifts and responsibilities, every member has the right and responsibility to share in the process (see 1 Cor. 12—14). Decisions of both faith and

practice involve the whole community. When the apostles in
Jerusalem saw the need for helpers, they brought the need
before the body, and deacons were chosen by the body rather
than by the leaders (Acts 6:1-6).

Although they should always be free to share their thinking and their advice needs to be taken seriously, emotionally
unstable people should not be burdened with a lot of
responsibility for decision making or be given the power to
hold back any decision on which the rest of the community
has clarity. People having deep struggles in their lives will be
excused from much of the decision-making process. This is
something that can be decided in relation to those who have
pastoral responsibility with these people. Usually the person
having such struggles will want to be excused from this part
of the community life.

There is nothing wrong with delegating responsibility. In
fact, it is important that responsibility be delegated, for too
often everyone's concern is no one's concern. The whole community cannot deal with everything. What cannot be delegated, however, is the communal discernment process. But
delegated responsibility is carrying out the concerns of the
community, not the authority to rule. Administrative decisions will be made by leaders, but the important decisions regarding direction and policy need to involve the whole community. It is not a matter of not trusting leaders to make decisions, but a more fundamental concern about the nature of
the church as a community rather than as an organization.

The congregational process may not be delegated to the
bishop, administrators, or scholars. The proper setting for
discernment is not formal ecclesiastical councils or meetings
of theologians. While these groups grind out "profound"
statements, they are often weak in conviction, commitment,
and grass-roots support. Although there is a place for
scholarship and expert witness, the proper setting for discernment is not an elite group of experts, but communities in

which all are deeply committed to God and each other and pledged to live out together the conclusions they reach. Expert analysis may be one contribution, but no expert as an individual is able to interpret the Word. That must be done by a community which seeks to hear and obey.

We cannot accept the idea that religious or political decisions should be kept out of the hands of the common people. There is a bigotry among some professionals which sees ordinary people as not intelligent or perceptive enough to allow the body to seek the truth.

It has been said that any study committee should have at least one member who knows little about the subject under study. This will help keep the rest of the committee honest and in touch with reality. Professionals fear the chaos that might develop, if more people were involved in decision-making, but that is exactly what has happened with organizations run by professionals. We have confused knowledge and technical expertise with wisdom and the leading of the Holy Spirit. The experts are wrong too often to trust the future to them.

Some say that we should have enough trust in our leaders to let them make the decisions. The issue is not trust, but the nature of community and how the people of God are together to test the spirits and seek God's guidance. Sometimes the community will make the wrong decision, but it is important that even our mistakes be made together. Then no one can accuse or blame anything on anyone else.

The process is important not only in making the decision, but in implementing it as well. The more people are involved in the decision-making process, the more supportive they will be of the decisions. This is because they then understand the decision and feel involved in it. Because of their seeking, they are committed to following through on the decision. If people are involved, decisions can be authoritative without being authoritarian or legalistic.

The Nature of Authority

This brings us to the question of authority, something that has been assumed thus far. By what standards shall our decisions be made? The question is not whether we have any authority, but what kind of authority and whether it will be dictated by the church or by the world. A fallacy of our culture is the idea that when we are grown up, we do not have to listen to anybody. But it never works out that way. One of the main problems in life is how to come to terms with authority. The heart of this question is deciding who is number one. It is the question of who is god, to whom or what can we give loyalty and allegiance. Will it be only to self, to God, or to some other power?

To reject all authority is to make oneself the ultimate authority, an illegitimate authority if there ever was one. So often the breakdown of authority simply leads to the blind acceptance of new authorities, however tyrannical they may be. People are hungering for authority and unless the Christian community provides it, some authoritarian structure such as the state will provide it.

We need to distinguish between legitimate and illegitimate authority, between authority and authoritarianism. Authority exists as a servant of the community. Authoritarianism is coercive, arrogant, and self-assertive. True authority can only be related to the truth, for any combination of authority with falsehood is bound to be authoritarian. True authority can be defenseless, for it does not need to be defended. It is self-authenticating. The use of coercion is a sign that authority has broken down.

Authority in Christian community is different from that of the state or voluntary associations, for rather than being based on coercion, the common good, or the majority opinion, it is rooted in the truth which is discerned by the whole community. Authority becomes repressive and constraining when not related to God or based on sharing, intimacy, and corporate discernment. In Christian community authority is liberating, for as we know the truth, the truth makes us free.

Community will have authority not in any sense of control or power to manipulate, but an authority that comes only from God and the integrity of our life and witness. Our authority is not what we create, but the One who creates us and our community. No other authority is legitimate within the community.

Never may we submit to the will of the group or even seek the will of the group. We are asked to give up our ego, but never our own integrity. Conformity must always be to the Holy Spirit and never to the spirit of the group. We may never submit to another person in our thinking. Submission of one's will can only be to God as understood through the community. There is a vast difference between a group gathered under the Holy Spirit and a peer group. The sociologists have rightly analyzed the strength of peer group pressure, but that may never be the basis of conformity in a Christian community. It must always be resisted. The important thing is not what others in the community think, but what we together discern to be the will of God.

Authority is found in community, but community is not the authority. The final authority is Jesus the Christ who lives and rules among us and is best understood by a community who earnestly seeks to follow Him in all things. Our concern is never the will of the community, but the will of God. Our commitment is not to the community's interpretation of the truth, but always to truth. Since Christ is the authority, the demands must come from Him rather than us.

*   *   *

It is not true that the individual is autonomous and can accept no authority without being oppressed. Rejection of any authority beyond ourselves may be a sign of arrogance and closedness, an unwillingness to consider anything that challenges our ideas. We are not a law unto ourselves. There is something higher than ourselves. The individual human spirit is not the same as the Holy Spirit of God.

Truth is not what each person wants to make it. Neither is authority something to be appealed to only when it serves my self-interests (the way those with wealth and power do), but also when it contradicts what I want. Sincerity is not the criterion of truth, for we can be sincerely wrong. The values one person accepts are not automatically as good or valid as another's. This would be to destroy any understanding of truth. We do not need to be chained to our own subjectivity.

Too much stress on the individual conscience denies any authority other than self, leads to a denial of Christian community, and ultimately ends in spiritual anarchy. Leaving everything to individual conscience is not a sign of a higher spirituality. One of the greatest enemies of Christian faith and community is the spiritualizers with their denial of historical revelation, rejection of any communal discipline, and stress on individual conscience. Christian faith is also much different from a self-centered mysticism which denies any outer grace, authority, and community.

We should always be suspicious of any special revelations or "new knowledge of God" which is something more than a deeper insight into the old. These new revelations will usually be quite vague, unconnected to history, individualistic, and without external authority. Usually they are quite dogmatic and cannot be tested in any way. Upon closer examination they often turn out to be a narrow expression of some current mood or fad. The latest revelation is not necessarily the best and purest.

This is not to deny the possibility of private revelation, but if true it will be submitted to the community for testing and critical examination. All kinds of crazy things have been done by people who claimed to be led by the Spirit. Without objective tests, the "spirit" can be used to justify anything from foolishness to criminality. If you have a private set of truths which no one can test, you are probably out of touch with reality.

* * *

The term "spirit" is vague and can mean most anything. All too often the term "spirit" or even "spirit of Jesus" is used to deny what Jesus specifically taught. It is important therefore that we be specific and make it clear that the Holy Spirit is the presence of God with us and is the same Spirit who was in Jesus of Nazareth and is consistent with Him. This roots the Holy Spirit in historical reality instead of seeing the Holy Spirit as a competing source of revelation alongside of Jesus and the Bible. Thus when we say "Spirit" we mean not a Christlike spirit, but an objective power working in our midst, a Spirit inseparable from Jesus Christ. We mean Jesus who is our living Teacher and leads into truth.

But who is Jesus? Well, obviously we mean the Jesus described in the Bible, for other than from that source we know virtually nothing about Jesus. The Bible then is another source of authority for the Christian community. We cannot separate the Spirit and the written Word, for both are witnesses to the same truth. The inner and outer Word speak consistently. They are one Word. Truth is not divided. The witness of the Holy Spirit, Jesus, and the Bible are one consistent witness to the truth. The canon is not closed to the extent that the Spirit no longer speaks, but neither is it open to the extent that the Spirit can contradict the written Word.

The authority of the Bible can best be understood in relation to discernment, for its authority is best understood as it is studied and used for guidance by a community as she seeks to discern God's will as related to specific issues before the community. This is what Paul meant when he said it is for teaching, reproof, correction, and instruction.

Each reading of the Bible must be a fresh one, seeking to be guided anew by the Spirit. The Bible is not to be used as a drunk uses a lamppost, for support rather than light. We read the Bible to be judged by it. When we become complacent and ingrown, the biblical message has its potential to disrupt our complacency. It jars us loose from our little idolatries and sets us free.

A faithful Christian community is a community encountering each other and God around an *open* Bible. The discerning community is a studying community. Often a Bible study will not seem to have much importance or relevance at the time, but then several months later the effect of a particular study will be seen.

The Bible is not a "paper pope," an infallible authority standing alone, but always to be interpreted by a community which is guided by the Holy Spirit. All Scripture and our interpretations must be judged by the norm of Jesus the Christ. Anything that contradicts Jesus is not truth. The Old Testament is interpreted in light of the New Testament and Jesus.

*   *   *

Our authority is found in the unified witness of the living Christ, the historical Jesus, and the Bible as understood by a community. This authority is truly a liberating factor in community, a real guard against any dogmatism of either our own subjectivism or group consensus.

We cannot emphasize too strongly how important it is to have both the inner and outer Word. A narrow biblical literalism that denies the living presence does not lead to life. But neither does neglect of the written Word. We need to struggle not only against the creedal establishment, but also the spiritualizers who may be an even greater threat to the faith.

The separation of Spirit and Word has a long history, going back to the early church with the influence of gnosticism. Its influence is destructive for community, for it is bound to lead to individualism and a spirit which cannot be tested. Following "only the Spirit" can soon degenerate into following the spirit of the times, making us victims of the dominant mood of the present age. Those who emphasize the Spirit over the Word usually are much more products of the present age than they would ever admit. When discussing specific issues with them it soon becomes clear that they "feel" more comfortable with many of the norms of current culture than the judgment Scripture brings upon them. Many of these people are completely closed. They will hear no words of judgment and criticism.

Each of us is conformed to the spirit of the times more than we want to admit. Twenty years from now much that seems so right to us now may appear totally false.

When we consider the realities of concentration camps, torture, war, massive oppression, and blind rage, we begin to realize that we can no longer tolerate the separation between mind and heart, of one having reasons the other knows nothing of. The mind and heart need to inform and check each other. The temptation to go one way or the other is great, but must be resisted.

We need to be keenly aware of our own fallibility and thus take the necessary steps to protect ourselves from self-deception. Our life and experience must constantly be tested by the Bible. When the Bible contradicts our most sincere convictions, we had better pause. Let us not assume too lightly that we have the truth. How arrogant and narrow it would be to think that our own age is the standard by which to judge truth. We judge the present age and current philosophy in light of the Bible, not the Bible in light of the spirit of the present age.

*   *   *

Authority also includes the testimony of Christians in

other places and cultures. God may be speaking to us through them. Sharing with those close to us is never enough, for the circle of conversation must continue to widen out to a broader circle of people. Unless we limit the work of the Spirit to our own group we are compelled to discern what God is saying through other people and groups. Discernment leads us to relationship with other bodies, for we are so in need of the witness of others.

An important part of this dialogue with others is dialogue with the past. Where we see ourselves coming from and going toward is a part of the whole discernment process. Although tradition may not be seen as an independent authority, how God's people in the past understood God's voice can be instructive for us. There is a consistency in how God relates to His people. The witness of those who lived before us may never be dismissed. What is happening now is only a small part of a larger story. We need to keep the present in perspective. How we respond to the past helps determine where we go from here. We are in dialogue with the past for the sake of the present and future. Tradition is not finished, but a living movement of which we are part.

We have so much to learn from the past. Too often the rejection of old ways leads to an uncritical acceptance of the new and giving in to the spirit of the times. We ought to be aware that the "new" ideas we come up with are seldom new. The "new" thing we suggest often has been tried over and over throughout history and because it did not work it did not become tradition. Most new fads are repetitions of the mistakes of an earlier century. Those who readily accept the latest fads are the ones who most quickly become outdated.

We might take another look at neighborhood churches with people from many denominational backgrounds who have no common heritage. Often their faith is a culture religion of the worst sort. It is those groups who have deep roots in the past without being tied to the past, that can respond most freely to the present and not submit to it. They may not always be in harmony with the times, but they are not necessarily outdated.

While the Christian community is not perpetuated by tradition, neither can she live without tradition. There needs to be an identification with those communities in the past which were created by the same Spirit, from whom insight and strength can be drawn. Tradition can be deadening or invigorating depending on whether it is dead or living. Tradition can be a dead weight or a constant reminder of our radical past challenging us to new life.

A significant concern is with which tradition we identify ourselves, whether it is faithful to the gospel and whether it has the power to speak to our present situation. This book is suggesting that our choice should be that heritage which goes back to the ancient Hebrews, came to new expression in Jesus and the early church, and was continued by radical groups like the Franciscans, Waldenses, Anabaptists, Quakers, and other radicals who in every century tried to live out the vision of the early church in contrast to establishment religion.

The true church in all times attempts to live the primitive Christianity of the early church. Because the early church was such a clear witness to the incarnation, the witness of the early church has special significance for us and in a real way is a judge of the church in later centuries. Since the church is fallible and apostasy always a possibility, restoration is an ongoing concern.

We really cannot start over with no regard for the past. We are products of the past. Each new expression of faithfulness is part of the past. Restoration is not merely a return to some ideal past. It is not going back to zero, but a new attempt *now* to be faithful. Restoration is always a new interpretation, for our view of the past is always different from the self-view of those in the past. While we cannot return to the beginning or make a new start without reference to what has happened since then, in a real sense we can make a new start from where we are. We can start over. Although we cannot return to the first century or the sixteenth century, we can start in the twentieth century and begin living what it means to be faithful now. We are called to be the New Testament church now.

Rather than being a denial of history, a concern for restoration takes history seriously, for rather than just affirm the present, we judge the present by norms from the past. To take the New Testament and the apostolic witness seriously as a norm and to follow it is not to be ahistorical, but rather is an affirmation of history. Identifying ourselves with the early church gives us historical stance and roots our action in a larger history.

Restoration is not an imitation of the early church, but a serious concern for her vision and witness. A restoration group is not seeking to follow the early church, but to be led by the same Spirit as she was. It is important that we not see any one form as the only possible embodiment of that vision, but to reject anything that is a contradiction of that vision. Important also is the warning that a restorationist group not center on a few important ideas neglected by other groups and make them the basis of their existence instead of seeking to live out the whole gospel. Neither is it possible overnight to begin a new tradition, symbols, and communal lifestyle that have depth and roots. It takes a long time for these to grow and develop.

Unity

One of the most precious gifts we can experience in community is unity. Community implies a common-unity. The deeper our commitment to Jesus the more we are drawn together in unity. If we are being led by the Holy Spirit, we will be led together, not apart. God is not a god of confusion, but of unity and clarity. The Holy Spirit does not point in many directions at once or speak with conflicting voices.

The New Testament emphasizes the importance of this unity for the Christian community. There is much stress on one Spirit. Much of the material in Paul's letters concerns division and unity. Nearly all the references in the New Testament to the church being a body are related to the problem of disunity in the church. The very idea of being members one of another implies unity. Paul wrote to the Romans concerning their disunity (Rom. 14:1—15:13) and told them of a power that creates a covenant so deep that it overcomes all divisions, bringing even Jews and Gentiles into the same community (15:7-13). Paul laid it right on the line when he wrote, "Complete my joy by being of the same mind, having the same love, being in full accord and of one mind" (Phil. 2:2; also see Eph. 4:3-6, 13-16). In His high priestly prayer Jesus stressed the importance of unity when He prayed for His disciples, asking

> That they may be one even as we are one. I in them and thou in me, that they may become perfectly one, so that the world may know that thou hast sent me and hast loved them even as thou hast loved me. John 17:22, 23.

Jesus prayed that the same unity would exist among His followers as between Him and the Father. Wow! We are to be "perfectly one." This is based on God's love for us. Love seeks unity. Love and unity go together and become visible. Jesus also makes it clear in this passage that unity is related to our obeying God, just as Jesus obeyed God. Sin and disobedience destroy unity. There can be no true unity where God's will is not obeyed.

Unity can never be imposed or created by ourselves, but is a gift of God to us. This unity is the living presence of God with us. There is unity in an ice cube, but it is cold. There is unity in a cemetery, but that is death. We do not want the unity of the false prophets who call for tribal unity by rallying around the flag of nationalism and support for the nation state, or the unity of a cultural consensus. Our unity must not be racial, cultural, philosophical, or even theological. Concern for unity may never replace concern for truth. It is the power of the Holy Spirit which creates a unity beyond anything we could ever build, a unity that breaks through all our efforts and struggles and makes us one. Any other unity is only partial and incomplete. We can have true unity only as God unites us.

If a community is the body of Christ, then there will be visible unity among the members. When this unity is given, the presence of the Holy Spirit is known in power and clarity. Sins are forgiven, demons cast out, sickness healed, and lives turned around. When we are given unity, then the world can know what God can do among His people. The church is to be a sign of unity in a fragmented world, a sign of the coming unity of all humanity. Whether the world believes or not depends greatly on the unity that can be seen among Jesus' followers. The problem today is not that the gospel is unbelievable but that the church is unbelievable.

When there is a lack of unity and morale is low, then in prayer and brokenness of spirit we need to seek the mind of Christ. There needs to be a hunger for unity and a clearer understanding of God's will for us. When we are not in unity, then more than ever we long for and pray for unity and the power of the Spirit. Lack of unity only makes us desire it all the more. The desire for unity must be a deep, burning desire, an unquenchable longing.

In times of disunity, it is important to keep in sight the unity we do have and daily praise God for it. We also should be sure that we seek unity in our own hearts and desires, and not only in the community. As we pray we will remember the promise that the Spirit is given where people earnestly seek the Spirit, always keeping in mind Psalm 133:1, 2. "Behold, how good and pleasant it is when brothers dwell in unity! It is like the precious oil upon the head, running down upon the beard, upon the beard of Aaron."

In our longing for unity, it is not so much to seek people of like mind, but diverse people seeking one mind. In this prayer and search we need to remember that God is able to bring the most diverse group of people in the whole world into perfect unity. God could take the most divided and broken congregation and bring healing and unity if the people would allow it. At this point we have a deep crisis of faith in God. Many of us do not believe that God is able to bring us into unity and so we accept our alienation, thinking that this is normal.

It should be noted that unity does not mean uniformity. No two people are alike. We do not think or act alike. Individuality may never be denied. But there can be no diversity of commitment, vision, belief, or spirit. Diversity has to do with different gifts and functions within the body. The different parts of the body do not mean conflicting ideologies and commitments.

Many people question whether it is even desirable for the church to have unity or speak with any voice that has authority. Some argue that we should all just accept each other and be friends. Some argue that the church cannot and should not speak with one voice, that the church will speak with many voices. We are even asked to celebrate our diversity. But diversity is not good in itself. We are not asked to seek diversity. We are to seek unity. We are to have one Spirit, proclaim one gospel, serve one Lord. This call for diversity is actually an escape from real dialogue and the need to really listen to each other and take each other seriously. It may also mean a lack of seriousness about truth and the demands God puts upon us. In reality this philosophy is divisive. It points away from unity.

Some will argue against the importance of unity, feeling

that there needs to be tension and conflict within the community for there to be life and growth. However, this in no way negates the importance of seeking unity. There is always enough tension between what the community is and what God calls her to be to provide for plenty of growth and life for a long, long time. In addition, there is the diversity of experience, personality, and gifts. Add to that the tension that exists between a faithful community and the pagan world, and you will soon see that we do not need to seek or create tension so that we can grow. If we are faithful, tension will be there.

In reality, living in community involves a daily struggle, a continual process of dealing with conflict. Where there is no tension or struggle there is death. True peace never means an absence of conflict but a way of dealing with conflict, a reconciliation of conflict. It is precisely in our conflict and disagreement that we daily seek unity. That is where the real tension, pain, growth, and life should be found. The more stable a relationship is and the more unity we have the more able we are to deal openly and freely with the conflicts and tensions that are with us.

*   *   *

In making decisions in community it is essential that the majority not rule through voting, but that we study, pray, and wrestle with each other until we come to unity. All decisions in community must be unanimous. We seek the will of God for the whole community and do not act until that is discerned by every member, until all hear the same voice. Taking votes which overrule minorities has no place in Christian community.

Apparently the early church made decisions by unanimity. Repeatedly the Book of Acts tells us that they were of one heart and mind, and various decisions are reported as having been unanimous (Acts 6:5; 15:22, 28). Edward Schweitzer argues that in the New Testament church there were no majority decisions. They sought together to understand God's will.[3] This has been true of many believers' churches since then, including for a time the Mennonites and the Brethren. It is the common practice of many Christian communities.

Sometimes we too quickly accept the idea that "there are two sides to every question" and so expect everyone to be either for or against. We then respond in this way, lining people up on sides instead of listening to them. Voting may force people to make a choice they should not need to make.

The decision-making process is vital to any community and is the point where many break down. Many communities have learned the importance of making decisions by consensus or unanimity. This can take several forms. One is that a decision is made at the point where there is no objection. Thus after full discussion, a few who still disagree but feel their concerns have been heard may withdraw their objections in order not to hold back the rest. This is the method still used by the Quakers.

A more radical form is to not make any decision unless there is wholehearted agreement on the part of all. This is the practice of many Christian communities like the Hutterian Society of Brothers. This approach reflects a deep uneasiness with moving ahead when some are not in full agreement, recognizing that something is wrong. When some lack enthusiasm, the Spirit may be saying something to the community. Some communities operate by the less radical consensus on issues that are not important and by complete unanimity on all important decisions.

Decision making in Christian community has little relation to democracy, a process of competing interest groups seeking either victory or compromise. Discernment is not each one having some power in the group and some say in running things, but rather all being sensitive and open to what God is saying and all obeying that. It involves coming to a "sense of the meeting." This is so often forgotten in the political world where decisions are based on majority rule. Freedom requires an ongoing dialogue among those who disagree. In fact, a test of how well a democracy is functioning is how well the minorities are being treated.

The Christian community can never be guided by majority rule, what most people want, but by the Holy Spirit and what is right. The hierarchical and authoritarian method of discernment has not done very well, but the more democratic churches have not done much better. Often it is the minority which will see the truth most clearly. We are not self-governed, but ruled by the Spirit and the Word. The voice of the people is not as important as the voice of God. We are not a democracy in that we merely share our opinions and best insights, or even choose the best insights. There is a big difference between making prudent and rational decisions with religious influence and discerning God's will in making our decisions.

Compromise must also be rejected, for we seek not the lowest common denominator, but the right decision. All too often compromise is a convenient way of not taking the other person or the issue seriously. Unity cannot be the result of compromise, for this implies no real unity but a disunity which will be the basis for continuing disagreement in other areas. Rather than compromise, as all opinions are taken seriously and out of the process of sharing, searching, struggling, and praying together a new answer can be given which is not only much different than conceived of before the discussion, but which is agreeable to all. How often in thinking through a decision we begin with a well-thought-out opinion, but because of the discerning together, we come to a totally different conclusion, realizing how far off our original opinion had been. By one person speaking the truth, the whole conversation may change directions. It is truly a miracle how God can work among those who seek Him.

A group should never be in a hurry to decide anything. Decisions made in haste are often not wise. What is desired is not consensus which comes through submitting to pressure, but a deep unity freely accepted by all. Even if there is no objection, but some are not wholeheartedly in agreement, at the very least the community should be sensitive to why all are not excited about the decision. This may be a sign that the decision is wrong.

Sometimes it may take years to reach unity, but then this decision is of so much more value than resolutions which are passed but never supported. The Quaker decision to reject slavery in the United States is a good example, a decision which took more than a century to reach. But when they did come to unity on this in 1776, there was a power there that tremendously influenced the abolition of slavery for the whole United States in the next century. They certainly could have voted through a resolution on slavery much earlier, but they still would not have had unity and their witness would have been weakened.

Some may object and see this way leading a group to an intolerable conservatism, that things would move and change so slowly that stagnation would result. They see it meaning a guaranteed victory every time for the conservatives who support the status quo. How can anything ever be changed if everyone must agree? The witness of groups like the Quakers who still operate by consensus points in the opposite direction. There is nothing radical in following the majority opinion, for the majority is usually more conservative than the minority. Only a continual search for truth is radical. When people are open to each other and the Holy Spirit, change can and will come much more easily.

In many groups some people are defensive and conservative because they do not feel accepted or listened to. To maintain their integrity and commitments, they feel the need to be defensive and stubborn. This can be broken down by love and trust and making sure everyone is heard. One reason why many have a fear of unanimity being too slow and conservative is that their experience has been in groups where people are not open to each other. If they would experience what God can do in a community of love and trust, they could be given a new understanding of how God wants to work among His people.

Some argue that this is impractical. But Quakers have been just as able to develop programs and operate institutions such as schools as anyone else. In fact, they have done much better than most. In the short run it may be quicker to have the majority decide, but in the long run this is the slow way when one considers all the resentments, hurt feelings, mistrust, lack of commitment, and policing that are connected with majority rule. How much more God can do with those who are in unity.

The Decision-Making Process

The process of coming to unity assumes a prior common commitment both to truth and to each other. Both of these are essential throughout the whole process. Without either one the process soon breaks down. Unless all are believers, there already is a deep disunity and insufficient basis for coming to a deeper unity. Unless we are totally committed to seeking only God's will in all decisions, the community will repeatedly go in circles around our own petty concerns. If we have divided loyalties, how can we all listen clearly to the same Spirit? Inability to clearly discern God's will often results from a duplicity of commitments rather than a simple commitment to do only God's will, or from mixing major with minor concerns.

It is essential that we not have any commitments, desires, or fears which would prevent us from being open to God's will, but that we be totally open to what God wants to say to us. This points to the importance of being in a right spirit before we may rightly participate in any meeting. Being in a spirit of rebelliousness, stubbornness, pride, or hate can have no place in seeking God's will, for whenever we are not in a right spirit, we lose our ability to think and perceive as clearly as we should.

Again and again in the process of discernment we are confronted with our commitment to Jesus and have to decide whether or not that commitment is total, whether self will be crucified. One of the most serious sins one can commit in the church or Christian community is to go to a decision-making meeting with one's mind made up, with the determination to push through one's own idea or program. That is a sign of being closed to the Holy Spirit and that is serious. We should be more eager to find the Lord's will than to express our own. Whenever we have an important decision to make, God has a will for us and our task is to find that will, that answer which is what God wants rather than what we want. That means giving up our will in order to seek God's will.

Another essential ingredient for the process to be valid is a readiness to act on what God wants. For us to be able to hear God, we must be prepared to do whatever God tells us to do.

Usually the problem is not with God's speaking to us, but with our listening and hearing. This points to the importance of patient waiting, silent listening, and prayerful seeking. Discernment needs to be done in prayer, searching, and opening ourselves to what God wants to give to us. This includes, of course, faith that God will guide us. Prayer is important for us, both as a whole community and as individuals. We cannot discern God's voice either communally or individually if we are not in tune with the Spirit. We must be sensitive to the movement of the Spirit in our souls. Prayer is essential in helping us to be open. Sometimes our prayer will include fasting, an important but largely neglected aspect of prayer.

Usually what we receive in prayer is light and clarity of sight rather than specific answers. Through prayer we are given the clarity to better see things as they are, to better understand our own motivations. Any specific answers received in prayer must be carefully tested.

Meetings for discernment can be among the most profound worship experiences of the Christian community, for here we gather to listen to what God has to say to us. Thus all decision-making meetings are meetings for worship, and any meeting for worship can become a decision-making meeting. Whenever God speaks to us, we must respond.

*   *   *

There is another part to this, for we will never be able to hear the voice of God if we cannot listen and be sensitive to our brothers and sisters. Part of the process of hearing God's Word is hearing what our brothers and sisters are saying. Dialogue has great theological significance, for it is an essential aspect of the search for truth. The possibility that God may be speaking through the other person makes that person's words precious and to be taken seriously by everyone. The voice and concern of each person is taken seriously, for what any person says may be the Word of God for that occasion.

True dialogue can take place only in a relationship of trust in which others are not seen as a threat and in which we feel no need to be defensive. Dialogue implies relationship in which everything that is said is accepted as sincere and properly motivated until there is clear evidence to the contrary. Trust and unity go together. If there are unresolved tensions, how can people openly seek together? Negative feelings will get mixed up with the issues. This must be straightened out before the people involved are ready to discern together. There needs to be a spirit of trust and unity for us to genuinely seek God's will together. Before we go to any meetings we need to ask ourselves if we can go in that spirit.

In many Christian communities it is understood that one must be in right relationship with everyone, including God, before coming to important community meetings. In New Covenant Fellowship at various times people have left the room or asked someone to go with them rather than continue in the meeting with any alienation. This process may seem to take a lot of time, but we have found that it actually saves time, for when relationships and feelings are cleared, then we can be most open to God's leading. By the way, Jesus commanded this very approach in Matthew 5:23, 24.

Discernment is best done by a people who share a broad spectrum of their lives together and know each other well and are thus able to relate the gospel to the needs and questions that arise out of seeking to live a Christian life together. This means more than a group of people who spend an hour together on Sunday morning. A group of people dressed to give each other the best possible impression is hardly the context for discernment.

Another factor in decision-making is to gather and carefully analyze all the available evidence that relates to the issue. Discussion is not a pooling of ignorance, but involves considering every angle and fact which is part of the context. As Christians, we will not fear thorough analysis, but neither will we take analysis and facts too seriously. They are, after all, only one aspect of the whole process.

How we feel is also significant and may never be ignored. Intuition, inner sense, subjective feeling, and human emotions are ever with us and God can speak to us through them. We must never confuse the Spirit with how we feel, but carefully test all our feelings. It is especially important to recognize how our feelings can become intertwined with the "afterglow" of an experience with God in prayer. As we grow in Christian maturity, our lives are shaped and bent toward

God. Our lives and inner feelings can become more and more integrated and harmonious with the call of God.

*   *   *

Discernment is a process of dialogue and therefore much different from debating. In dialogue the objective is not to win an argument, but to find the truth together. In this process eloquence and persuasive speaking are of little value. All must search deeper than persuasive arguments. We must even be careful in appealing to outside authorities, including the Bible, for these appeals can be a tool to avoid dealing with the other persons' insights and the real issues. Not that these are unimportant, but bringing in an outside authority or expert can depersonalize the issue and can make it more difficult to hear the Holy Spirit. Neither may the issue or other person be avoided through administrative or parliamentary maneuvers.

Disagreements should not be seen as two sides competing with each other, but rather as open, honest sharing done in a spirit of seeking. Competition has no place in community. When dialogue becomes a struggle between groups, then it is time to stop. Sometimes it is helpful to have a period of silence and prayer, or a time of reflection before the issue is discussed at a later meeting, or maybe to change the subject and begin to deal with the real problem that is dividing the two sides. Sometimes a point is reached where more discussion will be of little value. All points of view have been expressed and further discussion would be repetitious and could even harden positions. At that point the discussion should be stopped. A committee representing various views might be appointed to study the matter further or plan for more discussion later.

In working through a particularly difficult decision, sometimes it may be helpful to separate the discussion of the positive aspects from the negative by dealing with them at dif-

ferent times. This can be an aid in listening to all sides, since
one will not feel as much need to form counterarguments and
may help move the discussion from debate to dialogue and
allow all the issues to be focused more clearly.

Not only is it important to give up my selfish will and to
listen to the brothers and sisters, but it is equally important
that anything that I think or feel be expressed to the community. Everyone must speak what he/she thinks, even if it is
contrary to what everyone else is thinking. It may be that the
one person is right. Expressions of disagreements are to be
welcomed, for that may be God wanting to show us another
alternative or saving us from a serious mistake. Great care
should always be taken to be sure the prophetic voice is
heard. There must be a total rejection of the attitude so
common in schools, business, and government that one
should not rock the boat, that to speak up is disrespectful,
that one should fit into the way things are. We might note
here that the so-called "low churches" often are more authoritarian than the "high churches." All too often the style
of pastors and Sunday school teachers has been monologue,
with a deep fear of dialogue.

We need to be free to disagree with any other member,
including a person who has been given a position of
leadership. Frankness and complete honesty are imperative.
There is no place for flattery, pretense, or dishonesty. Any
disagreement or uneasiness must be expressed. One must not
hold back what may be the voice of the Spirit. Say what is on
your heart and let the community test whether it is of God.
Expression of disagreements after the meeting is not helpful,
unless it is part of the decision-making process. Sometimes,
though, ideas can be better clarified in a private conversation
than with the whole community.

One should not necessarily speak the first thing or even
everything that comes to one's mind. Before we speak we
must weigh and test our thoughts. This means neither blurt-

ing out the first thing that comes to our minds nor holding back what we need to share. What we say should take into consideration what has been said before and be an evidence of dialogue rather than monologue. In fact, the more we listen, often the less words we will need to speak. We especially need to listen to discern who has been given the most light on any particular issue.

Disagreements need to be voiced and should be expressed as clearly as possible, but should also be expressed with a humble attitude, with a readiness to be shown that one is wrong. The critic is always to be accountable for what is said. We need to hear Paul's advice: "Do nothing from selfishness or conceit, but in humility count others better than yourselves" (Phil. 2:3). Rather than violently objecting, one should state the concern in a humble and tentative way. Too forceful expressions of disagreement may be signs of a lack of trust. When we know the community will seriously consider anything we say, we can say it in a quite humble and tentative way. If we feel threatened or angry, we would do well to consider why. We would do well to remember that anger and defensiveness are signs that we are trying to justify ourselves, rather than being justified by God's grace.

When we oppose what the group wants, it is good to have a reason for our opposition and maybe even a better suggestion. Never should we oppose for the sake of opposition. However, sometimes we may not be able to give a good reason, but simply have an uneasy feeling about what is being discussed. This must be respected by all and the community will seek to understand more about why this uneasiness exists.

Sometimes in working toward a decision, people will say one thing with their words and the opposite with the tone of their voices. This is a sign of something deeper. With much sensitivity the community needs to help these people work through their ambivalent feelings or help them understand the contradiction that may not be conscious. Sharing decisions with the community involves counseling and helping people work through their own feelings to achieve clarity concerning God's will.

Prolonged minority resistance to a certain suggestion must be taken seriously. It may mean that the issue has not been adequately discussed, that the majority has been pushy in its concerns, or that God is speaking through the minority. It may be a symptom of a deeper disunity that needs to be dealt with. Unanimity is easy in a group that has unity, but if the unity is not there, then there is always a struggle to reach a decision. Sometimes someone needs to point out what is holding people back from unity.

We do need to ask whether any disagreement we have is important or whether it is a matter of taste or cultural difference. No serious disagreements should exist on matters of taste. These can soon be resolved by overlooking the matter or maybe even giving up one's own preference for the sake of the community. This may not be done on important matters, however. Sometimes cultural differences may point to more fundamental differences which may not be overlooked.

Neither may diversity ever be allowed to stand in the way of the Holy Spirit bringing us together. All must be surrendered. When we say that certain things are unimportant, we need to examine ourselves carefully and test whether this is just an excuse for being unwilling to let go of something unimportant that in fact is very important to us and we do not want to give up.

Forgiveness is an important part of this process. The ability to leave some concerns to individual taste is rooted in a loving and reconciling relation to others. The more forgiving we are toward others the less their peculiarities will bother us. We are much more critical of others when we have not forgiven them. In fact, it is difficult to agree on anything with a person whom we have not forgiven.

If a person appears stubborn or defensive this may be a sign of some deeper conflict in that person's life which first must be dealt with. In this case people should visit the person and talk frankly about what they see. Through listening to the person they may find that the reason is that there are still hostile feelings about something that happened in the past, maybe even relating to a decision which was made ten years earlier in which his/her views were not taken seriously. Or it may be some other problem that needs to be confessed and resolved so that there can be unity and all can respond freely to God's will.

There is always a real danger of stifling dissent or pressuring people to conform. This can be so subtle at times. Actually even the most anarchistic group cannot completely avoid group pressure. What others think and say does influence us. The question is whether these pressures are properly recognized and controlled. We especially need to be sensitive to the subtle pressures that affect different people in various ways.

The process of consensus actually gives everyone the power of veto and is a guard against forced conformity, although one should never think of having the *right* of veto. Actually giving each member this power itself can be a way of discouraging rather than encouraging disagreement and dissent. A lot of pressure can be felt by the lone dissenter if his/her dissent is holding back the whole community, but this can also be a way of ensuring that each person will be heard and no one run over.

It is important that every community be especially aware of this danger and be careful not to pressure anyone into conformity. People need to be reminded constantly not to agree unless they really do and never to try to convince themselves that they agree when they do not, nor to feel guilty about disagreeing. It is essential that one always remain true to what is in one's heart, unless what is in the heart is not of God.

When there is disagreement care must be taken to determine whether there is a substantial disagreement or merely a misunderstanding. When there is clear disagreement, deep patience and understanding are needed and faith that God can work His will through that discussion. Sometimes hostility and negativism will need to be confessed. But grace can be given, even and especially then, to come closer together. The more difficult a decision is, the closer together the community can be drawn.

Leadership is a vital part of this process. Leadership does not mean convincing or imposing one's will on others, but helping the community come to unity and clarity. One kind of leadership is to articulate a concern clearly. Another kind of leadership is for someone to be sensitive both to all the members and to the leading of the Holy Spirit so that after many opinions have been expressed, he/she can suggest a solution which takes into consideration what has been said and meets the approval of all. When there is unity someone will put into words what expresses that unity and captures what is being felt by the whole community. This task includes summarizing, but it is much more than this. It is also to sense what the Holy Spirit is saying to the whole community and to articulate it.

*   *   *

A decision has been reached at the point where a deep peace and easiness exists within the whole community regarding a particular decision, when there is a "sense of the meeting." It occurs when all want to say "amen," when there is a sense of deep gratitude to God. It is achieved when everyone can say, "It has seemed good to the Holy Spirit and to us" (Acts 15:28). The quiet and contentment that is experienced comes from knowing that we have correctly heard God's call and responded faithfully. This peace is not to be understood passively, for it will include a clear call to get on with the deci-

sion and live it. It may even include great excitement and
eagerness to get started.

Although this process is not perfect and the community
will often err in her understanding, what better way is there
for testing and discerning God's Word? When a unanimous
decision has been prayerfully tested with the authority of
Scripture and the presence of the living Christ, seriously taking into account subjective feelings, factual evidence, and the
testimony of other Christians and tradition, and the result is a
deep sense of peace, love, joy, and humility, we can trust that
we have discerned God's will.

* * *

We now come to a crucial point, for although we believe
we have discerned God's will, we must be aware that this decision is not absolute and always is open to new light and
further discernment. Never can we say that we have the final
light and that what we have seen never can be questioned. We
are always to be open to new light and truth, even if that
means a contradiction of what we have believed in the past.
Even after unanimity has been reached, anyone must feel free
to question that unity with no fear of rejection.

The Christian community is always a human community
and so participates in all the weaknesses and failures that implies. We need to be aware of how our discernment is always
colored by our social class, culture, history, and the makeup
of our community. No group can claim to have the whole
truth, no matter how faithful they may be. Although communal discernment is the best way we have for knowing the
truth, it is not perfect.

Because the believers' church tradition has recognized
this and because they saw the necessity for always being open
to new light, they have rejected the creedalism of the establishment church. Creeds tend to crystallize the faith into a
hardened system and discourage continued seeking under the

Spirit and the Word. Never may we put ideas into words and claim that to be *the truth*. Our only creed can be the New Testament.

Through wrestling with real problems, the community arrives at decisions and develops a group of testimonies, positions they have come to together which stand as a witness to the larger society. Testimonies are not rules we devise, but expressions of what we together have discerned to be true and what we are actually living. It is vitally important that these testimonies be the result of the discernment of the whole community and that they are lived, rather than being bold statements made by church leaders which do not represent any constituency. Testimonies are not statements about the perfection of the church, but what the church is earnestly seeking to live.

These testimonies need constantly to be tested and reexamined. Each time they are questioned, the community comes to a new decision either by changing or reconfirming her stand. Never may we use our interpretations and creeds to close ourselves to the Holy Spirit or as an excuse for rigidity, division, and bloodshed.

Not only are we open to new light, but we live in the expectation that it will come. We live with a continual sense of expectancy that the Holy Spirit will give us new truth out of the Word. The Holy Spirit does not create finalized dogmas or structures among us, for history is not yet complete. There is still more God wants to do among us. Since reality is not static, we expect our views to change. We do not expect, however, that anything new will be given that will contradict the final norm of Jesus Christ.

*   *   *

But what if the community unanimously says one thing and I still deeply feel and believe the opposite? I must always remain true to what is in my heart. Since there is always the possibility that the whole community may be wrong and one person right we have to leave open the possibility of practicing "holy obedience" in community, of doing the opposite of what the community discerns to be right. Never may we say, "My community right or wrong." Sometimes a person must call the whole community to repentance.

To go against the word of the community is extremely serious, however, and never should be done without first thoroughly working it through with the community, really hearing the community out with deep soul searching, prayer, and study. Let us pray that we will never need to make this decision, but that we can be part of a community that listens to the voice of the Holy Spirit and discerns together what is good and right. That is a wonderful gift.

Chapter 5

THE DISCIPLING COMMUNITY

Love is patient and kind.
—Paul in 1 Corinthians 13:4.

The Importance of Discipline

Any discussion of community soon leads to the question of how to relate to a person who falls from the faith. What is to be done about broken relationships?

Two of the important texts for this are Matthew 5:23, 24 and 18:15-18, NEB:

> If, when you are bringing your gift to the altar, you suddenly remember that your brother has a grievance against you, leave your gift where it is before the altar. First go and make your peace with your brother, and only then come back and offer your gift.

> If your brother commits a sin, go and take the matter up with him, strictly between yourselves, and if he listens to you, you have won your brother over. If he will not listen, take one or two others with you, so that all facts may be duly established on the evidence of two or three witnesses. If he refuses to listen to them, report the matter to the congregation; and if he will not listen even to the congregation, you must then treat him as you would a pagan or a tax-gatherer. I tell you this: whatever you forbid on earth shall be forbidden in heaven, and whatever you allow on earth shall be allowed in heaven.

These words of Jesus are vital for the life of the church or for any community. There cannot be a healthy, spiritually alive group that in some form or other does not practice these teachings. The work of the Holy Spirit is severely hindered if relationships are not straightened out in the church. All important revivals in the church through the years has involved restoring broken relationships. The Wesleyan revival is a good example of how concern for each other, including discipline, led to deep renewal. The weekly "class meeting" was an important part of the Methodist movement.

Jesus understood us well when He said we must first straighten out things with our brothers and sisters before we come to the altar. Hating another person makes it impossible to love God (1 Jn. 4:20). We cannot pray with people if we are not in right relation to them. The process of working through our problems may well include prayer, but that prayer is for healing and unity. It does not assume it. Prayer is empty in any group where relationships are not in order.

If we have negative feelings toward others, we should go to them and talk to them directly rather than talking behind their backs. If we hold back resentments and negative thoughts, even though we may forget them, they eventually come out in relation to something else, and often in destructive ways. Hostility and broken relationships must be worked through before we can continue as a full part of the community. True community cannot exist without working through broken relationships. If we see something wrong in someone else, but do not confront them, we will find ourselves backing off from them. There then can be no authentic relation with them. A relationship will not last if we are not honest with each other. Any group is crippled in which there is a lack of openness or anyone holds a grievance toward anyone else.

Although the main concern of discipline is with the people involved, the unity and witness of the church are also important. One of Paul's concerns in discipline was the effect brokenness would have on the fellowship. The actions of one person affect the whole body. A bit of leaven soon affects the whole loaf (1 Cor. 5:6 ff.). In the writings traditionally attributed to Paul, in five of the eight situations calling for discipline, Paul was concerned with the life of the church. We are not solitary individuals, but share together a moral responsibility for each other, for whatever affects one affects all.

Jesus said that if our brother or sister sins, we are to go to that person. The concern here is more than resolving differences or reconciling broken relationships. The concern is also with sin, for sin is always serious and cannot be ignored. While many translations of Matthew 18:15 include the words "against you," many of the most reliable ancient manuscripts do not include these words. Either way, similar passages in Luke 17:3, Galatians 6:1, and James 5:19, 20 do not include this qualification. We are to go to the other person, whatever the sin. We are not to go primarily out of concern for our own feelings and dignity, but out of concern for the other person. The main intent in all these texts is to deal with my brother's or sister's need. We are not to wait until we are offended before we go to the other person.

The basis for discipline is not a vision of a pure and perfect church, but rather a recognition that the church is not perfect. The issue is not perfection, but how we deal with imperfection. A perfect church would have no need for discipline. Rather, the purpose is to acknowledge the existence of sin in the church and to deal directly with it instead of ignoring it or pretending it is not there. Sin and broken relationships will not simply go away by themselves if we ignore them. The church needs always to be vigilant against all the possibilities of evil invading the community. We need to accept that the church is not perfect and act accordingly.

Little needs to be said to document the loss of discipline

in the church. The breakdown of community and discipline has been a common problem for too many groups. A Methodist statement would typify most groups:

> In the early days the Methodist was required quarterly to prove his faith and loyalty, else he was dropped. Today the Methodist is likely to find his name still enrolled, despite nonattendance, indifference, nonresidence, iniquitous living, or even death.[1]

Church discipline has often been misunderstood and misused. Much of this is because often the motive for discipline moved from concern for the person to something else. Often the chief concern was for standards or rules that were violated. The identity and standards of the church became more important than the person.

Sometimes the concern is more with the offense than the offender. Bigger offenses call for more concern than smaller offenses. The result usually is that the church deals only with "big sins" such as sexual immorality and stealing, or offenses such as dancing or card playing which can easily be dealt with, while ignoring sins such as pride, racism, greed, or gossip which are more difficult to handle. The sins of the weak and intemperate are overemphasized while the sins of the strong and proud are ignored.

At other times the concern shifts from reconciliation to punishment. This may be based on a desire to punish the guilty or at least humiliate them publicly. Often discipline has been based on hostility and a desire for vengeance, and sometimes even as a means of scapegoating.

The loss of discipline in the community of faith has been tragic both because individuals are not loved and forgiven as they should be and because it contributes to the loss of the church's sense of direction and mission. Intolerable situations are accepted, conflicts and factions go unreconciled. The result is that the church has little authority or power to witness to the world. Not only is the church unable to act because of lack of any common agreement, but more important, nothing about the Christian message is considered binding. Relativism and pluralism become the only norms of the church and sometimes these norms are very strict, so strict that people do not feel free to challenge the principles of relativism.

Rather than being legalistic, the problem for most of us is ignoring people with problems and struggles. We draw back from those in need and tell them to fend for themselves as best they can. We can hardly justify this by calling it love. The church with no discipline is no less cruel and unloving than the church with a harsh and legalistic discipline.

Churches often do not have a way to deal with problems in the church. When things get too far out of hand, church members feel they have to do something. They then act out of desperation, and their actions are often extremely clumsy and insensitive. Usually no process is involved, for they know no process to use. The ax simply falls and that is that.

Another alternative exists, however. The church can be a community of people who are both deeply committed to following Jesus and deeply committed to each other. In this context a new moral authority can emerge, based not on legalism, but one which grows out of a mutual concern and love for each other and the gospel. It is in this context that discipline makes most sense.

Although it is often forgotten, we still have heresy trials. The problem with them is that they are now too informal. When one goes against the prevailing values in regard to racism or militarism, for example, the person is often censured and ostracized. Many pastors know all about such "heresy trials." The problem is that the accusers and judges seldom come out in the open or are cross-examined, and the issues are not subject to the test of Scripture or prayer. The result is neither purification of the church or restoration of sinners, but a further accommodation to the world.

A common reason for dismissing the need for discipline is an unbiblical view of human nature. If we see people as basically good, the need for forgiveness, reconciliation, and guidance is needed only in exceptional cases as a last resort— and then only after the situation has become intolerable. First we hope the problem will go away by itself. We hope that discipline will seldom be needed and that we will never need it ourselves.

The demonic results of this view should be obvious. Since we consider the need for confession and discipline a weakness and look down on those who need it, we all try to make as good an impression as possible and hide our own weaknesses. With this view how can our relationships be anything but phoney? We all need help and the sooner we admit it the better off all of us will be.

One of the biggest shocks in community and a deterrent to further growth in community is learning how much sin is in the heart of each of us. When we begin to be honest with each other and put away all the masks and pretenses, we realize how much all of us are in need of divine cleansing. Rather than a source of discouragement to us, this realization should push us on to a deeper faith and more reliance upon God to sustain us.

Another common argument against church discipline is that we should not judge (Mt. 7:1-5). But closer examination of this text shows that Jesus meant that we should not judge with hypocrisy. Jesus didn't say never to make judgments, but rather, as Clarence Jordan puts it, "Don't act as a judge in order to escape being judged."[2] Any judgment we make will fall upon ourselves as well as others. In other words we may not set ourselves above others or make our own judgment, but use God's judgment which falls especially on us (Rom. 2:1-6). Jesus said to take the log out of our own eye first so that we can see more clearly to take the speck out of the neighbor's eye. Why not take the speck out of our neighbor's eye? That is the loving thing to do. We need to see clearly to do it, however. And we had better be very, very sure that it is not our own problems that we are projecting onto the other person. First examine yourself.

The point is not that we do not discern, but that there not be any self-righteousness in our judgments. We are to judge between right and wrong. Jesus asks us to know the difference between sheep and wolves dressed as sheep, but we may never put people in boxes or categories or consider them hopeless. Paul tells us not to judge those outside the church, but that we should judge those inside the church (1 Cor. 5:12, 13). The time is even coming when we will judge angels (1 Cor. 6:3). We are to pass judgment, but in humility and awareness of our own sinfulness. Jesus does not call for an indiscriminate acceptance of people where they are. We are to know swine when we see them and not throw pearls to them (Mt. 7:6).

It is true that it is easier to point out the sins of others than our own. That is why I need my brothers and sisters to come to me. I can rationalize my sin, but they will not let me. The point is not that I should only worry about my own sin, but that I need help in handling my own sins.

A related common objection to church discipline refers to the parables of the wheat and the tares (Mt. 13:24-30, 36-43) and the dragnet (Mt. 13:47-50). The classical interpretation of these parables is that they apply to the church and that until the end of the age, both righteous and unrighteous will together form the church. This would seem to contradict all the New Testament teachings on the importance of church discipline.

A brief examination of these parables will show, however, that they apply not to relationships in the church, but to the world. Verse 38 clearly states "the field is the world." There is no hint that saints and sinners are indistinguishable. Rather the assumption is that they are. Tares or

darnel are psuedo wheat whose differences from wheat become more obvious as they both mature. The point is that the
church should not use violence or coercion to root evil out of
the world, but rather call together a righteous community
that already is gathering the harvest of the faithful. "Lift up
your eyes, and see how the fields are already white for
harvest" (Jn. 4:35). We are called to reap the harvest that is
now ripe. The way to separate the wheat from the tares is
through proclamation of the gospel and the voluntary gathering together of those who hear the Word and obey it. There is
already a separation, but the work of the church is not to root
out evil people in the world. This in no way contradicts
church discipline. Rather, the point is that the church may
not impose her discipline on the world.

Although we are not basing our understanding of church
discipline on the concept of the purity of the church, there are
enough references in the New Testament to the church being
pure that we cannot ignore the idea or rationalize it away.
God keeps pruning His vine, cutting off the dead branches so
that the resulting plant may be strong and healthy and will
bear plenty of good fruit. God is preparing a community that
will be pure, holy, and undefiled.

The church is holy not because of her members, but because God is holy and calls us to be holy. We can be righteous
only to the extent that we recognize that God is righteous.
The purity of the church is not to be thought of as a gradual
achievement, but in terms of our relation to the One who is
pure and perfect. We are invited to participate in that completeness even now. It is a gift and promise which we can already claim and realize (Col. 1:12-23; 2:9-13).

The church is composed of those called to be saints. Although this term has moral implications, it is primarily one of
relation to God. It means to be holy, to be consecrated to
God alone, to be set apart. The saints are those who are set
apart to be God's own people. Thus seeking to be faithful

should not cut us off from mission. God's act of making us holy is a process called sanctification (2 Thes. 2:13). But it is also a task. "You shall be holy, for I am holy" (1 Pet. 1:16).

Church discipline assumes that true faith and discipleship do become visible. The problem is not in deciding who is a true Christian, but how to relate to those actions and attitudes in the church which are a clear contradiction of the gospel. Discipline is the way we help each other make our discipleship take flesh. The command in Galatians 6:2 to bear one another's burdens comes immediately after the command to admonish each other when we sin.

Although we never measure up to the command to be pure and perfect, we are always measured by it. The point is not that we are perfect, but that we as a community have submitted all to God and that we seek the admonition of the Word and of the brothers and sisters at any point where we are not faithful. Our weaknesses are being recognized and put in God's care. The unregenerate are not willing to admit their sin or seek this admonition.

Accountability

We need support not only when we fail, but even more to help keep us from failing. The recurring failure of most new-year resolutions raises not only the question of the sincerity behind them, but also points to the need for external support and accountability. Our record of achieving our goals is not encouraging. Disciplines are meaningless if there is no accountability. The church should not accept confessions of faith and commitments without providing nurture and support to help people keep their promises. We fail people by not supporting and helping them keep their commitments. The believers' church is not interested in any commitments except those which are lived. John Wesley said that to win people for Christ without providing a fellowship for nurture and discipline is to "breed children for the murderer."[3]

We need to be accountable for the commitments we make. It is more likely then that we will not make any commitments unless we fully intend to keep them. Rather than taking away responsibility from people, to make them accountable is to make them more responsible. Often accountability will encourage people to move ahead and be more faithful. It may be because of this encouragement that people will use their talents or that they will do what for a long time they felt they should. Through confession to others often we can be helped to see how we can be more faithful. Sometimes we keep compromising because we see no way around it. But if we share and confess this with our brothers and sisters, they may be able to show us an alternative that we had never seen before or help us find the courage to stop our compromising.

At times each of us goes through periods of personal struggle, dealing with inner feelings, frustrations, doubts, relationships, or deep searching regarding deeper commitments we feel led to make. At times these struggles become quite intense. Everyone faces these in one way or another, and often in community they are sharpened because of the intensity of relationships and commitments. In addition to this, in community we are challenged to wrestle with these problems, rather than avoid them. The pastoral dimension of community is extremely important.

A whole community will not have the time or energy to deal in depth with the needs and concerns of each person. Yet each person needs that. One answer is for each person to have one or several people with whom they regularly share what is happening in their lives. In New Covenant Fellowship each of us is accountable to another person with whom we meet for a sharing time at least once a week, and sometimes more often. This does not mean that we are no longer accountable to the total community, but is an extension of our relationship with the total community.

Some churches have developed an undershepherd program where the congregation is divided into smaller units with one person responsible for the people in each unit. Some work at accountability through sharing in small groups.

These sharing sessions will vary with each person, but will focus on what has been happening in the person's life during the past week, the state of one's spiritual pilgrimage, relationships, and attitudes. There will be a check on how well one is living up to the commitments one has voluntarily made. It will be a time of sharing needs, problems, and struggles, a time of building each other up in love.

This can help avoid the danger of dealing with persons or their problems only when they explode. People need help before their problems become major. Just as a child may misbehave in order to seek parental attention, so the sin of my brother or sister may be an expression of his/her alienation and loneliness. We need to respond to each other's needs before they become a crisis.

It is important that these accountability relationships be seen as more than opportunities for sharing, but also include authority. They are concrete expressions of our submission to each other, for in these relationships we are submitted to someone who is in turn submitted to someone else. It is another expression of the fact that our lives are not completely in our own control, but committed to doing whatever God wants with the help of our brothers and sisters. As we share our lives with the other person, that person has the authority to make firm suggestions on what steps need to be taken in one's life. There needs to be an openness to hearing those difficult things we need to hear but do not want to hear. Anything that doesn't seem right can be appealed to other persons, or the whole community if necessary. No one may ever have power over the conscience of another person or allow anyone else to rule over one's own conscience.

In many cases it is best for more than one person to be

involved in the sharing sessions. Deep counseling should not be done by one person alone, with no checks on what is happening. This is especially important in counseling between sexes, a relationship full of dangers. Many pastors and counselors are either seduced or do the seducing, and the counseling relationship becomes destructive for all. Deep struggles are best shared with a larger group of people who can give daily support. Although the community will be therapeutic,[4] she should not see herself primarily as a therapy group. The focus needs to be living out the gospel together.

The Authority for Discipline

The church receives the authority for discipline both from Jesus and from the members in their membership and baptismal commitments. Seeking membership means asking for discipline and being open to correction. It should be clear upon becoming a member that one is committed to giving and receiving counsel. Membership in the body of Christ includes asking my brothers and sisters to help me be faithful to the covenant I have made. I expect to be accountable to them and for them. Thus as we disciple each other, we are doing what our brothers and sisters asked us to do when they made their covenant with us. We can learn from the early Methodists. Some of the questions asked in Wesley's societies before admittance to membership included,

> Do you desire to be told of your faults? Do you desire we should tell you whatsoever we think, whatsoever we fear, whatsoever we hear, concerning you?
> Do you desire that in doing this, we should come as close as possible, that we should cut to the quick, and search your heart to the bottom?
> Is it your desire and design to be on this, and all other occasions, entirely open, so as to speak everything that is in your heart without exception, without disguise, and without reserve?[5]

That is putting it right on the line.

Ultimately the authority for us to exercise church discipline comes from Jesus. After Jesus gave the command to go to the brother or sister He said, "Whatever you bind on earth shall be bound in heaven, and whatever you loose on earth shall be loosed in heaven" (Mt. 18:18; also see Mt. 16:19). Church discipline is "binding and loosing." But what on earth does that mean?

To bind means to forbid or require while loosing means to permit or leave open. *The New English Bible* catches this meaning by translating it "forbid and allow." Binding and loosing were well-known terms in Jesus' time which referred to rabbis making decisions on moral problems brought to them. They would either forbid or allow, depending on how they saw the law relating to each problem. From these decisions developed a moral tradition called the *halakah.*

Binding and loosing means moral discernment, but there is another meaning, for the term also implies forgiveness. To loose means to forgive and to bind means to withhold forgiveness and fellowship. The theme of forgiveness can be seen in the parallel passages in Luke 17:1-4 and John 20:23. Also the context of the Matthew 18 passage is forgiveness: the hundreth sheep, seventy times seven, and the unmerciful servant.

Actually discernment and forgiveness need to be seen as parts of the same process. It was important that our discussion of discernment came before the chapter on discipline, for binding and loosing imply that sin can be identified and discerned. But correct discernment is impossible without forgiveness and love. Reconciling a difference requires both discernment and forgiveness, or maybe better stated, discernment and forgiveness are what church discipline is all about.

While binding and loosing were common terms in Jesus' time the scandalous aspect of this teaching of Jesus was His granting to others the authority which had been reserved for the rabbis. The Jewish authorities were offended by His claim of a unique relationship to the Father and His claim of the authority to forgive sins. But Jesus took the offense still one step further. He gave authority to His disciples and to us to forgive sins. The power of binding and loosing has been given to the congregation meeting in His name.

> As the Father has sent me, even so I send you. . . . Receive the Holy Spirit. If you forgive the sins of any, they are forgiven; if you retain the sins of any, they are retained. John 20:21-23.
> I will give you the keys of the kingdom of heaven, and whatever you bind on earth shall be bound in heaven, and whatever you loose on earth shall be loosed in heaven. Matthew 16:19.

The modern Protestant idea that only God has the power to forgive sin is hardly scriptural. He has given that power to us.

Actually the church does not have any authority of her own to discipline. She can act as a representative of Christ only as she is being led by Christ. Therefore, all authority to discipline comes from the discerning of the mind of Christ in every situation. The *ekklesia* then is a gathering for deliberation and discernment, the people of God binding and loosing. That is the church.

We are now ready to understand the meaning of the keys. The power of the keys is the authority to bind and loose, an authority given to Peter and the whole church. The charge Jesus gave to Peter in Matthew 16:19 has correctly been understood as a call to evangelism. Peter was given the authority to open the doors of salvation to all (both Jews and Gentiles) who would receive the gospel. This implies, of course, that all who would not receive the gospel would not be included.

Actually Matthew 16:19 concerns not only church discipline, but also proclaiming the gospel. The John 20:21-23 parallel is also a form of the Great Commission. This is further supported by the observation that the commission to evangelize is often connected with the forgiveness of sins (Lk. 24:47; Acts 2:38). Jeschke says, "The authority to bind and loose is first and foremost the commission to proclaim the gospel."[6]

Could it be, then, that binding and loosing in Matthew 18 actually is also dealing with evangelism? Exactly. The reason we go to the fallen brother or sister is to win that person. The basis for remaining in the church is precisely the same as for entering. Binding and loosing, love and forgiveness, define the basis both for entering the kingdom and the basis for life in the community. Evangelism and church discipline are one and the same thing. Jeschke makes this clear when he writes,

> Too often the meaning of the gospel, though recognized in missionary proclamation, is forgotten when it comes to discipline. Then the church is on another track—charges, courts, trials, condemnation, punishment—in short, legalism and casuistry. It forgets that what meets men initially as good news always remains for them the good news of the power of God's grace to free them from sin in order to live a life in conformity with God's gracious intention for mankind.[7]

Extending Forgiveness and Love

Discipline is not to be seen in contrast to forgiveness and grace, but as forgiveness and grace. Going to the other person must always be seen as humbly sharing the gospel with that person. Discipline will become legalistic only when it is not seen as part of the good news we have to share. Even God's chastisement of Israel in the Old Testament was an attempt to bring her back into covenant relationship with God. Discipline is redemptive, not punitive.

The desire to forgive is at the heart of God's nature. It may be incomprehensible to us that a holy and righteous God who hates sin would love and forgive sinners. That, however, is the gospel. Jesus illustrates this well in His reaction to the

woman who was caught in adultery. Although Old Testament
law demanded that she be stoned, Jesus offered her forgiveness along with the call to sin no more.

The motives in discipline are reconciliation with and restoration of the fallen brother or sister. The purity or image of
the church, an understanding of the righteousness of God, or
holding the line against relativism are not the goals, although
they are related to caring for each other. We discipline one
another because we love Jesus, because we love each other,
because we are members one of another. The concern is not
with the person's mistakes, but for the person's spiritual
health. The idea of punishment or revenge must always be rejected. Eberhard Arnold has said it so well:

> Woe to us if we become correct without having love. Woe
> to us if we say the right thing without having love. Then let us
> rather be silent; that would be better. One ought not to tell a
> person the truth until the Holy Spirit gives one this certainty:
> You love him with your whole heart, therefore you may say it.
> Woe to anyone who would say the truth to his brother or to his
> sister if he does not love them with his whole heart. He is a
> murderer. For truth without love kills. But love without truth
> lies.
>
> It must be given to us to grasp the full depth and whole
> breadth of the truth in Christ and in God's Kingdom. By no
> means are truth and love two separate things that we now have
> to bring into harmony. No! No! On the contrary God's heart is
> the truth. God's heart is love. The content of ultimate truth is
> nothing but absolute love. For God's truth is the essence of His
> heart, and the nature of His heart is love.
>
> Our love can only be such that it brings God's truth to
> men. There can be no other love for us—the love of soft com-
> passion, of diplomatic compromise, or of mutual concessions
> that loses the objectivity of truth for the sake of the other's
> soul. To this kind of love we must not pledge ourselves, but to
> that love alone which carries into the heart of the person we
> love the full depth of the truth and the whole, sweeping vastness
> of the truth.
>
> Truth, therefore, is truth only in love. For it is not the

truth to set forth a polished, dazzling theory with a cold heart. Nor is it the truth to smite men with a hard, stony orthodoxy that comes from a stern mind. That is not the truth. If we were to speak the correct truth exactly and accurately in every sense, it would be of the Devil if it were done without love.[8]

When a member of one group made a small infraction of the rules a leader suggested that they not do anything this time, but when they catch him again that they really nail him. Not only had this group missed the meaning of discipline, they had lost the vision of the redemptive nature of the Christian faith.

Forgiveness is at the heart of the Christian life. Jesus even links the command to forgive with the sending of the Holy Spirit (Mt. 18:20; Jn. 20:23). In the Lord's prayer Jesus links God's forgiveness to our forgiving others.[9] We cannot properly pray for someone unless we forgive them and love them. God is hardly interested in our condescending prayers. Our prayers should come out of concern for the other person, not self-righteous pride. "Hold unfailing your love for one another, since love covers a multitude of sins" (1 Pet. 4:8).

The emphasis in the past too often has been on what the guilty person should do to receive forgiveness rather than how the church could extend forgiveness and be an agent of reconciliation. Why should we offer forgiveness and liberation from sin to people outside the church, but not to those who are part of the church? The gospel concerns not only an initial commitment or conversion, but it is the good news by which we live every day.

Forgiveness is not some vague graciousness of God, but concrete love which comes to me and my neighbor, often through my neighbor. Just as the church must become visible, so forgiveness also needs to become visible. The church is God's way of making visible His forgiveness and love. In the church we experience God's forgiveness through the mutual forgiveness of each other.

We need more than self-forgiveness which can be self-justification, but also the forgiveness of God and our brothers and sisters. The idea that I do not need the forgiveness of others can soon lead to the popular idea that I can forgive myself through self-acceptance and not need God's forgiveness. The basis for self-acceptance is God's forgiveness and acceptance. We seem to have forgotten that there is a close connection between divine and human forgiveness. Sometimes we have even said that we can confess our sins directly to God and have no need for the help and forgiveness of anyone else. It takes at least two to right a wrong: the offender and the offended. Usually more people are involved, at least through knowing about the problem.

In many churches when someone sins there is no way to receive the forgiveness of the church even though the whole church knows about it. Oh, we have an informal discipline—gossip and social ostracism—but not a discipline informed by the gospel which offers forgiveness and acceptance. If a couple has to get married, thirty years later people still remember, but forgiveness often is never extended.

A story dating back to around the turn of the century is told of an unmarried member of the Church of the Brethren becoming pregnant. Because of this, she was called before the church (presumably the man was not a member) and the church voted to revoke her membership. Then, because of her confession, at the same meeting the church voted to reaccept her back into membership. The procedure for reaccepting fallen members at that time among the Brethren was for her to stand in front of the whole church where every sister in the church greeted her with the kiss of peace and every brother greeted her with a handshake. After this the elder of the church warned that anyone speaking of this again would be subject to discipline.

While this may not exactly be the way we would want to do it, we cannot help but be impressed that she received the love and forgiveness of the whole church in a way almost impossible today. She was able to raise her child out of wedlock with no stigma and with the full support of the church. Seldom is such deep love shown today.

More is needed than a call for the church to pray for someone without talking to them personally and offering them concrete help and support. Much attention needs to be given to restoring the person. If a person has certain weaknesses, ways can be found to help the person in that area. We are interested not only in forgiveness and confession, but also in bringing healing and restoring the person so that he/she will not fall again.

When we fail to forgive each other, we bind and lock each other into patterns of sin and broken relationships. But when we forgive, freedom and grace are given for people to be loosed from their chains of sin and alienation.

Without discipline we do not receive forgiveness or guidance. We seek this in many secular sources, but seldom are able to find what the church could be giving to us. Although there is a need for psychotherapy, the church should not see this as replacing the need for the church to be a reconciling, forgiving community. The church can provide a wholeness that therapy cannot provide. Much of modern psychotherapy stresses the need for confession. Its popularity is a sign of the inability of the church to deal with guilt, doubt, and lack of meaning. Secularized confession loses much of what it could mean in the context of a faith community—for example forgiveness, absolution, and support. How much the church needs people with spiritual depth who can get right to the heart of people's alienation and sin! People not only need counseling, but also the assurance of forgiveness.

We need to recover a proper understanding of both justification (God's gift of free grace) and sanctification (the new life we are to live).[10] By separating them we reduce justification to cheap grace and sanctification becomes legalistic obedience. But if both can be seen together related to discipleship, discipline is an aspect of grace. Discipleship then becomes an alternative to both legalism and relativism, to rigidity and license. Neither judgment nor grace can be understood unless they are seen together. When the sanctions of the gospel are applied within a loving community they can be both tough and liberating.

It is important that we not see love and forgiveness as a sentimental something with no demands, expectations, or responsibility. Often this is an excuse for not taking the other person seriously. It is time to reject the idea that we should never say no to anyone out of fear they may feel rejected. This ends with the view of trying to dispense grace in small amounts to everyone rather than clearly proclaiming the truth. Often those who are troubled by their present life appreciate talking to sensitive people who oppose their activities and can clearly point to a new way. Mowrer sees moral nonaccountability as part of the reason for the lostness of people.[11] Although he overstates the case, it is true that we have been unable to deal with people's guilt. Along with Freudian psychology we have often denied (or at least overlooked) the reality of guilt and so failed to deal with it very deeply. Forgiveness does not become real until there is repentance. It is meaningless if not accompanied by change in a person's life. The thief must stop stealing before there can be true forgiveness. Although forgiveness is offered before repentance, it is not effective until it has been accepted through repentance.

Forgiveness and grace are never cheap or easy. No one can simply forgive and forget. Sin may never be glossed over and it will not automatically go away. True forgiveness is experienced as we work through that which needs forgiveness. Reconciliation comes after facing our problems, after the cross. There is no cheap grace.

To forgive is not to overlook or forget, but is a deep experience that goes to the root of the sin and enables us to remember in a new way. Often this can be the occasion of establishing a deeper relation with the other person.

The Process of Discipline

Our failure to go to our brothers and sisters is an expression of our unfaithfulness to the gospel. We have not loved our brothers and sisters deeply enough and we have not believed sufficiently in the transforming work of the Holy Spirit to go to the other person, even when there was no doubt that this was needed. This is a serious matter, for it strikes to the heart of the Christian faith and the meaning of the church.

We can go to the other person in the confidence that the Holy Spirit will be in our midst and bring reconciliation and unity to us. We can go in the faith that there is a power which can take away our division and bring us together. Without this consciousness, discipline would soon degenerate into something ugly.

If we truly love each other we will speak the truth to each other, even if it is difficult. Love implies both forgiveness and admonition. Love is not weak. It confronts and does not allow us to evade our responsibility. If a person falls or does something that is destructive for self and others and we do not talk to that person about it, our love is lacking. If we love each other, we will help each other. This means taking each other seriously, deeply caring for each other, and taking responsibility for each other.

This process begins the moment a problem becomes known to us. The sooner we can get to the person who needs help the easier restoration may be.

This does not mean that only things which happened recently should be dealt with. If it happened a long time ago and it is still bothering you, that is a clear sign that it needs to be straightened out. If it is still causing you trouble, you cannot say it was not important enough to worry about. You may argue that things are going better now. That may be, but that is no reason not to get it straightened out. Besides, if things are going better now that may make it easier.

The responsibility for extending forgiveness and going to the other person is every member's responsibility, not just the task of church leaders. We need to know that everyone cares for us, not just the pastor. Paul saw this as the work of the entire congregation (1 Cor. 5:4, 5). Rather than exercise his own authority, he wanted the congregation to wrestle with the problem.

Church discipline has been distorted by shifting responsibility from the whole congregation and every member to an authority figure such as the bishop, pastor, or elder. This is unfair to the leader in that it hinders the other work of that person by making that person a disciplinarian.

There is no New Testament basis for seeing this as solely the responsibility of leaders. There may be times that leaders will be chosen to serve as mediators or "the wise among you" (1 Cor. 6:5), but only after other attempts to bring reconciliation have failed. To first go to church leaders destroys confidentiality and may be unfair to the other person. When we see someone sin, we are to go directly to that person. This is the responsibility of everyone; the offended, the offender, and any other person who is aware of any need to restore fellowship. If a conflict develops between two people, it is the responsibility of others to point out to them what is happening and help them come to grips with it.

But when do I go to the other person? I should not go for every little picky annoyance, should I? No. Obviously we cannot deal with everything every member does. Some things are better left to individual freedom. There will always be border areas where the church does not have clarity. That is a reason why discernment is an important part of the process. These border areas are areas of growth. They are a safeguard against a static dogmatism. Different communities will be specific in their discipline in different areas and at different times. What is normative is not always the same for all communities.

How then do we decide what is the concern of the church and what is not? The answer is not for the church to deal with the big sins and forget the little ones, for this focuses on the deed rather than the person and soon leads to legalism. The answer to this question is that we must be sensitive to anything that offends or raises concern among others. Anything that destroys fellowship is an important concern, even if it seems unimportant, for often it is the little things that bother us most. If it bothers you or hurts your relationship, then go to the other person. Always give the other person the benefit of any doubt, however.

Distinguishing between big and little sins soon distorts the meaning of discipline. Actually the "biggest" sins can often readily be forgiven and sometimes very "small" sins can exclude one from the community if there is no repentance. The real distinction is not in the degree of sin, but in the attitude of the person. A distinction should be made between a person who happened to fall and one who is seriously out of relation to the community and the faith. In the latter there is the need not only for forgiveness, but also for restoring a seriously broken relationship.

A serious blind spot in traditional church discipline has been to concentrate on items of personal morality such as adultery and stealing, and neglect the whole area of social justice. The church should be equally concerned about racism, economic exploitation, and support for war and violence. Let's face it: participating in economic injustice is every bit as sinful as robbing a bank, and expressions of racism are as serious as committing adultery.

All sin, both public and private, is a serious concern. Of

course, we cannot know the secret sins of others, but where they exist, their symptoms will soon be revealed. When something is wrong in our lives, even if it is secret, it will show. We cannot long deceive those who are close to us. When we notice something is wrong, that is the time to go to that person. We do not go around spying for secret sins. We look for discipleship and where it seems missing we offer our love and support. Discipline does not begin after one has sinned but is a continual process of mutual concern and love which begins before and continues after we have sinned.

At times it may be obvious that someone is resisting the Spirit or refusing to turn something over to God. With much prayer and love the situation must be confronted and the person helped to see that he/she no longer needs to keep holding back. Sometimes we need to stand up to certain people and say what needs to be said. The answer is not just to endure, for often this causes deep resentments. Sometimes "enduring" is little more than a noble excuse not to reach out to the other person with the help that is needed.

Let's look again at what Jesus said. I am to go *directly* to my brother or sister and raise my concern between the two of us *alone.* All our temptations to pass on what we hear or see are denied. Jesus' method insures that the concern remain confidential and not become gossip.

How much misunderstanding, conflict, and suffering could be saved if we stopped talking to a third person about the sins of others and instead went directly to that person? Much time and energy would be saved by not needing to repair all the damage done by gossip. If the person is guilty he/she already has enough of a burden without us adding still more condemnation. If we gossip to a third person who is no more responsible than we are, the story will spread in no time.

Of course it is difficult to go to another person in a spirit of forgiveness and humility. We are not as willing to extend forgiveness as we expect to receive it. We enjoy the sense of moral superiority which comes from condemning others. We enjoy still more the support we get when we tell others and they morally shake their heads with us. With this gratification it is not difficult to make the story sound even a little worse than it is. But if I go to the other person with forgiveness I have to give up my pride, and that is not easy. When Jesus commanded the disciples to forgive constantly, the disciples answered, "Increase our faith" (Lk. 17:5).

Each step of the way requires humility, prayer, and a readiness to learn how I have been wrong, or even the cause of another's stumbling. We are able to go to our brothers and sisters only to the extent we are open to hearing them. We need to confront each other directly, but we must be careful that it is always done in love and out of a deep sense of caring for the other person. Discipline needs to be seen as our suffering with the fallen person. We go to the brother or sister to bear the pain with that person. We take on the weakness of the other as if it were our own, willing to stand beside that person and give all of our strength to help overcome the problem, even ready to go through the struggle with that person. John Howard Yoder gets to the heart of the matter in his statement that

> Forgiveness is not a generally accessible human possibility; it is the miraculous fruit of God's own bearing the cost of man's rebellion. Among men as well it costs a Cross. Man can go to his brother only as God came to him; not counting his trespasses against him. Forgiveness does not brush the offense off with a "think nothing of it"; it absorbs the offense in suffering love.[12]

For discipline to be redemptive the person must realize love, understanding, and acceptance from the church. We should go to our brothers and sisters not only when something is wrong, but also when things are right. We need to build each other up in love. When someone is admonished we have the responsibility to show just as much love in the form of support as we did in the form of admonishment. Maybe we should be supporting and thanking each other at least ten times as often as offering criticism.

Care must be taken not to make the person defensive nor to strengthen defense mechanisms which deepen alienation. Care must be made to evoke a response rather than impose a response. Confession must be freely made, not demanded. Sometimes people are not ready to confess. Sometimes we can go to the other person asking help in relating to the problem or asking where we might have been wrong. We need to learn the best insights of counseling and pastoral care. This does not negate the necessity of at times confronting the thief with stealing even if the thief does not want to be confronted. But even this can be done with love and humility. Paul put it well when he wrote, "If a man is overtaken in any trespass, you who are spiritual should restore him in a spirit of gentleness" (Gal. 6:1).

We cannot excuse ourselves by saying that since we are not perfect we cannot go to the other person. No one is perfect. That is a reason why we should go. Those who know they are in need of forgiveness are the very ones to give forgiveness. It is a real asset to go to another person and realize that we are also sinners. We can be sensitive to our neighbor's sin because we are so aware of our own and so go in humility. In fact, before we go it is important that we always examine ourselves to see if we might be guilty of the same thing. In other words, there is no place for hypocrisy or being judgmental.

Care must be taken not to make false accusations against anyone. All of us have experienced other persons and groups making judgments against us without checking whether they are true. We know the pain and alienation that causes. Sharing a concern with someone must always include asking how that person sees things. No matter what the situation, we need to show openness and love to the other person or group. This will always involve a process. There is often the temptation to cut ourselves off from those who offend us without seeking understanding and reconciliation, but this desire is not of love and must be resisted.

If we hear something negative about someone and are unsure if it is true, we can go to the other person and simply say that we heard something and would like to check if it is true. We will do well not to harbor unproven suspicions in our own hearts.

We especially need to go to the other person when we realize that we have been in the wrong, even if it was only the way we said something. There is much truth in the saying, "It is harder to forgive those whom we have wronged than those who have wronged us."

If you were in any way wrong, go only to ask forgiveness for that. Do not go with the attitude that "I was partly wrong, but so were you." This is an expression of pride and a cowardly way of attacking the other person. All pride must be given up for confession to be authentic. If the other person was 90 percent wrong and you only 10 percent, go and make your part right. That will give the other person freedom to also confess. But be sure to confess. Do not just say you are sorry. Sorry for what? Be specific.

The process of discipline is a guard against self-righteousness, for if I become self-righteous my brothers and sisters will soon tell me about it. If I become picky, legalistic, or judgmental, it is the responsibility of others to come to me concerning that. Only in this way can any community deal with these tendencies which exist in every group.

I am to go to the other person to extend forgiveness and love, to work at strengthening our relationship. But that is quite different from going to the other person to vent my hostility. Discipline may never be done as a means of release of frustration and anger. Expressing hostility is usually to meet my own needs rather than concern for the other person. Someone has called this the vomit system of honesty. It does a lot for you, but not much for anyone else. Venting hostility does not necessarily mean a reduction of hostility. It may only encourage more hostility or even develop into a pattern of reaction.

We are not permitted to relate to others in anger, which is an expression of condemning judgment, the opposite of love and forgiveness. That is a right we do not have. In addition to being destructive, it is an expression of self-righteousness, placing the blame on others and evading our own problems and responsibilities.

Heated arguments, free expression of hostility, will not automatically bring healing. In fact, often this makes the wound deeper and prevents healing. We never have the right to violate anyone else in the name of expressing our own feelings. When a person does something that angers us, we need to first discipline ourselves so that when we go to that person we can care for that person's good. Hostility needs to be more confessed than expressed. Although anger needs to be controlled, it may never be repressed.[13]

There is a place for talking confidentially in a pastoral way to a third person in order to sort through one's feelings, some of which may be irrational and need not be worked through with the other person. The purpose of this should be seen as confession, recognizing that this is primarily for my own healing so that I will be able to reach out to the other person.

After we work through our feelings, then we may be better able to go to the other person and accurately express our feelings to that person. At this point the anger need not be denied, but can be confessed in a redemptive rather than destructive way.

There should be no secrets between two people about another in the community. It is understood that if someone in

the community talks to me about someone else in the community I will not necessarily keep that a secret. I will then
have a special responsibility to help bring reconciliation by
seeking to get the people to talk together.

Just as God takes the initiative and speaks to us before
we invite Him, so we can take the initiative and go to our
neighbor before we are invited. It is important to be humble,
but also open and direct. We do not have any right to coerce,
impose, or pry, however. The other person must always be
respected. If he/she does not want to talk, that must be
respected. Never do we have the right to force anyone to
share with us. This must always be voluntary. We do not seek
submission to any rule, but a change of heart. The other
person can always say no and that wish must be respected.

There may be some situations where the other person is
not emotionally able to handle something and we need to
bear the burden ourselves. This might be done with those
who are under the special pastoral care of the community but
should be only after consultation with others who are
responsible. It would be done in the hope that soon the
strength for reconciliation would be given. In most cases,
however, it is condescending to think that the other person is
not mature enough to listen to me or would not be able to
understand. We should not underestimate others. One may
need to display extra sensitivity, but if we go in a humble
spirit, the other person may well understand and be given the
strength to hear us.

If our effort to bring reconciliation fails, Jesus said to
take several others with us and try again. When it seems impossible to get through to the other person, we should go to
some others, not to gossip, but for help. It may be that they
will show us where we were wrong, either in our ideas or in
the way we approached the other person. Again the process
of extending love and forgiveness is repeated. It may be that
they will be able to reach this other person. If so, we have

gained the person. If not, then we bring it before the whole community and reconciliation becomes a concern of all.

Jesus' point is not that there are three steps rather than four or six, but that the first be in complete confidentiality and that other attempts then be made, including mediation, before the concern is brought before the whole community. Reconciliation is never easy and often takes a long time. Much patience is needed. Never should our actions be hasty.

Bringing a concern about someone before the whole community includes giving that person the fullest hearing possible. It means the whole commuity is ready to listen to that person.

If a person acts negatively toward the community, not only must that person be taken seriously, but there needs to be careful examination of how the community may be responsible for that person's feelings and behavior.

It will be noted that the gospel order runs opposite to the encounter group approach in which one is encouraged to bring out one's feelings immediately before the whole group, express as much hostility as possible, and pry and prod the other person until in desperation all the withheld feelings come gushing out. Further, the gospel order sees this happening in a covenant community rather than a group of strangers gathered together for a weekend. This order is also a guard against exhibitionism which can become a problem in group confession.

It is important that all communities follow the gospel order. In addition to being more redemptive, much time and energy can be saved if problems between individuals can be worked out privately, without involving the whole community. If relationships are worked out before meetings, it is less likely that the discussion will get hung up on side issues. It is doubtful whether we can improve on Jesus' order.

Normally all negative feelings need to be worked out one-to-one, but occasionally they may be part of a larger negative attitude in the community and will need to be worked out in the whole community. Sometimes these sessions will be a general cleansing for the whole community. There need to be times to clear the air. Whenever tension builds up in the community, it may need to be released by the whole community. In working through these feelings often secret resentments will be expressed. An expression of hostility by one person must not be seen as an excuse for others to vent their hostility. If handled with love and sensitivity the community can experience a cleansing. These situations do need to be controlled, for they can degenerate into destructive dynamics.

It may be that when you go to the other person he/she will maintain that there is nothing wrong with what was done. At this point the process of discernment is needed. Some problems may be the occasion for deep prayer and study of that issue before any action can be taken. It is important always to avoid the temptation to apply general principles uniformly and mechanically without regard to the context or the person's needs. Each concern must be dealt with as an individual case. No two problems are the same. The situation, motives, and weaknesses of each person must be taken into consideration. It may be that the other person was right.

This process is a safeguard against legalism and holding onto outdated rules, for each time the process is used, the stance of the church is tested again. Sometimes it will be seen that the community was wrong and needs to change. Other times it will be clear that the testimony of the church needs to be reaffirmed. The loving and discerning dealing with brothers and sisters in concrete situations is the way to change or reaffirm the stands of the church. Discipline is based on discerning the Holy Spirit, not a method of maintaining cherished ways in which the Spirit is no longer present.

If the position of the church needs to be reaffirmed, then the church has a responsibility to help the other person find ways to live with this position and find a solution to the problem. At this point the work of the community has just begun. The strong need to bear with the weak just as the weak need to bear with the strong. Dissenters must be respected. Think of God's patience with us! Loving discipline presupposes a redemptive fellowship of believers.

Although the process of Matthew 18 is primarily intended for the Christian community, much of it is relevant also in our relation to non-Christians. We can go to them also. Do not argue that since the person is not a Christian he/she may not understand. What better Christian witness could you ever make to that person? We do need to be especially careful and sensitive where there is neither a covenant or any expectation of mutual admonition. We can, however, go to anyone to ask forgiveness, and should do so whenever needed.

The Christian does not resort to secular authorities and courts to resolve disputes with other people, for we have been given a better way (1 Cor. 6:1-7). This way is to go to the other person in a spirit of reconciliation. If unsuccessful, then we take up the nonviolent cross, the way of suffering love.

Excommunication

There may be times where all efforts at reconciliation will fail. As a last resort, *at the end of a long and loving process,* the community may have to declare that that person is no longer part of the church fellowship. This does not mean that we kick that person out of the church, but simply openly recognize that he/she is no longer in fellowship. Sometimes we need to recognize that doors are closed, but we never close them. Actually, in many cases it is the individual who recognizes being out of fellowship and will want that to be recognized by the community.

Since the actions of the community may never involve coercion, anyone will have the freedom to reject the church. Rather than coercion or manipulation, recognizing that one is no longer a part of the fellowship is a sign of respect for that person's freedom to reject the love and admonition of the church.

Since everyone in the church is a sinner, it hardly seems right that anyone should be put out of the church for any sin. The church is one group that holds on to the fallen person after the rest of society has rejected him/her. If sin would permanently cut us off from the fellowship of the church none of us could remain. But there is more. Yes, the church is a home for sinners, but for *repentant* sinners. Simply being a sinner is not the basis of membership. The only way we can be cut off is by refusing to repent, refusing to accept the love and forgiveness of the church. Then *we cut ourselves off.* Excommunication is never for any particular sin or violation, but is the *result* of impenitence and rejection of forgiveness and grace.

The only sins that are unforgivable are those in which there is no repentance, in which there is no willingness to recognize the wrong, to be open to the Holy Spirit, receive love and forgiveness, and make the needed changes in one's life. Ultimately it is not our sins that separate us from God, but our unwillingness to accept the forgiveness God offers to us. At times we put ourselves in a position where grace cannot reach us. This is the true meaning of mortal sin. The suggestion not to pray for one in mortal sin (1 Jn. 5:16-18) does not mean unconcern, but not to offer or pray for forgiveness where there is no repentance. The process of church discipline is partly to help the church discern if the person is at that point forgivable. When the church discerns that the person is not open to forgiveness the person is no longer seen as being in fellowship with the community.

It is important for the community to be straightforward

in dealing with sin and brokenness in relationships, not so much because the rest of the fellowship will be tempted to sin (although that happens when moral standards are weakened), but because feelings and relationships become confused in this kind of situation. To give fellowship if one does not feel it is dishonest and creates great confusion, both within the community and in how the world sees the church. It also can give the impression that we do not really care about the person, that we do not take seriously the fact that the unrighteous will not inherit the kingdom (1 Cor. 6:9).

Excommunication is an awesome thing and can be done only with deep anguish. Twice in the New Testament excommunication is referred to as delivering someone to Satan (1 Cor. 5:5; 1 Tim. 1:20). This seems to refer to turning people over to the forces of the world without the support of the church, hoping that really experiencing the horror of life apart from the church will bring them to their senses and help them recognize their state.

One of the signs of the loss of community and of our humanity is our inability to feel anguish, to deeply hurt and feel pain for each other. We seem to have no fear for those who are lost. We have ignored the serious and terrible consequences of sin (Heb. 10:31). We smooth things over and take a tranquilizer. If we would fear and hurt more for each other, we would take each other more seriously. If community is important, if it is in community that the kingdom of God is breaking in, then it is horrible to miss out on it. To not be in fellowship with the community of faith is an awful reality. It is to not be in fellowship with God. In impersonal churches it is difficult for us to understand how serious this is. But if we are excluded from a community that means more to us than anything in the world, then the impact is tremendous. How can we help but anguish for those who are left out?

Excommunication is an extreme means of confronting a person with the truth, with the ongoing love of the community, with the fact that he/she is outside the kingdom. It is a drastic way of reaching out to the person who would respond to nothing else. It is a reminder to that person that he/she is not forgotten or ignored, an expression that we care so much about that person that we are even willing to suffer the pain of broken relationships. Excommunication is a means of communication rather than merely a cutting off from communication. It is not cutting anyone off from grace, but the final way the church offers grace to the unrepentant. It is the same message as to any sinner: "Unless you repent and believe the gospel, you will not enter the kingdom."

If a person will not listen to the church, Jesus said to treat that person as a sinner. But how are we to treat a sinner? We are not to reject that person. No, we love that person just as much as we would love any other sinner who is not part of our fellowship, and even more. In 2 Thessalonians 3:15 we are told regarding one who has been excommunicated, "Do not look on him as an enemy, but warn him as a brother." We seek to include that person again. But we do not delude ourselves. We understand and make it clear that he/she is not now part of our fellowship. Excommunication simply means out of communion. There cannot be two levels of fellowship: forgiven and unforgiven, faithful and unfaithful. Either a person is in fellowship or is out of fellowship.

We are talking not about a break in communication, but a break in fellowship. Although we still love that person as much as any member (and maybe even more), we are forced to recognize that our relationship cannot be the same as with any other nonmember, for here there is also a violated covenant to deal with. We will still reach out to that person, but we cannot have the deep relation we once had until there is reconciliation. We cannot pretend that everything is fine and be as warm and friendly as ever.

On the other hand, the church may never show hostility to that person. In every future contact it is important that the church communicate neither rejection nor an easy acceptance that would ignore the person's condition. All communication should show love, an invitation to come back, *and* a reminder of the need for reconciliation. Since this person had formerly been a part of the community he/she will understand the love and concern that this expresses. Exclusion from the church makes sense only if the church is a loving, life-giving, redemptive fellowship. In fact, the community will continually carry a deep concern for that person in their hearts and constantly seek to know how they may have been wrong or failed to reach that person. Repeated attempts at reconciliation will be made.

There are various degrees of being out of fellowship, depending on the attitudes involved and seriousness of the brokenness. This can extend anywhere from not participating in decision-making meetings to exclusion from the community.

But who is to decide this? The answer is the whole community. There needs to be unity to disfellowship anyone, and then the decision must be clearly within the bounds of the gospel. If a group is divided over this, there is a deeper problem of disunity that must be dealt with, and disfellowshiping one person will not solve it. No bishop or pastor has the authority to do it.

There are a number of New Testament texts which call us to avoid those who are excommunicated (Rom. 16:17; 2 Thess. 3:6, 14; 2 Tim. 3:2-5; Titus 3:10). These texts have been implemented in many ways. Some groups such as the Amish practice shunning, not speaking to that person. Other groups take the practice only as far as described above. This is an area which requires a deep discerning of the Spirit by each community. Jeschke expresses the meaning of this when he writes,

> Avoidance is that kind of circumspect relationship with an excommunicated individual which brings home to him the truth about his spiritual condition and does not permit him to escape

into self-deception. It means refusing to pretend that a person is a Christian after he has ceased to be one.[14]

This discussion of excommunication has not been a pleasant subject, but it is just as essential as honest diagnosis in health care. People need to be confronted with the truth. What integrity does the church have if it cannot do this?

Restoration and Reconciliation

The goal of all discipline is reconciliation. When that reconciliation happens, there is cause for great rejoicing. Forgiveness is an occasion of deep joy and sharing. Then the sin of a brother or sister becomes an occasion of reminding the whole community to praise God for His forgiving love to all of us, a reminder that all of us are weak and in need of God's grace.

Should confession be public and before the whole community? This depends on the nature of the sin, at what stage the restoration occurred, and the extent to which the sin had been public. Sometimes it may be better to keep an unknown sin in strict confidence, working it through with only one or two others. Any temptation to live a less than fully open and honest life must be resisted, however. Unless we are at least *completely willing* to have all who are close to us know *everything* of significance about us, there will always be that barrier of fear that they might find out about our past and reject us.

Communities have found that hidden things in one's past always come out in one way or another, either in the form of confession and forgiveness, or in fear, hostility, projected resentments, and inability to be close to people because it takes too much energy to keep up a front. Obviously every little thing does not need to be confessed to everyone, but no one should keep any secret that might cause one to wonder what others would think if they found out. At times at New Covenant Fellowship all the details are confessed to the one to whom one is accountable and then the general outline is shared with the whole community so that forgiveness and acceptance can be received from all. There is a good reason for the New Testament command to confess our sins to one another (Jas. 5:16). How can we be free and in right relationship with our brothers and sisters unless we know they have forgiven us?

It may not be necessary for a matter between two persons to be made public, although the joy of reconciliation may be so great that it will have to be shared. If the sin was known by all, then a public confession seems essential in order that all may know of the change and extend forgiveness. Obviously an excommunicated person would need to make a public confession and again be received by all. Never, under any circumstances may anyone bring up anything critical related to this from the past after there has been forgiveness. From here on, that has all been forgiven and taken away.

Confession involves both the admission of wrong and affirmation of what is right. The two can never be separated. When a confession is voluntary, it is an occasion of rejoicing rather than any humiliation. The emphasis is not on sin or guilt, but on the new life and forgiveness the person has found.

In a sense it is humiliating to confess our sin to others. It destroys all our pride. It means death for the old self. When we confess our sin to others the last possibility of justifying ourselves is surrendered. But we are then ready to receive the love and forgiveness of both God and the community. Confessing things to our brothers and sisters is a powerful way of confessing things to God. The sin no longer has the same power then, for the community bears it also.

Accepting one back into fellowship is similar to accepting new members, so the conditions should not be much different. Faith and genuine discipleship can be the only conditions for either. When there are real fruits of repentance (not just words or even tears), then the community can recognize that God has also given forgiveness in that person's heart. The forgiveness of the church then is an affirmation of God's forgiveness.

Rather than see discipline in conflict with freedom we can see the two as inseparable. Being a member of a loving and disciplining community leads to a new freedom. We are free to be open and honest. We do not need constantly to worry about what others think, for they will tell us. There is also the freedom to fail, to be wrong, because we know our brothers and sisters will correct us where we are wrong. And when we are corrected we will not feel rejected. We know they corrected us because they love us. We have a new freedom to be faithful because we know we are not alone. Our brothers and sisters are with us.

Church discipline is the expression of love and concern for each other within a community of love that knows her purpose and identity. It is the way a community relates to her members with integrity. Perhaps now we can understand John Howard Yoder's description of the believers' church, a community which he says

> gives more authority to the church than does Rome, trusts more to the Holy Spirit than does pentecostalism, has more respect for the individual than humanism, makes moral standards more binding than puritanism, is more open to the given situation than the "new morality."[15]

Chapter 6

THE VOLUNTARY COMMUNITY

Now the Lord is the Spirit, and where the Spirit of the Lord is, there is freedom.—Paul in 2 Corinthians 3:17.

Religious Liberty

The full process of church discipline must be limited to those who have voluntarily committed themselves to this discipline. Never may the church seek to impose her will on anyone outside the community. In fact, the church does not even have the right to impose her will on anyone in the community.

Since most discipline has been lost in the church, many church people look to the state to provide the moral discipline once provided by the church. The state and its police are expected to spy into the lives of the immoral and degenerate and enforce morality. The irony of this is that many of these same people do not want the church to exercise any discipline in their own lives. The state, yes, but not the church.

Puritanism is still with us, a desire to force everyone in a geographical area to conform to a certain prescribed morality. Those who cannot or will not conform are either crushed or expelled. Since inner thoughts cannot be controlled, the puritan approach concentrates its control over the more obvious and physical sins.

During the time of *corpus christianum* (the union of church and state), church discipline became especially severe, for the loss of privilege in the church also meant loss of civil rights. Luther advocated that the state discipline those unresponsive to the discipline of the church.[1] In the post-Reformation church the consistory soon became an arm of the state, forcing conformity. One Protestant statement reads,

> It is [the Christian magistrate's] most solemn duty to support the ministry in its exercise of the "key of discipline," by every lawful means in his power.[2]

It was the nonresistant sects which correctly understood the New Testament process of discipline in the church. They experienced the alternative to a church which wields the sword or a church which stands for nothing.

A brief look at history and what is happening today in the world makes obvious the importance of this view for the whole area of political and religious freedom. This becomes apparent when we read the history of how down through the centuries the established church murdered those who had the courage to reject the paganism which had infected the church. We need to remember Augustine's call to exterminate the Donatists, official support for the Crusades and Inquisition, and the slaughter of the Anabaptists because today church people still call for extermination of communists and justify killing those they consider their enemies. Many so-called Christians still would play God and attempt to mold others in their own image.

It is difficult for a true Christian to read the bloody story of church history. The transition from a persecuted nonviolent community to a persecuting establishment is a tragic story. The doctrine of no salvation outside the establishment church came to mean no existence as well. How painful it is to read of Protestants killing Catholics, Catholics killing

Protestants, and Protestants killing other Protestants.

The mainline Reformers failed to grant to others the religious freedom they demanded for themselves, agreeing that dissent was to be crushed by whatever means necessary. Calvin even insisted that in dealing with the heretics all feelings of humanity had to be put aside.[3] In justifying the persecution of the Anabaptists, Luther wrote,

> I, Luther, approve. Although it seems cruel to punish them with the sword, it is still more cruel to damn the ministry of the Word, to propagate false doctrine and spurn the truth. . . . [4]

With that view anything can be justified, but not by faith alone.

We can take it still one step further. That anyone would ever be punished for what one believes, or even for refusing to do something seems barbaric. If a society cannot get people to do what is needed without coercion, a deeper problem must need attention.

Christians will affirm religious freedom because of their understanding of the gospel and the Christian community. Freedom of religion includes the freedom to choose and change one's religion, to organize with others of like mind, to live one's faith and worship unmolested, to preach and publish one's views to others. Each of these points is vital and without any one of them, there is no true religious freedom. Without voluntary associations of believers, religious liberty has little meaning.

The Christian view of religious freedom is rooted in a concept of a voluntary community which receives her authority from Christ only, rather than in any toleration granted by the state. The Christian community is a representative of the universal church and is not dependent upon any government for her rights. The state has no authority to grant any freedom to the church. It can only protect or try to take it away. That freedom is prior to the authority of the state. The religious covenant and community came before the political system. The state has no right either to persecute or to support the church, either to prohibit or to establish religion. It has no authority in the area of faith or conscience. The church can be ruled only by Christ.

This does not include the right for the church to amass great wealth at the expense of the poor or to achieve great power for herself. No one should have that right. The state can deal with the church as a corporation or landowner, but may not have authority over the spiritual and moral concerns of the church.

Modern history has clearly demonstrated that faith is not dependent upon state support for survival. With all its faults, religious life in the United States compares quite favorably with that in countries which still have formal, established state churches. Our main problem in this area is that we have not taken separation of church and state far enough. Christian faith suffers from any control or help from the state. It is important that the church be supported only by voluntary contributions rather than by the state through taxation or from endowments.

Both the church and the world must be free of any domination of each other. If either dominates the other, both are impoverished. If the church either dominates or is dominated by the world, human freedom is greatly diminished. From the Christian point of view, however, the most serious domination is for the church to dominate the world by force, for then not only is human freedom sacrificed, but so is the vision of the kingdom and the soul of the church.

While there can be free churches without a free state, it is doubtful whether there can be a free state without free churches. To have such free groups in society is an important aid in ensuring freedom for everyone. A free church is an impetus for freedom in a society which desires homogeneity and centralized control. It is important to have centers in society other than the political. This is why totalitarian governments are so interested in destroying free churches. The Nazi party in Germany stated,

> We demand the freedom of all religious confessions in the state, in so far as they do not imperil its stability or offend against the ethical and moral senses of the German race.[5]

To accept this would be suicide for the church, whose prime concern should be obedience to God, not what produces stability or will not offend the tastes of unregenerate people. This view was not only a threat to the church, but to the freedom of all Germans.

The established powers fear sectarian movements, for they stand as a threat to the existing order. History is full of state attempts to destroy these developments of alternatives to the existing order which pose new possibilities of voluntary choice. The reason for the persecution of the sects and dissenters was grounded in the desire for a unified and uniform nation in which the cause of the church would be identified with that of the state.

To a large extent our present political freedom was won by religious nonconformists and noncooperators with the unchristian demands of the state. We owe much more to them than to the militarists who claim to have fought for freedom, yet are so ready to deny it to others.

As Christians, our understanding of political freedom is based on our understanding of community rather than on any abstract idea of individual liberty. In fact, at least some of the roots of modern democracy are in the voluntary gatherings of Christians. There the common people learned the art of responsibility and decision-making. When transferred to the larger society, the priesthood of all believers and the idea of voluntary church membership have tremendous implications.

Freedom and the Gospel

At the heart of Christian voluntarism is love, God's love as known in Jesus and in the love we share with each other in community. Coercion has no place in the Christian community, for it is a part of the old age we have rejected. Coercion is a contradiction of the center of our faith. God does not wish to coerce anyone. God constantly seeks us out and invites us to come, but always we can say no.

We are free not only because we have surrendered all and given up every human bondage, but also because that is the way God is. The closer we are drawn to God the more deeply we experience freedom. God does not desire any compulsion, but rather a free, loving response to His love in Jesus Christ. God is love. People can be coerced into many things, but love cannot be coerced. God wants our love even before our obedience.

The authentic life in Christ exists only as we freely accept God's love and grace to us. It is impossible to legislate or force Christian conduct. True faith must be free and voluntary. It cannot be imposed, but must be the work of the Holy Spirit who does the work of bringing people into the community of faith. Not long before he was beheaded for his Anabaptist faith, Claus Felbinger told the authorities,

> God wants no compulsory service. On the contrary, he loves a free, willing heart that serves Him with a joyful soul and does what is right joyfully.[6]

The way of the cross and the way of compulsion are diametrically opposed to each other and cannot be reconciled. How in the name of New Testament faith can people compel, with the threat even of death, non-Christians to attend church meetings as often has been done? Whenever the church accepts coercion she has rejected the heart of the gospel. Those who down through history used coercion and even sanctioned killing the "heretics" did so not because of a blind spot in their theology, but because something was seriously wrong with their whole understanding of the gospel.

A belief in the need to enforce faith humanly seems to be inconsistent with an understanding of salvation by grace alone. The desire to coerce others is a result of our lack of faith in the ability of God to work out His purposes, a feeling that we need to be in control. The more we know of God's truth and love the more able we are to be open and defenseless. The truth is that God has no need of human coercion for His will to be victorious.

Those who do not know the freedom of the gospel think coercion and force are necessary to maintain order. In the Christian community we experience a new order based not on force, but freedom in the Spirit. How different from the inauthentic life of the old society with all of its structured disorder. Life in community is love, freedom, and order.

The idea of voluntarism is deeply imbedded in the whole New Testament. John Howard Yoder points out that in a society where family ties were stable and binding, Jesus called for people to renounce father and mother, husband or wife, brothers and sisters (Lk. 14:26) not because He was preaching hate, but because He was calling together a new community based on voluntary commitment which needed to be prepared for the hostility that would come, including that from other family members.[7] The New Testament sees women and slaves (neither of which had any legal rights or moral status) as being able to make their own decisions rather than obediently following the religion and values of the husband or master.[8]

It is essential that we not lose this emphasis on voluntary decision, for if we believe we know the truth it is not difficult to move to the position that it would be irresponsible not to bring everyone to the truth, even through coercion if necessary. Rather torture a few dissenters than allow the whole body to be led astray.

To resort to coercion would be a denial of our faith, however. Even as God has given us the freedom to rebel against Him and to reject Him, so we must allow the same freedom to others. We cannot put ourselves above God. There can be no force in religion. People must be free to be pagan, otherwise they will not be free to be Christian.

Our commitment to freedom is not based on any view of the absolute freedom of the human will, but is rooted in the nature of God and the freedom we know in Christ and His community. We cannot accept coercion because of what we know of God's love.

Personal Decision

Christian commitment involves a personal decision concerning Christ and His kingdom. We do not enter the new covenant by natural birth, but through the new birth.

There can be no second-generation Christian, for God has no grandchildren. There is no second-generation faith. Each generation needs to weigh the alternatives and struggle with the faith just as did the generation before. Even in ancient Israel, each generation needed to respond anew to God's covenant.[9]

Faith is based not on ethnic birth (circumcision) but on a voluntary response to God's grace. Each of us must make a decision regarding the kingdom of God. No one else can make the decision for us. Faith is more than a gradual acceptance of Christian values through Christian education. There comes a time to decide for or against the faith. Hearing the gospel calls for a decision.

The believers' church's stress on personal decision should be understood in a communal rather than individualistic sense. Although this decision is personal, it is made in relation to God and others and involves a decision for Christ's body.

Although mass evangelism was originally an expression

of voluntarism and a rejection of establishment religion, now with its infatuation with numbers, it has lost much of its voluntarism. Since entering the faith is a journey whose destination is not known in advance, serious thought needs to be given to the decision. It cannot be an easy raising of one's hand or the result of pressure to repeat a simple prayer. The person needs to be given time to think and work it through and should not be hurried. It is essential that Christian commitment truly be a voluntary response to God's initiative and not due to any pressure, psychological manipulation, falsification, indoctrination, or any other attempt to circumvent voluntary decision.

Any action or program is not voluntary and is to some extent compulsory that encourages people to participate through any enticement or rewards that are not directly connected with the essence of the program. There is a big difference between working voluntarily or out of a sense of economic compulsion. High school dances and dating with all the pressures connected with them, including status, glamour, and fear of being excluded are not true voluntary activities. For the church to be truly voluntary, people must be attracted to her only because of what she is. Door prizes, gimmicks, and extending social status work against voluntarism.

It is doubly important that the principle of voluntarism be stressed in a society that takes pride in being voluntary. Just because the state does not enforce church membership is no guarantee that other means of pressure are not being used to bring people in. Participation should be a result of a desire to participate.

Becoming a member of any group is not voluntary unless one is clearly aware of the implications of one's decision. A free choice necessitates awareness of what the other choices are and the virtues of this choice over the other possibilities. Membership must be intentional. Each member needs to be a "convinced" member, to use a Quaker term.

A biblically informed membership which is capable of giving a reason for the hope they have is a necessary element for full and voluntary participation in community. If obedience is to Christ and not simply to the dictates of the community, it is essential that all, to the extent they are able, be well informed in the faith and understand the faith they submit themselves to. Voluntary membership requires a substantial amount of teaching and discussion in the community concerning the basics of the faith, helping to nurture people in their personal growth. Bible study, corporate worship, and personal disciplines such as prayer and fasting are very important.

The faith of the community is empty without the faith of each member. A group becomes authoritarian when the personal faith of the members is not strong enough to maintain the vision of the community and withstand the pressures of the surrounding society. If that is lost, either legalism comes in to hold things together or things fall apart. The church cannot freely hold any positions without teaching them. One result of the failure to teach is the church demanding that the members obey and hold to practices they do not understand or are personally not committed to. For people to hold to any position voluntarily they need to understand it and why it is important.

To be free the community must be composed of people who are free. True community is impossible unless the people are authentic persons and have an identity and integrity of their own. They need to know who they are in order to voluntarily become part of the community. Without this personal integrity on the part of each member there exists not community, but tyranny.

For any community to be free, all must be members because they genuinely want to be, because they made the decision to do it.

Community presupposes integrity and freedom on the

part of every member. There should be no compulsion to do anything. If people submit to the community because of coercion or fear, there can only be trouble for everyone. All commitment and conformity must be voluntary.

Although commitment to Christ and the community should be a total commitment of one's whole life, there also needs to be a real freedom to leave at any time. No one should be bound to the community by economic necessity or any other pressure, except one's voluntary commitment. For a community to be voluntary other possibilities must exist for the members of the community. An intentional community can degenerate into an ethnic subculture where acceptance of a cultural tradition passed down from past generations is the basis of membership. One is born into it and never wrestles with the concerns or values of the outside world. At this point the community reverts back to an establishment group, another Christendom.

Community does create ethnicism. The people of God are an *ethnos.* That is good. Many of Jesus' disciples were relatives. The ethnic flavor of many Mennonite communities is one of their strengths. This is bad when it becomes an end in itself, when it denies voluntarism and outreach, when it causes the community to become closed. It is important for members of the community to develop and maintain relationships outside the community. An open, outgoing *ethnos* can be beautiful. Having a distinct identity and maintaining voluntarism are in tension with each other but need not cancel each other out. Both can remain as important aspects of community.

The Meaning of Membership

Any group which has a clear sense of identity will understand the meaning of membership in that group, who is and is not a member, and how one can become a member. The first question, however, is not who is in the church, but what is the church. When we answer that, we will have answered who is in it.

Because of the new sense of identity and direction which comes from commitment to each other and the gospel, membership in a Christian community will have meaning and integrity. It will be understood that membership in the body of Christ involves commitment and discipleship. When the meaning of membership is not clear, many problems are created, both for the community and for those outside.[10] Unless there is a clear commitment of everything to God and the discernment of the body, the whole decision-making process is threatened and the authority for discipline is severely weakened. The result will be a weakening of the life of the community, because of the loss of unity and clarity of commitment. When this happens, the freedom of the community is also reduced, with informal discipline replacing the voluntary community of love. As Elizabeth O'Conner puts it,

> The refusal to grapple with the issue of entrance into the Christian church is not tolerance; it is betrayal of the gospel which we preach. No one claims that seeking to ensure integrity of membership is not frought with danger and difficulty, but the answer does not lie in skirting the problem.[11]

Who can respect the pastor or church who tells a prospective member, "Well, this is what the church has historically taught, but we don't expect you to accept it if it creates any difficulty for you"? In addition to being an insult to the person, it casts suspicion on the integrity of the whole church. The church that has no discipline gives the impression that church membership need not make any difference in one's life. The result is a church that demands nothing and expects little.

An association whose primary purpose is to abolish capital punishment does not seek to include people who actively are working to continue capital punishment. Any such association that includes the opposite persuasion in order not to be "closed" is not serious about abolishing capital punishment. Accepting people into membership who are not committed to following Jesus is a significant cause of spiritual decline in the church.

One of the arguments against the believers' church position is that it is better to have everyone in the church so that at least everyone will be subjected to a little faith than for there to be a faithful church of only a few. The judgment of history on the two approaches should be clear. Small faithful groups are able to confront everyone with an undiluted gospel, something the mainline churches cannot do. Conrad Grebel, the early Anabaptist, wrote,

> It is much better that a few be rightly taught through the Word of God, believing and walking aright in virtues and practices, than that many believe falsely and deceitfully through adulterated doctrine.[12]

One way to solve many of the problems of discipline is to make the expectations and meaning of membership so clear and specific that only those committed to that vision will join. If the church is clear in her identity, those opposed to it will not want to be members and so will exclude themselves.

If expectations and commitments are made clear, this gives a greater freedom not only to members, but also to nonmembers to honestly explore the meaning of community without fear of being given responsibilities they are not ready to accept. It assures people that the group is open to new members. One of the differences between a clique and Christian community is that one can easily learn how to be included in community while the clique is more vague and subjective. When membership is clear, nonmembers make the decision whether or not they will be included.

There will be many levels of association with the community. In addition to the committed members there will be serious seekers, visitors, and those on the outside who keep in touch in various ways with members of the community. When seen in this way, the circle soon becomes quite large.

Membership in the church should be open to all and determined only by the person's response to the gospel and never on the basis of class, race, or nationality. Jesus never turned anyone away for any reason, but He also laid down the terms for the relationship.

It will not be expected that a new member need be on the same level of maturity of faith as everyone else. The question of membership is not based on maturity, but whether you have given all you have to Jesus, however little that may be. The question is, Are you committed to share and grow? The biggest problem in the church is not with those sincere, yet immature Christians who continually keep stumbling and need the help of the community, but with those who are not committed.

In a believers' church the process of accepting new members is a creative and exciting process. Not only is it a time of examination of the prospective member, but a time of community self-examination and openness to what the new person can bring to the community. It is a period of giving and receiving and should be a growing experience for all involved. Anytime a new member is received the group changes.

During the process of becoming a member the community will probe quite deeply into the life of the prospective member, examining areas of faith and life, questions and problems. She will deal rather directly with any problems which could hinder full commitment to the community, in addition to what the person has to offer. The prospective member will also probe deeply into the community, learning to know the community intimately, sharing doubts and weaknesses and how he/she feels the need of the help of the community. The process of examining each new member will never be exactly the same. The strengths and weaknesses of each person are unique and with each person the community will see different areas that need to be explored more deeply.

The period of testing and questioning before acceptance into membership is a means of taking people seriously and helping them to think through their faith and commitment. In many churches where you would ask for membership, they would simply put your name on the roll and never take you seriously.

At any point where there is disagreement between the prospective member and the community the discernment process will begin to work. The community may realize her own need to change, the person may see and accept the insight of the community, or recognize that he/she does not want to be part of the community.

Some will want to join the community with the condition that they not need to change. "Why can't you just accept me the way I am?" We do need to accept people where they are, but a condition of membership must be that everyone be open to the Holy Spirit and that includes being open to change. Some may object to this and argue that they will be willing to discuss these matters gradually after they are members, but not before. This may be a sign that the community has been pushing too hard and needs to back off a bit, but the request to wait to deal with these matters until later cannot be accepted, for it probably is an excuse to avoid dealing with them at all. If a person is not willing to deal with something before membership, it is doubtful whether there will be more openness afterward. The problems will still be there and will deeply affect the community even though they cannot be openly dealt with. Taking in members who are either uncommitted or have problems that have not been faced will mean much trouble for that community. To spend the time dealing with differences before the person is granted membership will be liberating for all involved.

Some persons seeking for something solid in their lives or running away from reality may be willing to commit themselves to anything sounding at all idealistic. Bursting with commitment today, some may have little concern tomorrow. Any idealism needs to be tested carefully against the hard realities of community before anyone is accepted into membership, otherwise, later the person may feel trapped by the commitment. In this way the freedom of the person is respected. Verbal commitments are not enough. Their validity is tested by the fruits they produce.

It should be expected that before becoming a member, the person, in addition to making a complete commitment to following Jesus, will have experienced repentance, God's grace and forgiveness, and a new purpose in life. This will include inner healing of mind and heart. Eberhard Arnold described how this can be recognized.

> We recognize the following as clear signs that healing is taking place: joy in humble service and in working together with others; *freedom from self-willed plans,* from lust for power over others; truthfulness in judging our self; and above all, *faithfulness and endurance* on the way we have recognized before God.[13]

Some communities have a time of novitiate, a time when a person can fully participate in the life of the community before final commitment in order that a more intelligent and voluntary decision can be made concerning commitment. This was a common practice in the early church. The deeper and closer a community becomes, the more need will be felt for this.

One becomes a member when everyone is clear about that, including the new member. One is accepted into membership when, after taking each other seriously, there is unity between that person and the community.

Just as consent of the community is necessary in becoming a member, so leaving the community needs the consent of the community. To leave the fellowship, without it being discerned that it is God's will, is a serious violation of one's commitment to Christ's church. One should not decide on one's own to leave the fellowship. Most churches discover that when little commitment is involved in membership it is easy to come into the church. By the same token it is also easy to leave when things become difficult. The strength of any group is related to the commitment needed both to get in and stay in. Commitment to the church is similar to marriage. It is a commitment to each other for good and hard times. It involves commitment of our whole lives. Thus no one should ever leave the fellowship unless it is discerned that God is calling that person to leave.

Although this kind of commitment is binding, it is also entered into joyfully and voluntarily. Just as the wedding commitment to not cheat on one's spouse is not forced, but made eagerly and freely because of the love between the two people, so commitment in community must be deep and free. If one does not want to make that kind of commitment, then one is not ready to become a member.

No pressure may ever be put on anyone to join. Rather, each person is helped to examine carefully the meaning of his/her motivation for joining so that it will be a truly free act. If a commitment is made out of pressure, desire to be accepted, or any other involuntary reason, the person will probably come to the point of feeling trapped and may become resistant and hostile. Plenty of time needs to be given for new persons to come to know themselves, God, and the community.

*   *   *

At this point some will object and argue that the church is always to be inclusive and never exclude anyone. It is important that we understand the relationship between exclusiveness and inclusiveness, for they go together. Any group that includes some, excludes others. If a church were serious about not excluding anyone she would need to declare everyone in that town, no, in the world, a member of that church. That would be ridiculous for no one in reality would be included. Some may not even want to be included. To be included has no meaning if there is no possibility of not being included. That is the problem with so many churches who are so open and inclusive that they do not deeply include anyone.

We can use the illustration of marriage. Having an exclusive relationship with my wife does not keep me from having meaningful relationships with other women. In fact, the more exclusively I give myself to my wife, the more free I can be to share meaningfully with many people. But if I were to give myself promiscuously to every woman I meet I would not be able to give myself deeply to anyone. Soon all my relationships would be shallow. God is also exclusive in that He expects everything from us.

Biblical faith affirms that the universal is found in the particular. God called Abraham and a particular people, the Jews, to make known His universal will. He chose them to be a blessing to all nations. The more we learn to love particular people the more we can love all humanity. We should be more concerned about feeding particular hungry people than in feeding everyone, for if we are only concerned about feeding everyone, we end up feeding no one. Concern for the particular is the best way to express concern for the universal. As D. T. Niles put it,

> In the work of the Holy Spirit, then, there is a quality not only of comprehension but also of selection, not only of wideness but also of narrowness—a contradictoriness which ought to be no surprise for anyone whose faith is grounded in the Bible. For, as the Bible makes plain, the work of God is always characterized by universality of intention as well as particularity of method.[14]

The idea that we are superior to others is politically described as "elitism" and theologically as "gnosticism," a belief in a knowledge or strategy not available to all or in having the "whole truth." A community which only claims to know the truth partially, which is open to all, and has no secret strategy or knowledge cannot be considered elitist. If membership is limited on the basis of race, class, or any other discriminatory criteria, then it is elitist. As long as a community reaches out to others, is open to new people and new truths, she cannot properly be called exclusive.

Children and Commitment

Our discussion of voluntarism relates to children who are raised in the community. Here also we dare not pressure or coerce persons concerning Christian commitment and membership in the community. It should never even be assumed that the children will become members. That must be their own free decision. In fact, we do not want them to take this step before they have carefully considered both its meaning and other possible options. If they do not decide to become part of the community, hopefully they will still make a valuable contribution to the world and still live out many of the values they were taught. This may even be part of our contribution to the world. We must always accept the possibility that God may call our children elsewhere, and our children need to know we believe that.

Although we have a deep responsibility for the spiritual life of our children, it is important that we not make commitments for them or impose our commitments on them. Our children should grow up to please God rather than us. I have no right to impose *my* will on *my* children. Ultimately, they are not *my* children anyway; they are God's children. It is important that my children realize that they belong to God rather than to me. They are a trust from God and together the parents and the Christian community are responsible to

God for them. Children are always to be seen as gifts and never as possessions.

Children will never be able to accept the faith freely unless they are allowed to struggle through the issues and discover the vision for themselves. Many children are prevented from ever freely accepting the faith by parents who attempt to manipulate them into the faith. They then spend the rest of their lives either in an unhealthy submission or a compulsive rebellion against the faith. They should never be put in a position where they are forced to choose between independence and rejection of the faith, or submission to standards they did not choose. The church should not be an institution youth have to rebel against to establish their own identity.

There is no need to make adults out of children. Let them be children as long as they can be. The innocence of childhood is a beauty not to be destroyed by overzealous parents who want to force their children to be adults, molded in their own images. Children become adults soon enough.

It is important not to force a premature recognition of sin and guilt in children. That is better left in God's hands. Although children need to be confronted with specific wrongs, their awareness of sin at a deeper level and need for redemption should be prompted by God's Spirit at work in their lives, rather than our imposing it on their consciousness.

The less moral pressure put on children the better off they are. What they need is a clear, living example of what is right, not pressure. One reason many parents feel the need to pressure their children is that they know they are not showing them a good example and that their own faith is weak. It makes little sense trying to pressure the children to remain in the community. As a Hutterite told me, if the spiritual life of the community is in order, the children will stay. If not, they will leave. A spiritually alive group attracts people. A dead one repulses them.

The Hutterian Society of Brothers is right in asking their

children to have at least a year's experience outside of the community before they are accepted as members. How different from those churches who are scheming to find new gimmicks to get their children to stay. If they are to make a free decision, youth must become acquainted with other options and claims for their loyalty. It is important that the community help prepare the children for life in the world. Commitment must not be based on a feeling that leaving the community would be harder, less fulfilling, and more of a sacrifice than staying. These things may be true, but of themselves do not represent a significant commitment. Membership in the community should never be easy. Rather it should require a deep commitment.

When children are taken into membership, the whole process is threatened. Not having made a completely voluntary commitment, when they become teenagers and begin a period of questioning if not rebellion, many problems arise. The person then is caught between a desire for personal freedom and guilt feelings for questioning the covenant that was made. The community is also faced with the problem of choosing between legalism and compromise of her vision. Must a person remain faithful to that commitment even if one does not really believe in it anymore, or is Christian commitment not really that serious? No youth should be put through this turmoil. They should be encouraged to come to a free decision of their own as they struggle through their questions and doubts. That means an adult commitment.

Limiting membership to adults in no way denies the responsibility to nurture children in the Christian faith and community. In fact, the community has the responsibility for helping the child come to the point where he/she can make a free decision regarding the faith. This obviously includes understanding the faith.

When a child asks for church membership this may indicate a desire for social identification and security rather than any call from God. It is important that children be given a sense of belonging in the community, that their faith be accepted as valid, and that they be assured that their not having been baptized in no way excludes them from God's grace. Children can enjoy a sense of belonging to God's covenant people without being bound to any commitments.

We have a responsibility for teaching our children and helping them raise the important questions concerning life and faith. It is easy to teach children the Bible stories and give them a fairly good understanding of the Bible by the time they are six. All one needs is a good Bible story book which they will beg you to read, and some time in honestly answering their questions. Children need an identity and history from which they can relate to the world, a basis from which to make their own decisions, something to either accept or reject.

Neither does limiting membership to adults mean that children will be discouraged from prayer and commitment. Children at a young age become aware of God and want to respond. They have deep religious experiences which must be respected. Children can make commitments and can take the faith seriously. When a twelve-year-old makes a commitment, we rejoice and seek ways in which we can help the child grow in the faith. But we understand that this is a child's commitment and not an adult, final commitment. There may be fidelity in dating, but this is not yet a marriage commitment. Children can be encouraged to make specific commitments, but not more total, general commitments. A premature, forced decision will necessitate a later decision, which may be quite unfree because of all the guilt and unclarity related to the former decision.

Twelve-year-olds are not able to make a voluntary lifelong commitment. They do not know enough about the other options and are too much under the influence of their parents to make a clear decision on their own. Few twelve-year-olds differ from their parents' political views. They reflect their parents' social values *and* religion, unless they are operating out of a pervasive rebellion to parents which is equally invalid as a voluntary commitment. They have barely begun to think these issues through for themselves.

Most children of twelve have a deep desire to please Mommy and Daddy. They receive a good feeling whenever they submit to the desires of their parents. If they finally give in and clean up their room, they experience a good feeling. If they give in to Mommy and Daddy's desire for them to be good Christians, they experience that same good feeling. Fine, but that good feeling is not the Holy Spirit or the new birth. The psychological dimensions working here are too clear. A voluntary commitment is an adult commitment.

Believer's Baptism

This brings us to the question of baptism. A discussion of believer's baptism is not a discussion of proper age. It involves the meaning not only of baptism, but also our understanding of the church. We are not dealing with unimportant differences of form, but with radically different understandings of the church. Rather than being a peripheral issue as many today suggest, this question goes right to the heart of the meaning of the church and Christian commitment. We will begin by taking a careful look at the New Testament understanding of baptism and then ask what would be the most authentic expression of that understanding.

In a few places baptism is seen as a cleansing and washing (Acts 22:16; 1 Cor. 6:11), but there is not much emphasis on this and no hint of a magical washing away of sin in a self-operative way. There is no teaching that the water actually washes away sin. That can only be done by God as we respond in faith. Water can be a symbol of a deeper washing that has already taken place and is continuing to take place in our lives (1 Pet. 3:21).

The deeper meaning of cleansing is forgiveness of sins which baptism symbolizes. "Repent, and be baptized . . . for the forgiveness of your sins" (Acts 2:38). But there is a little catch here. The Bible ties God's forgiveness and baptism to the need for repentance. The primary meaning of John's baptism was repentance. Repentance must be voluntary.

Paul's distinctive contribution to our understanding of baptism is to connect it with the death and resurrection of Jesus (Rom. 6; Col. 2:12). Baptism is a matter of death and life, a symbol of our dying to our past and pledging to follow unto death. Before we can enter the new community we must die to the old. Baptism is a symbol of our dying and being buried and then being raised a new person in Christ. Jesus asked His disciples, "Are you able to drink the cup that I drink, or to be baptized with the baptism with which I am baptized?" (Mk. 10:38). Baptism is not kids' stuff. Whether we will give up the old life and be prepared for persecution is not something that children can decide. When this aspect of baptism is ignored, we seriously weaken the meaning of Christian discipleship.

The cross is not the end. We are also raised with Christ and delivered out of death into a new life. Baptism is a symbol of Noah's ark (1 Pet. 3:20, 21) and Israel's passing through the Red Sea (1 Cor. 10:1, 2). Water is a biblical symbol for chaos and death. The baptismal water symbolizes the grave out of which we have been delivered. It is a symbol of deliverance from sin and the beginning of a new life of love and joy in the new community.

Baptism is a sign of commitment to Christ *and* His body. Baptism is not an individualistic experience, for being baptized into union with Christ includes unity with others who are also followers of the way. There can be no real unity with Christ that does not include being part of Christ's body. We are baptized into the body of Christ, not just into Christ or into a mystical body. "For indeed we were all brought into one body by baptism" (1 Cor. 12:13 NEB). One of the commitments made in baptism is accepting the joys and demands of membership in a Christian community. Baptism is incomplete if it does not include membership in a body which will give nurture, discernment, and discipline to the new believer.

The theme which the New Testament most often connects with baptism is receiving the Holy Spirit. During Jesus' baptism the Spirit descended in the form of a dove. Jesus promised the disciples a baptism which would be more than John's, for this baptism would include the Holy Spirit (Mk. 1:8; Acts 1:5). At Pentecost Peter said, "Repent, and be baptized . . . for the forgiveness of your sins; and you shall receive the gift of the Holy Spirit" (Acts 2:38). Water baptism is no guarantee of receiving the Spirit nor is it always connected. Sometimes it is a sign that one has already received the baptism of the Spirit (Acts 10:47, 48). God comes to us when He chooses and cannot be manipulated by any of our rituals.

Baptism as a symbol of receiving the Spirit suggests an Old Testament parallel of anointing with oil, which was a symbol of receiving God's Spirit. When we are called out for a purpose we have the promise of being given the power to carry it through. This was symbolized in the Old Testament by anointing with oil. The New Testament clearly connects baptism with ordination. The laying on of hands which is a symbol of ordination is connected to baptism in Acts 19:5, 6; 8:17; 9:17-19. Jesus was baptized at the beginning of His ministry. Acts connects Paul's baptism with his call to be an apostle. Baptism is not only a symbol of initiation into the new community but commissioning the person to be a witness. Baptism symbolizes the commitment to make discipleship one's main vocation in life.

The New Testament understanding of baptism does not fit when applied to infants. Cleansing, forgiveness, repentance, dying to sin, and being raised to a new life, church

membership, receiving the Holy Spirit, and being ordained to witness cannot have any meaning in relation to infants. Not only does the New Testament understanding not
fit, but more importantly when we accept infant baptism we
seriously cheapen the deep commitment called for in the
gospel. In the context of *corpus Christianum* (making church
membership and state citizenship synonomous), infant baptism certainly makes sense. The idea that all the citizens are
expected to have the same religion as the prince is an extension of the idea that what the father believes the children also
are to believe. Infant baptism makes sense in a church which
sees herself as coextensive with society, spreading her means
of grace as widely as possible with minimum commitment,
but not in a gathered, voluntary community of believers.

If we take a historical approach we will not find any
record of any infant being baptized before the third century.[15]
In the fourth century there was a great amount of resistance
to the growing practice of infant baptism.[16] There is no mention in the New Testament of any infant being baptized.
Some refer to Acts 16:15, 33 and 1 Corinthians 1:16 where
mention is made of whole households being baptized. These
references tell us nothing about whether infants were
baptized because we do not know if they had any infants in
those households. Even if they did, this still tells us nothing
unless we first know whether or not they practiced infant
baptism in the early church. If someone raised in a church
which practices only believer's baptism said that a whole
family was baptized it would not be understood that infants
were baptized even if there were infants in the family. It
would be understood that this referred only to those who
were baptizable. These texts prove nothing concerning this
question.

The traditional sacramental view is that baptism is a
means of grace which overcomes the mark of original sin,
making it more likely that the child will respond to God's

grace. It is true, as infant baptism affirms, that God extends His grace to infants, that God seeks us before we seek Him, but nowhere in the New Testament is this one of the meanings given to baptism. Baptism refers to *our response* to God's grace. It is also true that the resurrection of Jesus has objectively altered the course of history and that all of us must respond to that in some way, but how does that justify or make necessary infant baptism? Yes, we want our children to accept this, but they must make that decision. We cannot decide for them. It is not that babies cannot receive grace, but that they cannot commit themselves.

Many supporters of infant baptism reject the sacramental understanding and see infant baptism as child dedication and an expression of God's love for all babies. Some see infant baptism in a covenantal sense, as a symbol that the baby is included in God's promise to the community. This is important but it has no relationship to the biblical understanding of baptism. It would be better for the children to be included in a real covenant community and be daily receiving the love, support, and guidance they need rather than having formal and empty ceremonies like child dedication.

A classical way to develop a biblical basis for infant baptism is to claim that baptism is the New Testament equivalent of circumcision in the Old Testament. It is interesting to note, however, that the New Testament never makes this connection. Only once are the two mentioned together and this seems to support believer's baptism.

> In him also you were circumcised, not in a physical sense, but by being divested of the lower nature; this is Christ's way of circumcision. For in baptism you were buried with him, in baptism also you were raised to life with him. Colossians 2:11, 12, NEB.

Rather than referring to an operation performed on male babies, the theme of being buried and transformed more likely refers to the Old Testament concept of circumcising your heart (see Deut. 10:16; 30:6; Jer. 4:4; 9:25; Lev. 26:41; Ex. 6:12, 30; Ezek. 44:7, 9; Acts 7:51). In all these texts the reference is to a radical change in one's life and implies a voluntary commitment involving repentance. Circumcision of the heart must be voluntary and so must baptism.

We might consider what Paul had to say about circumcision in Romans 2:28, 29, NEB.

> The true Jew is not he who is such in externals, neither is the true circumcision the external mark in the flesh. The true Jew is he who is such inwardly, and the true circumcision is of the heart, directed not by written precepts but by the Spirit.

How infant baptism is a sign of an inner response of the heart to the work of the Spirit rather than an external mark will take a lot of explaining. As Vernard Eller put it, "If real circumcision must be a matter of the heart, it follows that real baptism must be a matter for the believer."[17] Just as circumcision is impossible before birth, so Christian baptism is impossible before being reborn through faith in Jesus Christ. Although infant baptism expresses important truths and performs useful functions, it is not the baptism described in the New Testament.

Many in the free church tradition now baptize young children and in many ways have accepted the theology of infant baptism, denying their own teachings and identity. For many, baby dedication equals infant baptism and child baptism corresponds to confirmation. However, some so-called believers' churches now baptize children at a younger age than is acceptable for confirmation by churches that practice infant baptism, thus raising the question of whether they take baptism less seriously than do those who practice infant baptism and confirmation.

It is sad to see all the twelve-year-olds in some churches being baptized at the same time each year. The kind of decision inherent in the believers' church's view is never called for. When churches move to a position of baptizing children they have moved away from being a believers' church and the consequences will manifest themselves for a long time. The commitment and vision have been drastically weakened. During times of persecution the seriousness of Christian commitment is clear to all. But without persecution, often it is easier for children to stay with the community than to leave. Rather than a commitment to God's kingdom or separation from the world, baptism then becomes an act of conformity which will threaten the heart of any believers' church.

It is not far from the sacramental theology of infant baptism to believe that if a child is baptized by age fourteen there is then a far better chance that that person will stay with the church and be a Christian. To argue that children should be baptized when they are young and still willing, with the fear that they might change their minds when they are older, is both manipulative and an acceptance of sacramentalism, the idea that baptism itself will do something for the person and make the person more likely to accept the faith.

The New Testament does not teach that baptism does something for you, that it predisposes one to become a Christian. Baptism is not a means of salvation or grace, but a sign and testimony of the salvation, grace, and transforming power which has already occurred in our lives. It is an act of obedience, not a means of salvation. Baptism does not save. It can do little more than make a wet sinner out of a dry sinner with Baptists getting more wet than Episcopalians. In the New Testament, faith comes from baptism. We become members of the body of Christ through faith, not baptism. The biblical meaning of baptism is completely distorted if done without faith and discipleship.

*   *   *

If we do not baptize people when they are babies, then at

what age do we baptize them? Well, Jesus was baptized at age
thirty. Actually, the question is not age, but when is a person
prepared to make the kind of commitment baptism and
membership in the community imply? As pointed out earlier
in this chapter, this is an adult decision. It is a decision more
important than marriage and we do not let children get married. Baptism is not a puberty rite or a symbol of entrance
into adulthood, but an adult decision regarding Christ's
kingdom, a decision to put one's whole life under the lordship
of Christ and the authority of His church. Baptism symbolizes a willingness to give and receive admonishment and to
be part of the discernment process, a commitment children
are not ready to make.

This kind of commitment obviously must be voluntary.
Any voluntary membership in a disciplined church would
mean oppression. Since children cannot make this kind of
commitment, adult voluntary commitment is essential.
Seldom would anyone in a believers' church regret having
waited for baptism until it could be a more meaningful and
serious commitment.

Although the proper age for baptism is not discussed in
the New Testament, the concern did exist in the early church.
Tertullian writing around 204 urged that baptism be postponed until there is more maturity.[18] Many of the early
church leaders, although raised in Christian homes, were not
baptized until they were 20 or 30. These include people like
Ambrose, Gregory of Nazianzus, John Chrysostom, and Je-
rome. There was also the concern that people not be baptized
without proper instruction and teaching, sometimes lasting
two years.[19]

Vernard Eller has pointed to analogies with other decisions people face and suggests that the late teens or early
twenties might be an appropriate time for baptism.[20] He suggests that receiving the Holy Spirit and becoming part of the
body of Christ have the character of a deep commitment

similar to marriage. Ordination to a life of service and witness is analogous to starting out on a career. Dying to the old and beginning a new life relates to youth leaving home to become independent of their parents.

Maybe we need to develop another kind of dedication ceremony which would be available to children as they come to the age of puberty. This could be a way for the church to recognize the seriousness of intention on the part of youth and a method of showing support for the search they begin. It could be another way of helping children come to the point where they can freely decide whether or not to make the radical commitment which is necessary to participate in the coming of Christ's kingdom.

What should you do if you were sprinkled as a baby or dipped as a child? The important question is whether you have committed your life to God's kingdom, whether you have died to the old. If this has never been symbolized by baptism, then in reality you have never been baptized, even though you may have gone through the motions. You should then consider being baptized once and for all.

Since baptism marks the entrance of a new believer into the Christian community it is one of the most important occasions in the life of the community. What could be more serious and joyful than this? That baptism is not important in the church today is only a sign of how its meaning has been destroyed. Baptism is not a formality, but a significant event in the life of the community. It cannot be a minor addition to the regular Sunday morning meeting or even a formal ceremony in front of the congregation. It involves the whole community and the whole community should be gathered around the baptismal site, eager to welcome the new believer with hugs, kisses, and tears. How we have cheapened this and destroyed its significance! Seldom is baptism a time of great rejoicing or an occasion in which there is hardly a dry eye in the congregation.

In addition to entrance into the Christian community, baptism is a public testimony to the world of our pledge to follow Jesus even unto death. It is the seal of the covenant[21] we have made, similar to a public marriage ceremony. The public nature of the act is important. I once heard of a convert who postponed baptism because of the disapproval of his family. Eventually this person fell away from the faith, probably at least partly because he was not willing to declare publically his commitment to Christ. Because of the public nature of baptism and its relation to community, the idea of a private baptism makes as much sense as a square circle. Baptism cannot be private.

Maybe the best place for baptism would be a public swimming pool on a Sunday afternoon in the midst of all the bathers. That would strip away all the pagan religious trappings and bring us closer to the real meaning of baptism. Streams or lakes would also be fine. Probably the least appropriate place is at the front of the meetinghouse, apart from the congregation, making the people spectators rather than participants.

Although more emphasis should be put on the faith of the one being baptized than the form of baptism, it does seem to me that the idea of being buried and raised up a new person, as well as cleansing, are best symbolized by immersion. The Greek word *baptizo* clearly means to dip or immerse. Immersion was the practice of the early church and was probably dropped as a matter of convenience. The important expectation, however, is that our dying to Christ and His kingdom be a free response to God's work among us.

Chapter 7

THE ORGANIZED COMMUNITY

That the power of the God-head may be known in the body, in that perfect freedom which every member hath in Christ Jesus; that none may exercise lordship or dominion over another, nor the person of any be set apart, but as they continue in the power of truth . . . that truth itself in the body may reign, not persons or forms.—Letter from Friends in Balby, 1656[1]

The Need for Structure

Since the body of Christ is a visible fellowship, the question of form and structure is inescapable. Wherever people come together for a common purpose, order and leadership are inevitable. Although we may never identify form with the fellowship, the community must have form. All through the Bible structure and authority are accepted and assumed. We cannot accept the spiritualist claim that only the spirit and not the form is important. Even a concern with reformation is an affirmation that form does matter. Outward forms are significant, for they are subtle teachers.

It is essential that we come to terms with this aspect of community. Otherwise we become obsessed with avoiding it and we are unable to move on to more important concerns. Stable communities like the Hutterites have found a way to deal with these questions and with what needs to be done.

Our topic is not an easy one, however, since most of us

have had such bad experiences with leaders, authorities, and structures in the past that we want to keep as far as possible from them. When we think of them we immediately think of relationships of domination and authoritarianism. Indeed, there is a deep crisis in our society today because most authorities are disrespected if not despised.

If we look deeper, however, we will discover that part of the crisis is the lack of true leadership and authority. We have plenty of people on ego trips and power hungry defenders of little kingdoms, but few people who have the character to instill respect and point to anything resembling sanity and reality.

Hopefully we are not so dominated by our reactions to bad experiences with leadership and authority in the past that we cannot be free to find our way out of the wilderness. We dare not simplistically say that since we reject domination, therefore we cannot accept any authority. Our resistance is not to structure, but to domineering structures which are no longer servants, but have become ends in themselves. Only when structure replaces the Holy Spirit and the fellowship as the essence of community should we resist it.

Authoritarianism and disorder are not the only two options. There is also the possibility of order, direction, and purpose in the context of freedom. Lack of clearly defined structure and roles does not necessarily mean freedom. It can also mean the rule of the strong over the weak, the manipulation of the more committed by those who are less committed. It can mean an inability to implement what most want to do.

Spirit and Form

Although the New Testament has a lot to say about form, there is no command what that form must be. Paul has four lists of ministries, each of them different from the others (Rom. 12; 1 Cor. 12:4-11, 28-31; Eph. 4). There is no single normative pattern in the New Testament. Within the New

Testament church herself there was no common organizational pattern. Forms of leadership and order were diverse
rather than static and uniform. Structure must emerge out of
the life of the community as the community is led by the Holy
Spirit into mission.

The true church is not the one with the oldest organization, the one with the most historical continuity, or the most
modern and progressive, but any community formed by the
Holy Spirit and true to the apostolic faith. The test of our
faith and witness is not in any organizational succession, institutional ordination, or unbroken chains, but in our faithfulness to the living Word. The question is whether we are
hearing and obeying the same voice as did the apostles. Those
who hear and obey today are those who are in apostolic succession.

We mock and profane the reality of the church when we
see it perpetuated by some sacred hierarchical structure. The
church is always born of God's free acts of grace. God gives
that grace as He wills, not as we control it. If apostolicity
were based on hierarchical succession or a fixed rite, then the
Holy Spirit and faith would not be necessary. There is much
biblical support for institutional discontinuity in the history
of the people of God. God moves and acts when, where, and
as He wills and cannot be captured by any of our institutions
or forms. The question rather is whether our forms are in
tune with God's Spirit.

The question of apostolicity is whether any particular
group was started and now is being led by the same Spirit as
was the early church. The nature of the early Christian community needs to be taken seriously. Are we faithful to that vision or have we strayed a long way from it?

Our faith needs historical emphasis and content. The
Spirit we know is the same Spirit we see in Jesus of Nazareth.
We are part of a movement that has come down through his-
tory. There is a theological succession in which the Holy

Spirit is seen as doing the same things over and over throughout the centuries. In this we do have continuity.

Order is a spiritual issue rather than a legal one. The Spirit gives the gifts and positions. Jesus is the Head and Leader. He orders the community, not we. The New Testament speaks in terms of spiritual gifts rather than legal structure or formal authority. The early Christian communities were ordered by the Holy Spirit through gifts distributed in the body and it actually worked. Even Paul was amazed by this miracle.

Although there is a different form in the pastoral epistles (1 and 2 Timothy and Titus) than in Corinthians or Ephesians, we need not see in the pastoral epistles the development of "early catholicism" and an emerging hierarchy as distinguished from the earlier writings of Paul. We should note that the pastoral epistles were written to very young congregations who were just beginning to form a structure of leadership, rather than to developed ones. It is striking to note that the movement is toward a multiple ministry with Timothy, for example, taking less of a monarchical role. Timothy and Titus hardly represent the beginning of hierarchical bishops. We should not see the pastoral epistles negating the vision in Corinthians of each member expressing their gifts, but another expression of the same thing.[2] The hierarchical view of leadership is a perversion of the New Testament understanding of leadership, not a logical development of it.

The development of hierarchical church organization came later as the vision of a radical community began to fade. There is a vast difference between the view of "where two or three are gathered together in my name, there am I in the midst of them" and the idea of the church existing only under the properly constituted authority of a bishop.

The amazing fact of the early Christians is not the development of the hierarchy, but that it took so long for it to develop. The fact that this took so long to develop indicates significant delaying factors. The early Christian *koinonia* and understanding of the presence of Christ as Leader made the development of a hierarchical institution slow and difficult. The sacerdotal (priestly) and sacramental developments met strong resistance every step of the way.

The struggle between structure based on faithfulness to the leading of the Holy Spirit and structure based on rationality and competence is still with us. Today in a world of bureaucratic relationships, the church has tended to follow the corporate, bureaucratic model and become a secular, democratic organization with boards, constitution, and administrators, with computer readouts the basis for determining policy rather than a body listening to the voice of the Holy Spirit. Service and office in the church are based on proper certification as in the educational or medical world. Church boards function more as business organizations than as spiritual leaders.

Structures of relationships and decision making should be more analogous to the family than to the bureaucratic world. We are a family, a community, a body—not a bureaucracy. We are a new people, not just another of society's institutions. The new life in Christ cannot be put into the old wineskins of the old society, be that bureaucracy, humanistic psychology, or service club models.

Another current tendency is to continually seek change and something new. Every few years we reorganize and restructure. Of course, we should not keep something just because it is old, but that is no excuse for uncritically accepting the new. It is not always necessary to give up forms that have been meaningful to us.

The wine of our faith does need to be put into wineskins, for it cannot be held in our hands. But we must be careful not to concentrate more on the wineskins than on the wine. The structures must be kept secondary to the main purposes. In no way may the community be structured to limit the freedom of the Spirit to lead in new directions. We do well to be aware of how forms become static and closed, including new ones.

We need to be careful that the power of organizations not take the place of the power of the Holy Spirit. The better the organization, the less need we may feel for the Holy Spirit. An efficient organization is a poor substitute for the Holy Spirit. Yet that is the state of most of our denominational structures. We have efficiency experts and management consultants, but little spiritual power.

Structure is important but must always be an expression of a deeper reality which no structure can perpetuate. Faith comes before order. Order is given by God, not something for us to create or impose. The faith of the community is primary, not method or structure. Without the Holy Spirit the best methods and structures are empty.

The outward form must correspond to the inner nature of the community. The form of the community is derived not from some formal concept, but from an attempt to live faithfully to what Jesus teaches us. The doctrine of the church is the doctrine of Christ. "Ecclesiology is Christology."[3] Everything else grows out of that and is defined by it. The presence of the Spirit enables the form and essence to correspond.

Again we must say, the church is a community, a people, and can never be equated with any institutions. The essence of the church is in the faithful people who are gathered and bound together by the living Christ. The church is the people, not the structure.

Leadership and Servanthood

In Christian community no master is recognized but Jesus, for we are all brothers and sisters (Mt. 23:8-10). This does not deny that God gives gifts of leadership to people in the community and that we participate in Christ's leadership.

Leaders receive their authority from God, however, not from themselves or even from the people. They are not laws unto themselves.

The purpose of leadership is for the building up of the whole body, for enabling and preparing all the members for ministry (Eph. 4:11, 12). The purpose of leadership is to enable all to exercise the gifts they have been given rather than take away initiative and responsibility from the rest of the community.

Maybe we could overcome our fear of leaders if we understood the nature of leadership in the New Testament, one of the most anti-authoritarian books ever written. Although the need for strong leadership is assumed, there is no acceptance of it being domineering or manipulative. Jesus' response to the question of who would be greatest in His kingdom was to say,

> You know that the rulers of the Gentiles lord it over them, and their great men exercise authority over them. It shall not be so among you; but whoever would be great among you must be your servant, and whoever would be first among you must be your slave; even as the Son of man came not to be served but to serve, and to give his life as a ransom for many.—Matthew 20:25-28.

There we have it. The leader is a servant rather than a master. Even as Jesus humbled Himself and took the form of a servant (Phil. 2:5-8), so we are primarily to be servants. Jesus particularily applied this to leaders. At the time of His temptation in the wilderness He rejected the ways of worldly power. In 1 Corinthians 12 Paul discusses leadership and authority in the community and then goes on to say that the greatest gift of all is love and in 1 Corinthians 13 describes this gift which applies to all leaders. In passages like Ephesians 5:23—6:9 or Colossians 3:19—4:1, it is striking to note what is said to husbands, parents, and slave owners.

There is no hint of condoning any domination. In 1 Peter 5:2-5 elders are told to

> Tend the flock of God that is your charge, not by constraint but willingly, not for shameful gain but eagerly, not as domineering over those in your charge but being examples to the flock. . . . Clothe yourselves, all of you, with humility toward one another, for "God opposes the proud, but gives grace to the humble."

The character of Christian leadership is distinguished by service to others. The greatness of leaders is found not in their power, but in their serving. Leaders are servants, having the lowest position in the whole community rather than a position of prestige. Leadership is never a position of honor, status, or superiority, but of servanthood. It calls for humility rather than pride.

Often when people are given a little authority, it goes to their heads. They begin to talk and relate to people differently and generally take on an artificial role. They begin to feel superior to others and expect to receive honor and praise. They become insensitive to prophets and to the gifts of others. In Christian community this pattern must be totally rejected. Authoritarian styles of leadership are out of keeping with both the letter and spirit of the New Testament.

One of the greatest evils in the world is seeking power over others. There may be none of that among Christians. In Christian community everyone needs to relinquish all personal power. Rather than seek control we submit ourselves to Christ and to each other. Love evaporates the will to power. Power struggles are a part of the old world we are to leave behind. We are called to give up the desire to seek power and to reject any position which involves "lording it over others." How offensive it is to watch people jockeying for power and position, strategizing how they can rise to the top. Some even think they are the best.

Even those with the best of intentions, if they seek to lead the community, are in effect replacing the leadership of the Holy Spirit. It is disturbing to see how often when people want to make a deeper commitment to God, the immediate first step is to seek some leadership position. Positions of leadership are not to be sought, but are to be accepted only as the community asks them of us.

Anyone who is given leadership responsibilities must be ready at all times to give up those responsibilities. In fact, a position is always something one would be happy to relinguish. One's position can never be defended. Leaders should understand that the future of the church is in God's hands, not theirs.

Never may leaders seek to secure influence, admiration, or a following for themselves. That is an expression of egoism rather than the leading of the Holy Spirit. We can influence others to submit to our wishes and sometimes overpower them, but since this kind of following is unstable, constant control needs to be maintained. Its effect is to erode the life of the community. When this happens the whole community is violated and the level of love and trust is reduced.

Good leaders use their gifts to build up and encourage others rather than build up themselves or tear down others. They help develop courage and confidence in others and have no fear of the abilities of others. Leaders can do much to prevent hero worship or development of a personality cult. If responsibilities are continually shared, the help of others sought, free discussion encouraged, a community need not center around certain leaders. Instead of building up a good image of themselves, they will allow others to see them as they are, including their weaknesses and mistakes. Leadership requires an extra amount of humility to overcome all the temptations that come with it.

Hero worship will be rejected by the whole community. So often because of our spiritual weakness we seek to establish a visible human authority, a hero figure whom we can admire. This is to lose sight of God, the One who is the Giver of leadership gifts. The more God is at the center of our lives, the more personal power of individuals fades away. Gifts of leadership are from God and focus on the Giver rather than the receiver of the gifts. When leadership is seen as a gift, there is no basis for pride.

Shared Leadership

Paul's understanding of the ministry and working of the Christian community is that many functions and tasks need to be performed and that the Spirit distributes the gifts needed for these tasks throughout the whole community, giving at least one gift to each member. The purpose for the distribution of gifts through the community is that the body may function properly (Eph. 4:16), that all the needs in the community may be cared for. What these gifts are will vary according to the makeup and needs of the community.

It is essential that we have some understanding of the leadership functions needed in the community so that all are cared for. So many churches emphasize only a few and neglect the rest. Some pastors keep preaching on evangelism and never nurture or disciple their people. Others counsel but never evangelize. People with leadership ability in one area may have none in another area. The teacher may not be a good counselor and the administrator a poor teacher.

We do not have the same gifts. Some gifts do not even fit well together in the same person. The prophet and the moderator roles will probably not be shared by the same person. The ear cannot do the work of the stomach or the stomach the work of the eye. But each of us is part of the same body and has an important place in the body.

What are some of the leadership roles that are essential in Christian community? We will list a few but it should be noted that this list is neither complete nor is it the only way of listing these roles. There is no one way to categorize these functions. In some cases some of them may be combined.

•There are those who are overseers, people the New Testament variously calls elders, shepherds, or bishops. These people have the responsibility of general spiritual oversight and have the gift of being able to discern what is happening in the community. They will keep in touch with what is happening in the whole community. They should not be power figures and it may be best if they not be the more charismatic persons in the community. Spiritual depth and sensitivity are essential.

•There are those who are prophets. They are the ones with vision, people who can both focus and articulate the hopes and desires of the community and see beyond where the community is. They have a special sense of direction and can boldly communicate it to others. They are not afraid of pointing out the weaknesses and sins of the community or to call for repentance.

•There are those who are mediators and moderators. They are able to sense and articulate the consensus of the meeting. Their work is aiding communication and reconciliation. These people do not just support all positions equally or never let it be known where they stand, but are able to help others work through the hard issues to come to the truth. They are not wishy-washy.

•There are those who are teachers, those who can communicate to others the content of the gospel. Their work is spelling out the meaning and implications of the gospel, helping people see more deeply the meaning of the faith.

•There are those who have the gift of discernment, who have special insight into problems that arise in the community. Sometimes this will be in the area of understanding what God is saying to the community. Other times it will mean seeing clearly what is troubling someone with deep problems.

•There are those who are counselors. They may have a special ability to visit and bring hope to those who are in need. They may spend some of their time visiting the elderly and shut-ins. Some of them will have special ability to help people work through personal problems or difficult decisions.

•There are those who are evangelists. Their gift is in communicating the meaning of the gospel to those outside the community. They have a special ability for dealing with non-Christians and calling them to decision. They will often be sent out by the community to proclaim the good news to others.

•There are those who are coordinators and administrators. Their ability is in the area of practical details, seeing that what needs to be done gets done.

•There are also those with special gifts such as healing, tongues, prophecy, and an extra measure of faith. They are a special blessing to the community.

Again it needs to be said that these are not clearly defined roles. In fact, all should feel some responsibility in most all of these areas. All should in some way be both prophets and mediators, dreamers and doers. But all have particular gifts which need to be recognized.

All of our references to leaders in community are in the plural because that is the way it should be. Leadership must always be shared. In the New Testament church there was more than one bishop or elder in each local community, chosen by that community. This is important. If there is only one leader, there is too much danger of the community centering around that person and taking on too much of the imprint of that person's personality. This may hinder the gifts of others from being recognized. In multiple leadership, the leaders need to learn humility and to submit to each other. Having more than one leader is a check on the pride of all the leaders.

Part of the problem in the professional pastoral ministry is that we have taken most of the tasks and made them the responsibility of one person, the paid pastor. This is not only unfair and destructive for the pastor, but stifles the ministry and gifts which have been given to the whole body. The life of the body is the concern of the whole community of faith, not only of certain specialists. Full participation should be expected of all members.

The nature of the Christian community and ministry is such that there is hardly a place for a paid, professional clergy, at least as we know it today. A salaried person hired to run the church is a contradiction of community. So often the clergy are hired to be administrators and promote active and successful programs rather than serve as teachers or evangelists. Often this person turns out to be more of a public relations person than a shepherd, or more of a counselor than a spiritual guide. Not that there is anything necessarily wrong with these roles, but when this person is seen as "the minister" then something is truly wrong.

Rather than professionals, the community is composed of amateurs, not in the sense of unqualified, but in the sense of doing it for the love *(amour)* of doing it. There are no professionals among the people of God. All God's people are amateurs. Maybe a good secular analogy is the Scouts and 4-H programs. They have a very active program with very little paid leadership.

There is nothing wrong with releasing people to give a major amount of time to some concern or mission of the community, but in no way should this replace those gifts already given and being exercised in the community. Nor should these people automatically be considered *the* leaders or authorities. This will be a supplement to the ministry of the community rather than a replacement and should result in the gifts of others in the community being better discerned and utilized rather than no longer needed. It is disastrous for a community when the Spirit has given a gift to someone in the community and instead of recognizing it, they hire someone to come in and do the work for which that gift was given.

Examples of the kinds of persons who might be released for a particular service are persons whose primary work would be outreach, pastoral care, or teaching and study. A theological seminary may have its place, if its purpose is to provide theological training for the whole church rather than to produce a professional ministry. The primary work of seminary graduates would be teaching others, not being leaders or administrators.

It is possible to not have a special clerical class. Groups like the Quakers, Plymouth Brethren, and Jehovah's Witnesses have demonstrated that a clerical class is not necessary for the life of the church. In fact there is so much more flexibility with the New Testament pattern of leadership.

Which form of structure is the stronger and more stable can soon be seen when a people are under persecution. During persecution a bureaucratic or hierarchically organized church is an easy target for subversion and control. A believers' church movement is almost impossible to control as has been demonstrated over and over under oppressive governments. The Ye-Su Chia-ting in China is a good modern example or the Pentecostal or Plymouth Brethren movements in Latin America.

One of the reasons the Anabaptist movement in the sixteenth century was so flexible and able to spread rapidly even under severe persecution was because it was not headed by one leader on whom the movement was dependent. Since the heart of the movement was small communities corporately seeking the leading of the Spirit through the written Word, all that was needed for a church was a small group of Christians anywhere.

An important difference between the sixteenth-century

Anabaptists and the other Reformation groups is that the
Anabaptists developed a group charisma rather than being
the result of an individual charisma. There was no clear
leader of the movement, and where there were leaders, they
were called by the community rather than a community forming around the charisma of one person. Ministry was the
work of the community rather than individual leaders.[4]

The Ministry of All Believers

When the New Testament talks about the gifts of the
Spirit, it emphasizes that every Christian has at least one gift
(1 Cor. 7:7; 12:7; Eph. 4:7; 1 Pet. 4:10). No person has all the
gifts and everyone has at least one. The mandate to proclaim
the gospel and minister according to our gifts is binding on all
believers. This is the meaning of the priesthood of all believers. Luther in his manifesto *To the Christian Nobility* proclaimed:

> All Christians are truly priests and there is no distinction
> amongst them except as to office. ... Everybody who is
> baptized may maintain that he has been consecrated as a priest,
> bishop, or pope.[5]

This idea is not a rejection of priesthood or the individualistic idea of each person being one's own priest, but
rather the communal act of being priests toward each other,
everyone having a ministry in the community. Although the
Reformation talked about the priesthood of all believers, for
the most part it has not been taken seriously in practice by
Protestantism.

This does not mean that we will eliminate the ministry,
but that we will abolish the category of laity, at least if that
means people who are ignorant or incompetent in a certain
area as opposed to trained professionals. God does not call
some to be lay people and others not to be lay people. The
word "laity" comes from the Greek word *laos* in the New

Testament which refers to the whole *people* of God rather than a particular group in the church. The ministry may not be a unique, minority group in the church. It is the calling of all. Every baptized believer is a minister.

It is questionable whether God ever intended for most Christians to devote themselves primarily to "secular" concerns and delegate "spiritual" concerns to a small group of religious specialists. The leaders of the church are not called to do the work of the whole community.

It is striking that the Bible does not identify work with calling. There is no mention of anyone called to a particiular profession. Our call is not to a job, but to discipleship (see 1 Cor. 7:17-24; Eph. 4:1). Our work is subordinate to our call as Christians and our life together in community and will be determined and discerned by the community. This will be determined primarily in light of the kingdom and the needs of the community rather than by psychological tests, best offers, or personal dreams. We are called to be ministers, not farmers or factory workers, although we may work out that calling as farmers or factory workers. In fact, our varied skills and jobs may be useful in fulfilling our calling to ministry.

Much of the current ecumenical emphasis on the "laity" actually does little more than reemphasize the Reformation idea of ministry to the world being one's occupation. It keeps intact the unbiblical assumption of a special ministry of the few and preserves the distinction between a clergy class and a laity class. That everyone has a gift does not mean that some are butchers, bakers, and candlestick makers, or that some are husbands and others wives, but that each has been given at least one spiritual gift. These spiritual gifts are for building up the body of Christ and are more important than any occupational abilities we may have.

We need to be critical of the worker-priest movement which actually continues the clergy-laity split rather than overcomes it. Why not have "worker-laity" in the factories?

Why are priests working in the factory different from Christians working in the factory? Why? Because some believe the clergy are a special class different from most Christians. The same thing is expressed in the desire to have chaplains on college campuses in order for the church to have a "presence on the campus." Why would a group of Christian students and faculty not be a Christian presence on the campus?

The question is whether all Christians will live out their whole lives as a Christian vocation or whether most of their lives will be spent as part of the world with a few hours set aside for "church." This does not mean more members to assist the pastor when needed or to help in the work of the church by being committed members, ushers, and song leaders, but being fully ministers according to the gifts which have been given to them. This means not an added responsibility for "those who are not ministers," but a whole new understanding of ministry and the nature of the church.

Discernment of Gifts

When the gifts of leadership are given in the community, it is important for these gifts to be discerned, recognized, and named by the community. It is unhealthy for leaders to exert authority and be neither recognized nor accountable to the community. Since every group does have leadership, if the leaders are not able to use their influence in formal, accountable ways, either their gifts will be wasted or they will use their influence in more subtle ways that are not easily checked by the community. Informal power often is more dangerous than formal power. It has been pointed out that the charisma of the Baptist preacher may lead to a more authoritarian role than that of the hierarchical system.[6] Nothing may exist in Christian community that cannot be checked by the discernment and discipline of the whole community.

In Christian community we do not choose leaders, but rather discern to whom God is giving gifts, and to name, make use of, and give support to those gifts. We do not give authority to those we choose as in the democratic way, but recognize to whom God has given authority.

In this process it is important that we focus on the gifts of the Spirit rather than on natural talent, or academic training, for they may not always be the same. Many times the uneducated can be more perceptive and speak the Word of the Lord more clearly than the intellectuals. The best-trained specialists are not necessarily the ones with the best vision or sense of direction. Those who best know how to get something done may not be the ones to decide what needs to be done. There may be people within the community who have more compassion, sensitivity, and gifts for pastoral work than people who have received much training in this area.

In the descriptions in the New Testament of the qualities of leaders there is no mention of worldly power, brilliant minds, or charming personalities. Neither will leaders be chosen on the basis of who are leaders in secular organizations. The successful business person or president of a service club is not necessarily the one with the deepest spiritual gifts needed in the community.

We are concerned with the person's character and gifts, not with any credentials. This is not to deny that training may be of help in our ability to use our gifts, but gifts and training should never be confused. No one should be appointed to any position unless it is discerned that God has prepared that person for that office. New Christians should not be given heavy leadership responsibilities until they have matured in the faith. In all cases, the concern must be with how the use of these gifts can build up the body.

It is essential in appointing people to positions of responsibility that they understand and be committed to the vision and faith of the community. Too often people are chosen on the basis of ability more than belief and commitment. Often youth leaders and Sunday school teachers are

chosen without anyone even knowing what they believe. This
not only denies the integrity of the community, but will lead
to the disintegration of her unity and witness.

One aspect of discernment of gifts is to uncover each
other's gifts and help each other to be aware of the gifts we
have been given and then to nurture and support those gifts.
Sometimes a person will not recognize his/her gifts, but the
community will name the gifts and help develop them. When
people are unaware of what they can contribute, they will not
feel as deeply a part of the community and may even resent
others whose gifts are more obvious. If some of the gifts are
not used, the whole community will suffer.

Rather than vaguely talk of the ministry of the "laity"
we can begin to discern and state what each member's specific
ministry is and how that person will be accountable for the
gifts which have been given. Thus we do not do away with the
specialized ministry, but relate it to everyone. Our servanthood will be related to the gifts we have been given.

The gifts of the Spirit are given and discerned in the
context of a community of believers, rather than each individual discerning one's own gifts. It is important that no one
in the community have an understanding of one's own gifts
or any sense of calling that is not tested by the community.
What good is it for us to use our talents, except in the way
God wants them used? We are asked to surrender everything,
even our best ideas and callings. This does not mean that we
deny their existence, but that *I* am no longer *in control* of that
call or commitment. It is important to follow God's call for
our lives, but also that *I* not be in control of that call.

An especially dangerous idea is the thought that "I know
more than others" or "I can do it better." Even if, and especially if, it is true, this leads to seeking power, destroys humility, and leads away from seeking together. This is destructive, for what better rationalization can we find to deny our
commitment to be servants of God and each other.

Although we cannot give up a call or leading from God, any call or leading must be submitted for careful testing. The community must carefully discern whether this is actually a call or an expression of ego or an unwillingness to give up some selfish ambition. A "sense of calling" can be a convenient excuse for holding back and not being fully committed to the community. Any sense of call must be taken seriously by the community. If it is a genuine call, the question then is how that call relates to the whole community and how the community can participate in that call and be supportive of it. Leadership does not exist in isolation from the community, but is an expression and function of the community and her mission.

Since gifts are named by the community, it follows both that the leadership of a local community will be named by that community rather than being assigned to a congregation by a hierarchy and that the leaders are accountable to the community they serve. What a servant does is determined not by the servant's own will, but by those whom he/she serves. Just as the apostles in the New Testament were accountable to congregations (Paul to Antioch and Peter to Jerusalem), so leaders today should be. Their power and decisions are always to be checked by the work of the Holy Spirit through the discernment process and the practice of church discipline.

In a real sense Christian ministers cannot be professional as that is usually understood. They cannot be ideologically and theologically neutral. Rather than being responsible to their peers as lawyers are responsible to the bar association, they will be primarily responsible to the people they serve. Since their particular gifts are taken seriously, their role could not be readily exchanged with someone else in the same way that surgeons are interchangeable. Since the qualifications listed in the New Testament can be discerned only by people who know each other well, intimacy of relationships and sharing are essential. Since leaders are servants, they are not above those they minister to, but are one with them.

It is important that recognized leaders be given support by the community. Their gifts cannot be used in their fullness unless they are accepted by the community. Theirs is a heavy responsibility which should be shared by all. They will not be in a lonely position if they are given the love and care they need.

When people are recognized as having leadership and authority, that needs to be respected and taken seriously. We cannot live in community if we cannot accept the authority of anyone else. For example, when someone is given responsibility in the kitchen, then we need to learn to accept that authority. Hebrews 13:17 even calls for us to obey our leaders and submit to them. This means more than to obey whenever we agree and not obey when we disagree. It does not mean that what leaders say should not be checked, but that what they say will have real importance and authority for us.

When leaders are servants who love and care and put others before self, it is possible to respect and obey them. We can then overcome our tendencies to project our problems with authority on authority figures and make them scapegoats. We will then no longer need to play "kill off the leader," a game destructive for all involved.

Women Too

The gifts which are distributed throughout the community are given to women and men. Women can do more than serve church dinners, work in the nursery, and support missionaries. The spiritual gifts given to women are just as important as those given to men. We commit a serious error if we refuse to recognize the gifts which are given to our sisters. How can we reject what the Holy Spirit has given? What injury, frustration, and bitterness we cause for women as the result of stifling their gifts.

The Bible does seem to teach that there is a basic difference between men and women (not a difference of inequality, however) and maybe also a particular role for male authority, but this may not be used to deny the clear teaching that in Christ "there is neither male nor female" (Gal. 3:28). The Bible does not say that women are inferior, that they should take second place to men, or even that they should be subordinate to all men. They are commanded to be submissive to their husbands, but there is no hint that either men or husbands may demand submission from women. In fact, husbands are told to also submit themselves to their wives, even as Christ gave Himself for the church (Eph. 5:21-33).

It is important to recognize the contrast between Jesus' attitude toward women and the general attitude of His day. In a time when women were not respected as persons, Jesus always treated women with respect and even spent time teaching women although it was against rabbinical law to teach women in spiritual matters. Jesus is not recorded as ever expressing any negative ideas about women.

This attitude carried over into the early church. It is significant that in a culture where women were property and expected to be silent, when women heard the gospel they were liberated, even to the extent of needing to be told to be more responsible. The New Testament position on women must be understood in relation to the struggle with a culture that would not allow women to enter the synagogues or speak in public. On some issues, the leaders urged the use of restraint in regard to violating the taboos of that culture. Yet in many cases women were allowed to speak and give leadership. They were allowed full participation in meetings for worship.

Although largely overlooked, there is much evidence of women's leadership in the New Testament. Acts 2:18 notes that the Spirit will be poured out on men *and* women. The first outpouring of the Holy Spirit in the New Testament was to women (Luke 1). In Romans 16 Paul acknowledges various

women leaders. 1 Corinthians 11:5 accepts the fact that
women have been prophesying and Acts 21:9 tells of Philip's
four daughters prophesying. Priscilla was a teacher (Acts
18:26) and called a fellow worker by Paul (Rom. 16:3), as
were Euodia and Syntyche (Phil. 4:2, 3). Women were involved in the administration of the early church. Pheobe was
a deacon (Rom. 16:1) and a leader in the Christian community at Cenchreae. From other sources we learn of the
tremendous importance of women in the early church.

It is also significant that in the believers' church tradition
women have received much more recognition and equality
than in the establishment church as can be seen in
Montanism, Anabaptism, Quakerism, or the Holiness movement. Hearing the gospel brings liberation for women as well
as for men.

Although this discussion raises many other questions
about male/female roles which we will not deal with here, we
can be clear that women may not be dominated by men and
that their gifts need to be recognized. When the Spirit gives
gifts they are to be used. In this area, there can be neither
male nor female. We can only accept what God has given.

Laying on of Hands

As gifts are named and people are called to particular
tasks within the community, it is proper to consecrate
persons for those tasks. A traditional ceremony for this consecration is the "laying on of hands." Having the community
together lay their hands on the person's head in a prayer of
dedication and support can be an especially meaningful and
significant ceremony within community.

The laying on of hands and calling of a person to a
specific task has a different flavor in the believers' church
tradition than where a whole class of seminary graduates are
together ordained to a new status. But when that person
kneels and the hands of his/her brothers and sisters are laid

upon him/her is a moment of high drama as moving as any ritual found in any other tradition.

This laying on of hands and consecration is different than the traditional Protestant and Catholic understanding of ordination. This consecration is symbolic of a commissioning for a special task and is meant to last for only as long as the task continues or until it is fulfilled. No permanent or indelible change takes place within the person, nor is a special status granted for life, no matter what the person may do in the future. All hints of sacerdotalism are to be rejected.

The traditional understanding of ordination to a "set apart" ministry cannot be found in the New Testament. The laying on of hands was a form of consecration but in no way implied a lifelong setting apart or giving a person a special status. If that was what the early Christians intended, anointing might have been a more appropriate ritual of consecration for a special office. The laying on of hands was used in many forms of consecration for many callings, including baptism. It was used in commissioning of the seven (Acts 6:6) and of Paul (Acts 13:3), but also with an entire congregation (Acts 8:17; 19:6) or individual converts (Acts 9:17). It could be done more than once as with Paul. It was not meant to make one different from one's Christian brothers and sisters.

The early church rejected any priest/people distinction although later a new clerical class did reemerge. While the church is described in the New Testament as a royal priesthood there is no suggestion that this refers to a special group in the community. There is no office of priests in the New Testament, except that all are priests. There is not a hint that elders, teachers, or apostles are priestly in function or position. To the extent that there is still a priesthood, it applies to the whole people of God.

We need to make a radical break with the tradition which sees the "minister" or "priest" as having special priestly powers that other Christians do not have. Why can only clergy lead in the Lord's Supper? Why do they have a special status? It should be noted here that many "low" churches have also accepted the idea that special power is conferred to a person through a ceremony of ordination which makes that person different from "normal" Christians. The country preacher is expected to be more moral, holy, and committed than the rest of the congregation.

There can be no distinction between leaders and the community except for tasks and functions. In every way they are part of the community and participate in her life as any other member. There can only be one standard for members and leaders. There can be no double standard. However, the standards may not always be applied in exactly the same way to both. For example, a test of membership can never be maturity, strength, or wisdom, but rightly expect these of leaders. Everyone should be seeking to grow toward these same goals, however.

There is no basis in the New Testament for the idea that the majority of the congregation has no specific calling for ministry or for a special category of people different from the rest. There were various leadership positions in the early church, but these people were not considered set apart from others or forming a special class of Christians. In 1 Corinthians 12, Paul warns against thinking some gifts are of more importance than others, except for the gift of love. Although some ministeries have more responsibilities than others, one is not more important than another. There is no hierarchy of gifts. One function is not more important than another. Ministry is a matter of tasks, not position. Special privileges and double standards are out.

In the past, before the Church of the Brethren was protestantized, the Brethren did not have an elevated platform from which the preachers would preach. They spoke from the same level as the congregation to minimize any distinction between them and the rest of the congregation.

When I refused official ministerial status in the Church of the Brethren after completing seminary, I wrote to the church that I considered myself a minister and intended to be active in the work of the church, but that "I do not wish to be considered different from the rest of the people of God." This act was to reaffirm my belief in the ministry of all believers.

The key to a faithful ministry is the gift of the Holy Spirit. Without that, no matter how many official and correct ordinations and degrees one has received, one's ministry accounts for little. But with that, even with no official accreditation, one can move the world. The Holy Spirit is one gift essential to ministry and this gift cannot be monopolized by any structure. The Spirit is the gift to the whole community.

The Holy Spirit is not tied to any office or guaranteed by it. Leadership in the community is not based on office, but on the gifts which come from God. Although discerned by the community, leadership is given by the Holy Spirit and not conferred by the community. In the New Testament, authority comes not from the position or person, but from God. Bishops or administrators have no authority in themselves or from the office, but the authority that comes from God as discerned by a community. Position, leadership, and gifts are not transferable. They can only be given anew by the Spirit.

Gifts and office are not two distinct categories with gifts being spontaneous and charismatic, and office being based on some ordination, ritual, or administrative ability. The New Testament is concerned with functions and tasks rather than the office determining the task. Rather than structures seeking a mission, structures are formed to aid in mission.

The Larger Church

Thus far our whole discussion of structure has related primarily to the local community. This has been necessary, for the essence of the church is in the local fellowship. The Lutheran idea of the church existing where the "Word is

properly preached and the sacraments properly administered" focuses on the preacher or officiant and how properly
they are speaking or acting rather than focusing on the congregation. This understanding says nothing about the attitudes, commitment, response, or relationships of those
present. The congregation is considered secondary. Even the
Reformed addition of "proper discipline" focuses on organizational controls rather than the community of faith. Recent
definitions of the church as witness, service, and fellowship
are a significant change in the right direction.

The local congregation is not just a fraction of the whole
church, but is fully the church. What can be said of the
universal church can also be said of the local congregation. In
fact, rather than the local community being part of the
universal church and receiving her life from it, the universal
church is composed of local congregations which are her life
and ministry. The local community is primary.

This is not to deny the importance of structures beyond
the local level. In fact, this aspect of the church is also
essential. The biblical understanding of the church includes
the total church. Each local community is part of the same
body as other communities. They are each manifestations of
the same body.

The centrality of the local congregation may not be used
to negate the mutual responsibility that exists among different communities. There also needs to be a community of
communities, something like current denominational group-
ings. There is the need for other communities with whom to
share and discern, to receive and give support and discipline.
We cannot be faithful by ourselves. The support and correction we receive from other communities is essential. This
should be the basis for "denominational" structures.

The basis for an association of congregations or communities must be the presence of the living Christ, the same as
for the local community. This means that a larger group is

more than a meeting of individual congregations, but also a community under the command of the Holy Spirit. Intercongregational meetings can be guided by the Holy Spirit just as local communities. A covenant can exist also on that level. What the Spirit says in the larger meetings is just as binding as what the Spirit says in the local community.

We need to come to the understanding that each level of the church is fully the church. The Quakers have understood this as well as anyone. They have their weekly meetings and this is the church. Their monthly business meetings are meetings for worship and they are the church. Then they have wider associations of meetings (districts) which meet quarterly and these Quarterly Meetings are considered fully the church. Then there is a still wider association of meetings which meets yearly. The Yearly Meeting is also fully the church.

When Quakers meet in their yearly meeting, they are primarily not representing their local meetings, but gathering together from far and wide to discern corporately what the Spirit is saying to the whole meeting. Rather than represent someone else, each participant is expected to be fully open to the leading of the Holy Spirit in that meeting.

Each level of the church is fully the church. The particular congregation and the universal church each exists only as a gift of God. The expectations at every level are basically the same. The universal church is visible just as is the local congregation. Each is called to the same faithfulness under the same Lord.

The association of communities or "denomination" must have authority and its judgments be listened to and taken seriously. On the other hand, each local community has her own integrity and cannot be coerced or ruled over by any other community or structure. Worldly power may not be used. Actually no statement or action of the larger group can be fully authoritative unless it wins the approval of the local groups. However, these decisions may not be easily dismissed by the local groups if they do not agree.

Suppose the larger community makes a decision with which a local community cannot agree. What then? At that point the process of discernment continues. First the local community will seriously consider the decision that was made and the reasons for it and prayerfully consider if this decision was really not correct and change needed. In an open, prayerful way the matter will be reviewed. The community may change or the community may go back to the larger community and ask that the matter be reconsidered. It may be that the decision was wrong and with the new light brought by the local community the decision will be changed. Or the larger community may discern that their original decision was correct. At this point all involved will patiently work with each other and try to come to unity, respecting and bearing with each other in love while continuing the process of discernment.

In the larger association of communities it is likely that some structure and staff people will be needed to coordinate and carry out the decisions of the larger community. It is essential, however, that bureaucratic models of structure and corporate management mentality be rejected. Hierarchical relationships are to be avoided.

There is always the danger of staff losing contact with the people, and the community feeling distrust toward the staff. Staff and community should not have conflicting goals for the church. Never may staff put their own positions and future ahead of the good of the whole community. They are always to be ready to relinquish their positions.

Frequent gatherings and conferences for worship, study, and decision making are important. They are times not only for sharing, communication, and worship, but an important channel for the Holy Spirit to bring unity to God's people.

Another important form of communication between

communities is that of the itinerant, traveling preacher. This was Jesus' pattern of ministry, the way the early church spread, and has been important in almost all renewal movements. The established church will often oppose and criticize these people. This was one of Luther's criticisms of the Anabaptists. Wandering preachers do not fit traditional understandings of proper church order. Among other things, they are considered irresponsible.

It is essential that itinerants not be irresponsible, but be sent by a home community and accountable to her. Itinerants all the way from Paul to John Woolman neither spent all their time traveling nor went out on their own. They were disciplined members of local communities.

Itinerants have an important role in evangelism, in building bridges between communities, and in speaking prophetically to other communities. A "visiting brother or sister" often has more freedom and authority to say what needs to be said than do members of the community. A fresh voice who does not need to worry as much about hurting anyone's feelings is needed in all communities. The itinerant is important but should not be given any leadership position in the community he/she visits.

Radical Ecumenicity

It is not enough to talk about the need for communities to be related to each other. Associations of communities (denominations) also cannot be faithful by themselves, but need the support, counsel, and discipline of other denominations. Unless we claim that our group is the only group of Christians in the whole world, we are faced with how to relate to other Christians.

We have the responsibility and biblical mandate (Jn. 17:20-26) to come to unity with all who claim to be followers of Jesus. Ultimately there can be no acceptance of divisions in the body of Christ. At any point where there is disagreement, we have the responsibility to dialogue with the other until we come to unity or until the other stops the dialogue. The basis for ecumenical relations is simply the application of Matthew 18 and the discernment process on a larger scale.

The real issue is what we can learn from each other. It may be that when there is disagreement we are the ones who are wrong. In fact, that is one of the first questions to ask. Since that must always be seen as a possibility, we will always be open to change and to what we can learn from others. Ecumenical dialogue is based on a recognition that we are not totally faithful and are in need of repentance. Rather than arguing from fixed positions, we are always to be open to more light.

We are compelled to be in dialogue with those with whom we disagree, for if what our brothers and sisters believe is right in the sight of God, then it may also be right for us. If their or our faith is incomplete, then we have the responsibility to share more fully with each other. We cannot accept disunity as normal.

Just as God took the first step in reconciling the world to Himself, so we always reach out to others. There will be times when the other side may be completely closed, honestly unable to accept what we say, or may agree that we are right but decide not to act upon it. In these cases we need simply to recognize that we are not in unity and not pretend that we are. But we will still seek more dialogue. Never may we break off dialogue with anyone. The other side may do that and at that point we will recognize that there is no dialogue, but even then we will go out of our way to maintain relationships with those with whom we disagree and seek to overcome the division.

We can learn from the early Anabaptists who never broke relations with Zwingli or any of the other Reformation leaders.[7] It was Zwingli and the others who forcefully and violently broke off dialogue. Even as the Anabaptists were being killed, they still sought out and pleaded with the Reformers for dialogue and ways of seeking together. It was only at the point where there seemed to be no other paths open that they began new congregations, but this did not decrease their desire for dialogue. The attitude of "break-to-be-faithful" is not the way, for this only leads to more splinters. Even after the break seemed irreversible, still the Anabaptists refused to accept it as final and sought renewed dialogue which was repeatedly rejected by the Reformers.

To be truly ecumenical is more than being nice to each other or even cooperating together. It means to be open to discerning God's will with others. Groups gathered for ecumenical discussions should be seen as meetings for discernment. This means that every meeting together is a meeting for worship if we are honestly meeting to seek God's will, for wherever two or three are gathered together in Christ's name, there is Christ in the midst of them. There is no need for academic or ecclesiastical arguments of whether such groups can worship together. How could Christians gather together without worshiping together? All that is needed is an openness to God's Spirit. But that openness is essential.

If the parties are gathered in the name of Christ and under the authority of the Word and are open to the leading of the Holy Spirit, they are an authentic expression of the reality of the church and are in themselves a powerful testimony of unity in a divided church. If, however, their primary concern is institutional structures, winning points in parliamentary debate, and jockeying for power and position, the meetings only reflect the divisiveness of the world and cannot be considered worship. Unless there is genuine openness to God's Spirit, worship is not a possibility.

The unity we seek is based not on completing claims to a valid ministry or correct doctrine, but in a common commitment to Jesus and His kingdom. It is not the unity through force and political manipulation found in the church councils like Nicea, not hierarchically controlled unity or the result of organizational mergers. No group, no matter how brilliant, can come up with a new creed or plan of union that will be accepted by most Christians. That is a gift that can only be given to us by God as we give up our stubbornness and open our lives to His will. Unity is a gift, not something we create. It comes before our recognition and expression of it. As John Howard Yoder has put it, "Christian unity is not to be created, but to be obeyed."[8]

There is a need to affirm and celebrate the things we do agree on. Any expression of unity must be an expression of real unity, however. Playing games and pretending are out of place here. If someone of a very different faith and I together help disaster victims, at that point we have a kind of unity in our action. But we cannot use that to cover our deep disunity in other areas.

If we are serious about seeking unity we will need to deal with some of the hard issues that divide us. There may not be any topics on which we are closed to dialogue. To take each other seriously, we need to grapple with our points of disagreement. Unity will be found on the other side of our disunity, not on this side. Real unity does not involve dodging the important or touchy issues. We cannot, for the sake of unity, avoid dealing with Protestant oppression of Roman Catholics in Northern Ireland, Roman Catholic suppression of Protestants in Spain, or Greek Orthodox persecution of free churches in Greece.

We do need to be careful in considering what the important issues are on which there needs to be agreement. The National Association of Evangelicals is clear on aspects of the inspiration of the Bible, the nature of Christ and the Trinity, but they are very unclear in the areas of discipleship, nonconformity, baptism, and the nature of the church—issues which are at least as important as the former list.

For the early Christians unity in ethical commitments

was at least as important as unity in doctrine. Jesus said, "Not every one who says to me, 'Lord, Lord,' shall enter the kingdom of heaven but he who does the will of my Father who is in heaven" (Mt. 7:21). Much more important than what we say is what we live; whether we will live the life Jesus calls us to. How is our obedience reflected in our daily lifestyles? Disagreements on some subject of church polity is not more serious than Christians being separated from each other by racism. The nature of the faith of the one to be baptized seems more important than a discussion of the sacramental nature of baptism. Not only is there one faith and one Lord, but also one obedience. Could we move beyond ethical pluralism and diversity to a position of Christian unity? What about unity in areas like sexuality, violence and war, race relations?

Although it is possible that two positions could both be right, there is also such a thing as apostasy. Admittedly, this is not a popular subject, but if we are to have dialogue, there must be a willingness to accept the possibility that some positions might be wrong. If this possibility is not accepted, there can be no serious dialogue. One reason for division in the past has been that some positions taken by the church have been seen by others to be irreconcilable with the claims of Jesus Christ.

This brings us again to the question of authority. Can we have dialogue based not on fixed historic positions but on the basis of hearing what God is saying to us through the written Word and the Holy Spirit? Can we allow all our perceptions of truth to be questioned? Can we allow our tradition to be judged by the standard of Jesus Christ? Dialogue will be difficult with those who have a philosophy, book, or assumptions other than the Bible that cannot be questioned. Unless Jesus is the final authority we have little basis for dialogue as Christians. We can have other kinds of dialogue such as philosophical discussion, but not Christian discernment which is the essence of being ecumenical.

There is another serious point to be made in this respect. Unless we are committed to abide by what we have discerned and live it out, we have reduced the whole process of ecumenical dialogue to a farce. Are we open to what God wants to say to us? Are we ready to obey?

The unity we seek must be based on faithful discernment of God's will for us, not on some fuzzy lowest common denominator. Probably most dangerous of all on the ecumenical scene is a vague "nonsectarian" and confessionless religion which sees religion itself being the important concern rather than the content or object of religion. This is expressed in anything from interfaith chapels to politicians praising the importance of religion for national survival. A more demonic form of this kind of religiosity is Hitler's "German Christianity."

One curious brand of sectarianism, and often a quite narrow one, is nonsectarianism. This is a narrow and excluive universalism which includes only those who are "nonsectarian." Often those who claim to be the most open are the most closed and judgmental toward those who are not open in the same way they are. They want everything reduced to the lowest common denominator and cannot tolerate any consistent group that has its own integrity. Authentic pluralism implies various groups having integrity.

Christianity is not an umbrella so broad that it includes everything, a fake pluralism. It is too easy to accept many creeds but be committed to none. We must oppose any religious movement which results in a loss in clarity of the Christian witness.

It seems to be true that the more exclusively we are committed to Jesus the more universal is our outlook and concern. In fact, our concern then goes even to our enemies. The more we are open to following human desires, the more narrow and exclusive we become. Rather than being a narrow exclusivism, an emphasis on the exclusive lordship of Jesus Christ is the only basis for a true universalism.

Because of her commitment to the coming kingdom, the Christian community has the possibility of being free of control by the narrow perspectives of one's race, class, or nation. Because of our vision of what is coming, we can view *what is* much more realistically, for we see no need to justify it. Because the present has little seductive attraction for us, we can be free to see the status quo as it really is. Because we are not bound to what is, we can see beyond it.

Questions of class, nation, race, and sex are to be clearly subordinated to the call to live in God's kingdom. Every claim of persons, ideology, or institution is subordinate to that kingdom. Because God's truth is universal it can never be restricted or identified with the attitudes of any locality. This naturally leads us to a vision of a universal community, a church not bound to its own narrow view, not captive of a particular time and place, but moving on toward a promised land. Radical free church groups have shown that it is possible for communities to be more than a reflection of the surrounding culture.

Syncretism, the blending of all religions, is not as universal as it sounds, for it rejects all that disagrees with its assumptions. Syncretism does not take seriously the real and important differences between world-views. All roads do not go in the same direction. Faith is not essentially an expression of culture and seeking truth an intercultural debate. Revelation judges culture. Ultimately syncretism denies revelation. Syncretism soon becomes a natural theology in which people determine truth for themselves.

Usually syncretism is a reversion to a watered-down moralism with little spiritual depth. Morals with no spiritual depth are ineffective or tyrannical. People again become enslaved to impersonal cosmic forces rather than liberated by Jesus Christ. The gospel is that one need not be controlled by impersonal forces, but can be liberated by a personal God. Biblical faith affirms that rather than speaking in an infinite variety of ways with little authority, God has spoken decisively in Jesus Christ. Thus instead of having a religion of concepts and insights we are in a living relation with a personal God. Truth is a "Thou," not an "it."

The Christian faith is universal for Jesus died for all. All barriers are broken down. All may come. The more seriously we take our center, the more universal we become in our outlook. This is the true meaning of universal, for our loyalty is not to any nation, tribe, or ideology, but to God. What else can unite all people?

Having a clear stand and knowing where we stand, rather than cutting us off from others, provides the basis for meaningful dialogue. How can dialogue take place when we are not sure where we are or what we believe? Commitment to Jesus Christ is the basis for reaching out in love to all people.

It is not an accident that down through history, for the most part it has been the believers' church groups that have been most open to dialogue. The Franciscans and the Moravians are two good examples. A major source for ecumenical relations, including the modern ecumenical movement, has been these voluntary groups.[9]

Although at times they have become divisive and closed, at their best, the believers' churches should be ecumenical and well-prepared for dialogue. At their best, they know who they are and can speak from that identity, are always open to new truth, respect dissent, and recognize the right of all groups to exist. They have not been willing to respect territorial limits nor define the church according to national boundaries. They refuse to use coercion or engage in violence against those who are called their enemies.

It is ironic that many who speak most loudly against church division refuse even to recognize the validity of ministry outside their own tradition and in church mergers have demanded a new ordination for the other clergy to make them legitimate.

Jesus' prayer for unity (Jn. 17) was not primarily for some institutional unity, but for a unity of heart and mind. Our unity is in Jesus Christ, not in institutional identities. In fact, a multiplicity and diversity of institutional expressions can be seen as a sign of vitality and creativity. Unity may dissolve denominations, but mergers do not necessarily bring unity. An insistence on institutional unity comes from the mistake of identifying the institution with the essence of the church. Our unity is in our brotherhood and sisterhood, our visible communities of faith and love. Our approach should be based on the understanding that the closer we walk to the light, the closer we will be drawn to each other (1 Jn. 1:7).

This is not to deny that our unity must be made visible and concrete and expressed through structures. Unity will include a tangible relationship of mutual discipline. We will do well to reject the spiritualist approach that structures are unimportant and need not concern us. Most of those who argue thus are deeply involved in structures themselves. Our unity must be visible and our structures must come under the lordship of Christ. If we have unity it will be expressed in structures.

If one focuses on organizational mergers as the locus of unity then one is bound to keep asking the wrong questions and thus come to the wrong conclusions. In fact, rather than create unity, often mergers bring about more disunity and new divisions. Any organizational unity that compromises basic convictions or covers up disunity is only a facade and no unity at all.

Mergers should come from the leading of the Spirit and be the result of deep renewal. If a denomination is not distinctive enough to justify her separate existence, then on what basis can we say that she has any reason to exist if she merges with another denomination which also has little reason for existence? Mergers which cut people off from their heritage can make them more susceptible to the spirit of the present age.

If examined, one will soon see that most all of the arguments for church merger are actually Constantinian, establishment arguments. One church will have a more powerful witness, more influence on government, be more efficient, and inclusive of many viewpoints. The goal of merging institutional structures in the name of greater efficiency and more power in society is completely at odds with the believers' church perspective.

An especially dangerous and serious flaw in the present ecumenical movement is the tendency to merge and reorganize churches on the basis of national boundaries rather than along confessional lines. We now have a united church of Canada, South India, North India, and in many other countries. Any church reorganizing which strengthens the identity and boundaries of the church with existing geographical, racial, or political boundaries is anti-ecumenical and not Christian.

It is easy to make fun of pan-Methodism, pan-Lutheranism, pan-Mennonitism, and question why in any one country there should be Methodists, Lutherans, and Mennonites. Why not have all the Christians in each country united? United on what? The present arrangement may not be very faithful but it is no worse than national churches. It is significant that in the most closed, oppressed, and dictatorial nations there are Christians who feel a particular bond with other Christians of like minds in other countries.

In an age of idolatrous nationalism those bonds are precious and need to be strengthened. Better to have the church organized around honest differences of understandings of the gospel than around national identities. Although cultural differences need to be respected, the unity of the church may not be based on any local or national loyalties. Commitment to the unity of the church in Jesus Christ must come before any national commitments. All other loyalties must be rejected if we are to be serious about ecumenical dialogue. Ultimately there cannot be a Nigerian church, an Ecuadorian church, a United States church.

Where then do we begin to seek unity? It is in our own particular community where we need to find unity and be the one true church. Unity must begin at home with the particular and lead to the universal. It is interesting that some of those who push hardest for institutional unity have little concern for unity within a local body. Rather, they have stressed the importance of diversity. How many ecumenical leaders are part of either a denomination or congregation that has unity? If not, how can they call for something on a grand scale that has not yet been possible on a small scale? How much better if our reaching out in search of unity with others can be an expression of the love and unity we have within our own fellowship which results from hearing the same voice and together being faithful to that one voice.

How true it is that "unity must come out of mission." This popular phrase has seldom been taken seriously, however. We should not seek unity for mission, but unity in mission. Our deepest unity comes as we obey and live out the gospel together.

It is not true that all division is sin. Although we seek to overcome all division, sometimes in order to be faithful we need to separate. Often we are called in different directions for different tasks. Multiplicity is not necessarily evil. The emergence of new Christian fellowships can be viewed as schismatic (and sometimes they are), or they can be joyously accepted as new evidence of the creative work of the Holy Spirit.

Although sometimes the cause for new groups is a search for personal power or divisiveness, often it is because new life has emerged which cannot be contained within the rigid old structures. Often it is caused by the unresponsiveness of the old structures. Rather than condemn the new groups, we need to be more critical of the old groups which make the formation of new groups necessary. Form and structures are necessary, but they can be shaken and destroyed by the One who can never be limited to any structure.

Chapter 8

THE WORSHIPING COMMUNITY

To worship rightly is to love each other, Each smile a hymn, each kindly deed a prayer.[1]—John Greenleaf Whittier.

The Meaning of Worship

It has been said that while Roman Catholics gather to receive the sacraments and Protestants to be instructed from the Bible, those of the believers' church tradition meet to visit with each other. Or to put it another way, while Roman Catholics need to see an altar to worship God and Protestants a pulpit, those of the believers' church need to look into the face of other Christians. While these are stereotypes, they do contain an element of truth. At least we can say that our understanding of the nature of the church will imply a particular understanding of worship. Those living in Christian community will develop an understanding and form of worship different from those of other traditions. Their worship will have an integrity of its own rather than be copied from others.

Vernard Eller suggests that rather than being a divine institution (commissary) for the purpose of dispensing spiritual merchandise, the church is a group of people (caravan) together walking toward a common destination. The primary concern of the church is not the quality of her merchandise, the credentials of her employees, or the nature of her franchise, but the quality of relationships among the people and whether they are on the right road going in the right direction. Worship then is not gathering to dispense blessings, but a conversation of all the travelers with the Leader concerning deployment of people and checking the maps.[2]

Worship is an important part of living in Christian community. How could we continue together without consulting regularly with the One who guides us and draws us together? In addition to the details of living together and reaching out to others, there needs to be a time of praise, thanksgiving, inspiration, nourishment, and recovenanting.

Christian worship is God-centered. It is to acknowledge and affirm the supreme worth (worthship) of God. Worship is more talking with God than about God. It is the conscious relationship of a community with God. Worship moves beyond the rational and intellectual and speaks to the depth of our being.

A currently popular word for worship is "celebrate," a good word and rich in meaning, but a word almost completely ruined by people who use it with religious meaning but without reference to what is being celebrated. Sometimes what is meant is to celebrate life, but usually this is so vague that it can include celebrating unregenerate life. Celebrate is a transitive verb and needs an object. As Christians we will want to be quite clear about what it is that we are actually celebrating.

Too often meetings for worship[3] focus on ritual and ceremony or feeling and experience, and these become the focus of worship rather than God. The result often is either feelings of warm togetherness without God or ritual with little content. Christian worship may never be just a package of nice sounding words and rituals to which people can give any meaning they wish. Neither is it a smorgasbord where all kinds of goodies are offered and all are free to choose only what they like.

While there is a place for aesthetics and beauty, neither may these be the center of worship. Appreciation of art forms and beauty are of themselves not Christian worship. After an impressive program, are we more aware of God or of the performance? It is not enough even to ask whether it is inspiring, for even pagan exercises may be inspiring.

Worship is more than a rededication to moral ideals. Neither is it centered on peace of mind, self-realization, or social justice. The question always is whether it points to God and the coming of the kingdom.

Christian worship takes history seriously, for a large part of our worship is taking into account and remembering what God has done in the past in order to get a better perspective for the future. We recount what God has done in the past, both in ancient Israel, in Jesus, the church, and in our own lives.

Remembrance of God's acts in the past means more than recalling them, but also real involvement, participation in history and reliving it, values, commitments, and vision that are important for the community. This relates to our daily lives as we seek to discern God's leading among us, as we struggle for justice and pray for the kingdom to come.

The God we worship is more than an unknowable mystery, but a risen Lord whose presence is made known in community, wherever two or three are gathered together in His name. Although God is a great mystery whom we can never fully comprehend, Christian faith and worship are centered more around that which has been revealed and what we do know (namely Jesus Christ) than any unfathomable mystery.

Mystery points to an unknown God while biblical faith reveals a God who makes His will known to us. Those eras which most emphasized "the sacred" did not necessarily have the clearest understanding of God or Christian love. In fact, emphasis on "the sacred" often detracts from love and righteousness. Harry F. Ward once said, "Mysticism is the refuge of the tired radical."[4]

Christian worship is our response to God's initiative among us. Rather than a reaching out and trying to find God by human effort, Christian worship is a grateful response to what God has first done among us. We need not seek to climb up to God through prayer, meditation, or good works. God has come to us. We need only receive Him. Christian prayer and worship is not a way to salvation (as in Eastern religion), but a result of salvation. Spiritual disciplines will not bring salvation.

This means a rejection of all human religious attempts to reach God through ritual or ceremony. Too often our rituals are not empty, but are filled with the works/righteousness and egoism of pleasing God and doing things correctly. Not that rituals and ceremonies are wrong, but they are not means to God. At best they can only help prepare us to be open to God. While there is much liturgy in the Bible, it is instructive that Jesus never showed any intention of beginning elaborate liturgies and rituals and that this was not the concern of the early church. The New Testament shows little interest in ceremonies. The rituals Jesus began were rather simple.

A clear distinction must be made between Christian worship and superstition or magic, which is the belief that if we do the correct action, God will automatically perform a desired response. There is nothing we can do to put God's actions under our control. Neither can we dictate how God will speak to us. God is not to be turned on or off as we please. There is no ritual that can make us more acceptable to God.

Our worship is our response to God. This is possible only as long as we both hear and respond. When we do not respond, our worship has ceased to be Christian. Worship is dialogue between God and us. Worship then cannot be separated from our obedience and response to the light.

Related to Life

Rather than isolated from the rest of life, Christian worship is an involvement in life at its deepest levels. More than a preparation for life, worship is the climax of a daily walk of faithful service, a concentrated expression of a larger life of discipleship. But this assumes that our daily life is an expression of Christian service and faith. If we are not daily living the new life Christ offers to us, then worship can hardly be more than an escape or retreat from life, unless it is an act of sincere confession and repentance, asking God to help us live more faithfully.

For our worship to be valid our lives must be valid. God will not even listen to our prayers unless we cease our evil ways and do good (Is. 1:10-17; Jn. 9:31). The Bible claims that there is a close connection between working for social justice and knowing God (Jer. 22:16; Hos. 4:1, 2). The prophet Amos reminds us that our worship is illegitimate when we are not living up to the covenant. Worship and prayer are a mockery unless we earnestly want to open our lives to the living God. The worship of God is not primarily participating in religious ceremonies.

It is so easy to shift the concern of faith from life to the sacramental and divorce faith from ethics. As the Hebrew prophets made so clear, God is not interested in any rituals which are a substitute for obedience and justice. The same Hebrew and Greek word is sometimes translated in the Bible as "service" and sometimes as "worship." Worship and service are one. We present our bodies as a living sacrifice, which is our reasonable service/worship (Rom. 12:1).

After defeating the Hebrew army, the Philistines took the Ark of the Covenant back and, to honor the Hebrew God, set it in a place of honor beside the statue of Dagon in their temple (1 Sam. 4—6). But God rejected this type of reverence by breaking the statue of Dagon into pieces. The Philistines got the point and sent the Ark back to the Hebrews. More than our reverence, God wants our obedience. Worship must be an expression of our obedience to God.

The goal of worship is not a great mystical experience or new insights into the essence of the supernatural, but rather more clarity and strength to live more faithfully. The Quaker contributions to social justice are the most complimentary commentary one can make concerning the power and significance of Quaker meetings. Evelyn Underhill misses the point when she criticizes the Quakers because, although they stress meditation, they have not produced any "great contemplative or made any real addition to our knowledge of the soul's interior life."[5] Worship includes a group of Mennonites and Brethren cleaning mud out of people's houses after a flood or American Quakers sending medical aid to "the enemy" in North Vietnam during the Vietnam war.

All of life is to be worship. We cannot separate the outer from the inner, relationships from prayer, action from devotion, material from the spiritual. Worship is not a distinct area of our lives. Worship is life. Rather than the Buddhist approach of escaping time and space, Christians know God in the midst of time and space and daily events. Worship is not to ease the pain we feel or to escape from life, but rather to be reminded of the hope and reality of the kingdom we experience in the midst of pain and suffering. Worship makes us more, not less, aware of the world. Worship anticipates the fulfillment of God's purposes both in our own midst and in the world.

The sacred and holy do not refer to special objects, persons, places, times, or words, but to a new quality of life that permeates all of life. All of our objects, places, times, words, and persons are to be devoted to Christ's kingdom and seen as sanctified.

So away with the mystique of worship, the sweet music, sermons unrelated to life, stained-glass attitudes, grim faces, or fake smiles. Away with all ritual and ceremony that are not a living expression of our response to what God is doing among us and calling us to.

This does not deny the importance of having times of concentration to remind us of the holiness of all of life. The particular is essential for the universal. All of life can be a prayer only if there are also specific set aside times of prayer. If all our meals are to be agape meals, some need to be specifically called agape meals. If every day is the Lord's, then we need a particular Lord's day to remind us of it. Set times for worship are not religious points in a secular life, but rather points of concentration where we focus, develop, test, and confirm what God is doing in all our life.

While we must get rid of any distinction between sacred and secular (more on this in the next chapter), this does not mean that everything we do is worship. Not everything we do praises God.

An Expression of Community

We respond to the light and worship God not as isolated individuals, but as a community. Worship is an expression of the community, the response of the community to what God is doing in the community and in the world. The biblical understanding of worship is primarily corporate and is a response to God's covenant.[6] Even personal prayers are seen as part of the life of the whole community and related to God's work among His people, rather than primarily concerned with personal piety. This can be seen clearly in the prayers of Jesus. Although private meditation is essential in community and a measure of the depth of the community, more is needed. The fullness of Christian worship is found in combining an intense personal relationship with God with a deep sense of belonging to each other and hearing God together as a community.

The early Christians understood the importance of gathering together for worship. In fact, they gathered for worship every day, giving time for prayers, fellowship, breaking bread together, and learning from the apostles' teachings (Acts 2:42).

Paul repeatedly states that one of the purposes of worship is to build up the community (1 Cor. 14). The primary concern is not personal fulfillment or whether it makes me feel good, but whether it builds up the body. The test of true worship is not goose pimples or chills up and down the spine, nostalgic emotions, or music and words that make us feel good. The question is how worship helps us walk more faithfully together. Not that there is anything wrong with nostalgic or warm feelings, but they should not be confused with the Holy Spirit. The issue is mutual edification and support rather than private enjoyment.

Corporate worship assumes a visible, believing community. Meetings for worship cannot be a series of cultic practices independent of who attends. In the rural communities of the past the Sunday morning meeting for worship meant something very different from what it does now. Then people whose lives were intertwined through a variety of social, economic, and religious activities met on Sunday morning not as strangers, but as neighbors and brothers and sisters. Today, in many cases, strangers gather together once a week for an hour of what they call worship. Since they share practically none of their lives together, how could their worship have the meaning it should have? Worship must come out of the experience and needs of the people. Without a faithful and believing community the meaning of worship is limited.

The fullest expression of worship comes when a community is completely united in listening to God's Spirit and desires to accept whatever God gives. It is an expression of a united desire to be one body, to really be brothers and sisters. The importance of unity that we discussed earlier in this book is also essential in worship, and so it is important that we be both in a right attitude and in right relationships with others before we come to prayer together (Mt. 5:23, 24). This concern of Jesus was continued in the early church as can be seen in these words from the Didache:

> On the Lord's own day come together, break bread and give thanks, but first confess your transgressions so that your offering may be pure. No one, however, who has a quarrel with his friend shall join you until they are reconciled so that your offering is not defiled.[7]

It is also important that when we pray we have unity on what we are saying to God. If there is the confusion of each person asking something different, then God can listen only to individuals and not to the church. There is special significance to a united prayer of the church (Mt. 18:19).

Worship is more the authentic expression of a community of believers than a creative attempt to impress unbelievers. Unlike evangelism, worship is primarily for committed Christians who are able to gather together in unity. Perhaps we need to recover the early church practice of having two types of meetings, one for committed Christians and one for all who are interested. Also, some subjects are best considered apart from nonmembers and children.

Worship will reflect the nature of relationships in the community. If the community has no life, the meetings for worship will be empty just as if there are no meetings for worship, the community will be empty. How a community worships will tell much about her life. The worship can only be as deep as the depth of the community. When a person has been giving the same testimony for the last ten years, you know not much has been happening in that person's life. Rather than the Sunday morning meeting for worship being what holds the congregation together, worship is to be an expression of something deeper in our common life together and an outgrowth of it.

When worship is an expression of a loving community, then every meeting for worship takes on a new significance, and especially special occasions. In weddings the yes of the bride and groom is the yes of the whole community, for they are being married after the community discerned this was right for them. In times of death the mourners do not weep alone, but with the whole community. At important times like this everyone stops work. Everything comes to a halt and the community gathers together. When people cannot even take off a few hours from work for these occasions life is out of focus.

Places to Meet

Maybe our meetings for worship should be in places like homes, places closely tied to the daily lives of people rather than in buildings set apart only for worship. It is significant that in the Bruderhof, meetings for worship are held in the same room used for their common meals and social activities. They have no set-apart "sacred" places for worship.

Here again it is instructive for us to look to the early church. The early Christians understood that there is no special place where God meets us (Jn. 4:20-24). God may be encountered anywhere. Stephen proclaimed that "the Most High does not dwell in houses made with hands" (Acts 7:48).

The early church did not have set-apart buildings for worship. It was through a network of small house churches that the Christian faith was spread throughout the Roman Empire. It was when the church began to compromise with Constantine in return for security and respectability that not only was the faith distorted but also a new day for "church architecture" began. After Christianity became the state religion, sanctuaries sprang up everywhere, beginning a pattern that has prevailed ever since. Just as we have not recovered from the civil religion started at that time, neither have we recovered from the architecture that came with it.

Consider what has happened. Huge ornate buildings, symbols of luxury, pride, and insensitivity to the needs of the poor stand in the midst of areas of poverty, of little use other than to stand in constant judgment on those who built them and then neglected the poor. People have even called these buildings "churches," confusing them with the body of Christ.

Our fancy buildings witness more to the influence of the sinful world and our own pride than to the leading of the Holy Spirit. They are more a testimony of our wealth and exclusivism than an expression of the gospel. Some have suggested that movements and institutions build their biggest buildings and bureaucracies after they have reached their peak of influence and vitality and have begun their decline.

If we do have meetinghouses, they should be simple and serve to encourage rather than discourage community. Their very shape and style should express the idea of family, community, and love. Meeting places should not be designed like concert halls or auditoriums in which people are expected not to share with each other but face the performers up front. In concert halls they even turn down the lights so that you will not give attention to others around you. Formal and spacious buildings encourage passivity and formality and discourage the mutual sharing and family atmosphere that should pervade our gatherings for worship.

One of the great abominations of the church is the modern innovation of pews. H. A. Reinhold stated it well when he wrote,

> Fixed pews are a nuisance; they turn the church into a lecture hall or auditorium. They not only immobilize the congregation physically to a high degree, but they bring in psychological elements of regimentation. The congregation becomes an audience, spectators. The celebrating throngs are gone, the informality so much needed to create ease and enthusiasm, the groupings of families, are made almost impossible.[8]

There ought to be flexibility to rearrange the room to fit the nature of the occasion or size of group. If chairs are used they can be easily put in rows, circles, or any other shape. Since the locus of God's presence is in the congregation, not the altar, pulpit, or worship leader, the layout of the meeting room should suggest this.

Our places of worship should not be set off from the rest of life. When we put a steeple on a meetinghouse we have perverted it by making it distinct, holy, and removed from life. The setting apart of special rooms like a small prayer chapel is an expression of a division between sacred and secular that is hardly biblical. The phony atmosphere created in these rooms is more sentimental than Christian. The true beauty of any meetinghouse is to be found in what is happening among the people who meet there.

Any art used in the meetinghouse should be good art and preferably created by the people themselves. Away with all *kitsch,* the fake art of carnival souvenirs. Artifical flowers are a poor symbol in a place for worship, suggesting that maybe other aspects of our life together are not real either.

A serious problem in the United States is the practice of so many churches putting the flag of the nation in the front of their places for worship. Could you imagine the early Christians putting images of Caesar in a prominent place in their meetingrooms? But even more horrifying is where it is put. Almost always it is put to the right of the speaker, just where the Boy Scout manual says it should be. The American flag is to be put to the right of the speaker in the place of honor and all other flags to the left of it in an inferior, subordinate position. That's right. Caesar's flag is in the place of honor and the "Christian" flag is in an inferior, subordinate position. Caesar first, then Christ. How any committed Christian can tolerate that is difficult to understand. Actually the "Christian" flag, stained by the blood of the Crusades, has no place in the meetinghouse either.

Spirit and Form

As with organizational structure, there is no one form to be found in the Bible or tradition which is the correct form for worship. We will reject the idea that if we do it in the correct order with the right gestures, colors, and sequence then we will have worshiped rightly. Worship is a matter both of the heart and of relationships of the community to each other and to God. To worship God we must worship in Spirit and in truth (Jn. 4:21-23).

There is nothing wrong with introducing new forms, but the new forms should be carefully tested, including their meaning and implications for the community. Nothing should be accepted just because it is new, or rejected just because it is not explicitly approved in the Bible. The question is rather what is in harmony with the Bible.

There is no point in creating new forms to bring a new spirit, but a new spirit may bring new forms. New forms without a new spirit are probably more empty and phony than the old ones. The answer is not to hire someone creative enough to dream up new worship forms. They must arise out of the life of the community.

We do need to get rid of empty forms that seduce us into thinking we have done something we have not. Many meetings for worship begin with the call, "O come let us worship and bow down, let us kneel before the Lord our Maker," but no one kneels. Why cheapen worship by saying what we have no intention of anyone following? We read in unison a ditty concerning confession of sins and think we are confessing our sins when actually no sins have been confessed. Even worse is a general assurance of pardon if it is little more than cheap grace. A formal litany of confession and assurance of pardon may never be a substitute for the real thing. There should be integrity in all that we do. A Quaker tract says it so well.

It is not honest to give expression to exalted sentiments which

are contradicted by one's actual condition. To sing of moun-
tain-top joys, when actually in the valley; of the banquet, when
starving in a parched desert; of glorious liberty, when in reality
in bondage to the lusts and cares of this passing world, is not
from the Spirit of Truth.[9]

It is ironic that worship is the area in which many are
most conservative and closed to change, even though it is
here where we are supposed to be most clearly open to and
led by the Holy Spirit. "Where the Spirit of the Lord is, there
is freedom" (2 Cor. 3:17).

It is essential that any forms we use in worship allow
freedom for the Holy Spirit to move as the Spirit will and the
freedom for all to respond as they feel moved. Any form that
does not allow this is more a hindrance than help. There can
be real freedom in fixed forms, however. The Old Order
River Brethren have great freedom in the set form for their
testimony meetings which is a hymn followed by sharing of
personal testimony, concerns, or insights, followed by
another hymn.

All worship must be open and sensitive to the leading of
the Holy Spirit. Genuine worship is not dependent on fancy
trappings or ecclesiastical pomp and proud displays, but is
centered around the presence of the living Christ in our
midst. Formal meetings with no room for the Spirit must go.
Simple and spontaneous worship forms are often more helpful than formal ritual. On the other hand in 1 Corinthians 14
Paul warns against the dangers of free worship, problems like
egoism, pride, exhibitionism, emotionalism, individualism,
and disorder. Paul does not prescribe an order, but does ask
that there be order.

Our meetings for worship should be something similar to
that described in 1 Corinthians 14. However, we cannot
simply copy form, for unless we are responding to the Holy
Spirit this also will be an empty routine. What is needed is not
new instructions on how to conduct more Spirit-filled meet-

ings, but to open our lives and meetings to the Spirit. Free church forms can soon become as fixed and inflexible as any formal liturgy. Spontaneous prayers also can be quite empty.

Since worship is a dialogue between God and His people this needs to be reflected in the structure of the worship. Rather than a monologue, there will be adequate opportunity for the response of the community. It is tragic that in most churches the entire meeting for worship is dominated by the person in the pulpit with the rest of the congregation reduced to silence except for singing and an occasional litany. Worship never was intended to be a spectator sport.

We can learn from the Balokole movement (the East African revival fellowship). In each community a fellowship group meets together several times a week. The service normally includes a time of spirited singing, several people leading in prayer, a sharing, testimony period to bring fellowship in the Spirit up-to-date, a Scripture lesson and response, an attempt to come to a consensus on what the Spirit is saying to them, then a time of prayer, followed by people bringing problems or decisions to the group for discernment.[10]

It is questionable whether it is ever legitimate to have a meeting for worship in which people are not given an opportunity to respond or share as they may feel led. Even in weddings and funerals opportunity should be given to share, for someone may have something important to say. In a wedding in which I officiated, at one point in the ceremony I asked if anyone in the congregation had anything they wanted to share with the bride and groom. A number of people responded with expressions of love, support, and admonition that I am sure were more significant than anything I said. How can we not give people the freedom to respond as they are led? Who are we to muzzle the Spirit?

Worship is expressing our love to God and also experiencing His love for us. But how can we do this following a script that outlines what will happen for the next 50 minutes and has our responses all carefully worked out in advance? Too often we read creative litanies but do not share with each other what is on our hearts. Worship is a response to God, not following an order of worship. There is something seriously lacking if there is a need to create worship experiences.

There is always the danger of substituting human creativity for God's initiative, of building defenses against the invasion of God's Spirit into our meetings, and using planned programs to hide the nakedness of our lack of sense of divine presence. Too often we do not actually believe that God can and will break into our lives and meetings, and so we try to fill the emptiness ourselves. Rather than drinking from the well, we add water to it.

The normal pattern of worship should tend to be unprogrammed and led by the Spirit. This is not to say that there is no place for planning, ritual, or for people to present prepared talks to the community. There is much value in this, but this cannot be the heart of the community's worship. How tragic it is that many people attend a formal meeting fifty-two times a year and passively listen but never gather together to be guided by the Holy Spirit, never are silent before the living God. No wonder the church plays such a minor part in their lives and they feel so little responsibility for the church.

This is not to question whether the Holy Spirit can work in the planning of worship, but whether we can consider that the end of the Spirit's work and not expect the Spirit to lead in the meeting other than secretly move people's hearts. The point is that we may never say that now the leading of the Spirit is finished. We never know what God will do or give to us. One can never know ahead of time how a meeting for worship will end. One can make plans, but we never know what to expect. We only know whom to expect and so come together with great expectation.

We have moved from the early church position of worship being the expression of a close fellowship of believers with free sharing, to worship centered around a professional religionist with a formal liturgy. In 1 Corinthians 14:26 Paul tells us, "When you come together, each one has a hymn, a lesson, a revelation, a tongue, or an interpretation." The prayers, songs, confessions, and testimonies are expressions of the people rather than the tastes of the leader. The theology and form of worship will be more an expression of the congregation than the individual tastes of a pastor. In some churches, the theology and form of worship change everytime a new pastor comes. This is a violation of the integrity of the community.

The church is to be more like an old-fashioned hymn sing than a string orchestra. Rather than professional expertise and quality of performance, the emphasis is on the joy of participation. The performance may not always be smooth and precise but all are involved. There is no distinction between performer and audience, for the people are the performers. Orchestras are fine, but not a good model for the church. The priesthood of all believers should be visible in the worship of the community.

A well-trained professional taking major responsibility for worship can retard the growth and maturity of the whole congregation. A smooth worship leader can create a fine atmosphere and even much fervor, but the true spiritual quality of the congregation is reflected in those meetings for worship which are led only by the Spirit. What happens when the professional is not there is a truer test of the spiritual condition of the community.

With this understanding of worship the use of robes is impossible. If all gather to worship God together why would someone be dressed differently to show that person is different even in function from anyone else? It is important to not give undue attention to those giving leadership in worship, or to see them as separate from the rest of the people. We can learn from camps and retreats where distinctions, titles, and clerical garb are put aside in order that there be no barriers to fellowship and worship.

*   *   *

There are many forms and moods of worship. We shall mention and comment on only a few. Very important is praise. We should spend much time in thanking God for all He has done for us, for giving us spiritual brothers and sisters, for the presence of Christ among us. No matter how weak we are, we can still give thanks to God for the fellowship and new life we are privileged to share. It is especially important that we thank God for all the little gifts and blessings that we constantly receive. The extent to which we give thanks for little things is a good indication of the depth of our gratitude.

There is a time for celebration and festivity, but also a time for fasting and mourning. Not only do we share the hope and joy of the kingdom, but also the pain and turmoil of the old world. The anguish of the world is our anguish, her pain our pain.

An important but terribly distorted aspect of worship is prayer. All too often it is a series of clichés, a sermon with our eyes closed, or an attempt to communicate something to others rather than to God. Often it is general and abstract rather than specific and concrete. Although every church has the formality of prayers, in most churches people never pray together.

Since prayer is something that must come from the heart we can pray only when we are moved to pray. We cannot begin to pray aloud because now is the time to pray or "someone asked me to." In our meetings for worship time should be given for prayer, but only those genuinely led to pray should pray aloud.

The same is true for singing. Rather than sing when it is
time to sing we should sing when the time is right to sing.
There are special dangers in singing. Do we believe the words
we sing and does that matter? Since worship is an expression
of the community, congregational singing is much more important than solos, choirs, and instruments. Although there is
nothing wrong with these things, the dangers of profession-
alism, pride, and entertainment are always there. Meetings
for worship are not the place for displaying the musical talent
of a few. It is significant that among groups like the Mennonites who have in the past rejected these things, we find the
most beautiful congregational singing.

Another important aspect of worship is silence. How
much we have to learn from the Quakers here. Often we need
to clear the clutter out of our minds and wait for God to
speak to us. Too often we speak to God but never take the
time to listen. In most churches in order to have silence, we
will first have to overthrow the tyranny of the organ. It seems
that even moments of silent meditation and prayer have to be
interrupted and dominated by it.

We cannot forget preaching. Protestantism in its extreme
reaction against the lack of preaching before the Reformation
put almost its whole stress on preaching. In reaction to this
some now see little value in preaching. At least we can say
that preaching is in a poor state. As William Stringfellow ob-
served,

> Instead of the exposition of the Word of God in the Bible in
> preaching, laymen [sic] are subjected to all manner of speeches,
> diatribes, commentaries, newscasts, patriotic declarations,
> poetic recitations, aphorisms, positive thoughts, social analysis,
> gimmicks, solicitations, sentimentalities and corn. ... The
> unbiblical tenor of much of Protestant preaching is strange, of
> course, in Protestantism because the opening of the Bible
> within the congregation was one of the historic premises of the
> Reformation.[11]

The presupposition of preaching is that there is a Word from God. Preaching is more than lecturing. It declares a verdict and has a binding quality. It is more than a discussion of various options. On the other hand, too much preaching is indoctrination in a particular theology to encourage sectarian loyalty rather than preaching the Word. Often this takes the form of proof-texting to support a particular position rather than allowing the Word to speak and judge. Often this means preaching some ideology, be it the American way of life, patriotism, or either a conservative or liberal social philosophy. Much preaching is lecturing on some important contemporary issue. These sermons are often quite informative and illuminating but they contain little gospel, authority, or food for hungry souls.

At times preaching is inspirational, intended to give the congregation a lift. Inspiration should come from the Holy Spirit, not our creative or emotional preaching. More important than sermons being polished and uplifting is that they be rooted in the gospel, to the point, and related to life.

How could anyone have gotten the idea that only properly ordained men can have a message from God to share with the community? The only authority needed to preach is to be moved by the Holy Spirit to preach. What is said will then be tested by the congregation.

It is important that preaching not be neglected in community. In a fellowship of informal sharing, it is tempting to replace preaching with discussion. To neglect preaching can lead to shallowness, however. The Word also needs to be proclaimed.

Preaching and prayer, confession and singing, praise, remembrance, and response all lead to an invitation to renew the covenant with God and the community, to reaffirm our commitment to God and His people. Meetings for worship are meetings for covenant renewal. Like ancient Israel, our worship is covenantal in nature and at regular times we will emphasize this with festivals that have covenant significance.

The Lord's Supper

Two of the most important worship events for Christians are baptism and communion. Since we discussed baptism earlier we now turn to communion and see its relation to Christian community. First we need to say that any theology of communion that is so complicated that simple fishermen could not have understood it is probably not the same as what Jesus had in mind at the Last Supper.

It is striking that neither the word nor the idea of sacrament can be found in the New Testament. Communion is explicitly mentioned only twice in the New Testament outside the gospels (1 Cor. 10:16, 17; 11:20-29). If it were a means of salvation or grace, certainly somewhere this would be spelled out and emphasized. It is questionable how any objective reader of the New Testament could conclude that the Lord's Supper is a decisive means of grace.

The whole idea of sacrament runs counter to biblical thinking. Judaism has always been very anti-sacramental and there is no hint in the New Testament that the early Christians were trying to convince Jews to be sacramental. The word "sacrament" means mystery and comes from the influence of the pagan mystery religions. The New Testament understanding of mystery must be understood in relation to Hebrew thinking rather than the thought of the Greek mystery religions. The New Testament never uses the word "mystery" in relation to communion. Even though some theologians may make a distinction between sacrament and mystery, for most people they carry the same meaning.

Communion symbolizes and points to grace rather than gives us grace. Never may we say it is *only* a symbol, however. Symbols point beyond themselves to a deeper reality. They are where spiritual truth and the material world meet. God speaks to us through the physical. Through a physical object or action we comprehend a spiritual reality. To confuse or identify the two, however, is idolatry.

There is an objectivity to grace, a grace offered to us in community regardless of our response. In addition to our subjective response, there is the objective reality of Christ's death and resurrection. But the community is more a means of grace than any cultic rituals. The miracle of communion is not what happens to the bread and cup, but that God offers His covenant to us and again binds us together in His grace. The transformation is not in the elements, but among us. We become the very body of Christ. When Jesus said "this is my body" He may have been referring more to the disciples than to the bread.

The real presence of Jesus in communion is essential, just as He needs to be present in all our worship. But Jesus is not present in communion in any way different than any other time. It is a time when we become more aware of Him and symbolize His presence more vividly. The purpose of communion is not to make Jesus present, but to heighten our awareness of His continual presence among us and an invitation to be part of His body, the new covenant. What higher understanding of the real presence of Christ is there than that based on the resurrection which makes Christ available to us at all times and especially when two or three are gathered together in His name?

Communion is often called "Eucharist," which means giving thanks, and should be an expression of gratitude by the whole community for God's grace. At the point we are supposedly most aware of the presence of Jesus and that we are the body of Christ we have the least need for a priest or mediator other than Christ. There may need to be someone to help coordinate and keep things in order, but it is the people who respond to Christ and give thanks. Rather than "administered" by a set-apart priest, communion is to be celebrated together by the community.

Communion, like baptism, is not a means of salvation. The bread and cup are not a "spiritual medicine." The transformation of communion into a sacramental means of salvation was an important part of the fall of the church, for with this shift came a new understanding of the nature and purpose of the church. The church became a conservative, sacrament-dispensing institution rather than the radical body of Christ. Then legally appointed priests began to dispense the "means of grace" to passive recipients who were not committed to God's grace nor bound together by it and did not see themselves as a covenant community.

* * *

Our understanding of communion should be an expression of our understanding of the meaning of Jesus Christ and what it means to be part of His body. In Jesus, God acted in a special way to make Himself known to us, to break the power of the old age of oppression and death, and to create a new people who would live in the new age of Christ's kingdom. Jesus came bringing a new covenant. This new covenant was formed by Jesus giving Himself for us, by His body being broken and blood spilled out. The broken bread and cup symbolize the new covenant and new life that God offers to us.

This covenant and new life are not possible for us without our being redeemed (set free from the slavery of the old age of sin) and so communion always looks back to the source of our new life, namely Jesus and what He did for us. But it does not end there. We are set free for a purpose, to be God's people, to be the body of Christ, to live in the new covenant. Communion is always a celebration of and recommitment to this body and new covenant.

That the Lord's Supper is a symbol of the covenant is made clear both in the Gospels and in Paul. The cup is especially a symbol of the covenant. "This cup is the new covenant in my blood" (1 Cor. 11:25). Communion is a "participation in the body of Christ," the community of faith (1 Cor. 10:16). Communion is a symbol of our *koinonia* and sharing. Jesus' last supper with the disciples should be seen as a covenant meal, just as in the Old Testament repeatedly covenant meals are connected with covenant ceremonies (see Ex. 24:9-11; 2 Chron. 34:29—35:1). As Vernard Eller put it,

> The Supper is a covenant meal celebrating the new order of relationships which has been established by virtue of the body of Christ which was "broken for you."[12]

Communion is a memorial of Jesus' death, not in the sense of a funeral, or the somber occasion we too often have made it, but a celebration of the victory of Christ on the cross which brings us together in the covenant community of the new age. In communion the covenant is renewed with the living Christ who is present and a Partner in the covenant.

As we participate in communion, we are confronted not only with what Christ has done, but also our response to that covenant. The meaning of communion is not individually or orally taking in the substance of Jesus into one's own self, but a communal act which centers around covenant and our together being the broken body of Christ. When we participate in communion we are accepting community. Communion is an objective sign of the unity we have with Jesus *and* each other. As Peter Rideman, the early Hutterite, put it, " . . . all who eat of the loaf with him are one loaf and body with him, he the head and we members one of another."[13]

Vernard Eller suggests that the emphasis in the New Testament is on the "breaking" of the bread rather than "eating" it.[14] Eating is a private experience while breaking and sharing it are communal. The character of Jesus and the body of Christ are represented as being broken. The broken body is given for all. We break the bread instead of biting it because we intend to share it. The breaking of the bread symbolizes what Jesus and His community are all about. The cup says the same thing: His blood (life) is poured out for others. Communion is not for the private inspiration of individuals, but for building up the corporate body of Christ. As Eller describes it,

> The me-by-myself consumption of a nubbin of holy bread cannot—simply cannot—be the correct expression of what the New Testament talks about.[15]

* * *

If communion is a communal celebration of the new covenant, then why not do it that way and celebrate it like the early church did? The New Testament knows nothing about the bread and cup separated from an agape meal. Originally the eucharist was part of a meal (agape) and the two were closely tied together.

The separation of the eucharist from the communal meal, rather than dropping an unimportant element, tore the eucharist apart from its meaning as a celebration of community. In tearing it away from its context, its meaning was drastically distorted and the way opened for the sacramental understanding.

Without a communal meal as the context for the bread and cup, it will be much more difficult to recapture their meaning. Without the meal, the covenant nature of communion is not as evident and more easily missed. The Lord's Supper really needs to be a supper. It is to be celebrated as a fellowship around a table, rather than individually at the altar. In a community of love communion will be a love feast.

Archaeologists have found that to work closely with Arabs in the Middle East, it has been helpful to share a common meal with the local sheik. This symbolizes an acceptance and incorporation into his people. The Lord's Supper is a reminder to us of our incorporation into a new community.

As we focus on this in communion, it will be possible that all our common meals can be agapes, love feasts, breaking of bread. Remember that Jesus' last supper with His disciples implies that there were many other suppers. Their common meals must have been significant occasions as ours can be.

There is yet another meaning of communion. Not only does communion look back to Jesus and reaffirm His community, but it also is an anticipation of something greater to come. As often as we eat and drink together we look forward to the fulfillment of the covenant in the kingdom to come. Jesus repeatedly connected communion with the future kingdom.

> I have earnestly desired to eat this passover with you before I suffer; for I tell you I shall not eat it until it is fulfilled in the kingdom of God. And he took a cup, and when he had given thanks he said, Take this, and divide it among yourselves; for I tell you that from now on I shall not drink of the fruit of the vine until the kingdom of God comes. . . . And I assign to you, as my Father assigned to me, a kingdom, that you may eat and drink at my table in my kingdom.—Luke 22:15-18, 29-30.

How can we capture this meaning without a meal? Communion is an eschatological banquet which anticipates the marriage supper of the Lamb, that great banquet when the kingdom comes in its fullness (Rev. 19:9). And so communion is a great celebration of hope and joy, celebrating the triumph of the resurrection, a victory feast which looks forward to the fulfillment of all that has been promised.

* * *

In the context of the Last Supper Jesus engaged in a scandalous act. He washed the feet of His disciples. Foot-washing was a common practice at that time, but it was done only by servants—never, never by a master. How shocking this was for the disciples. And it is still offensive for us. But that only adds to its importance.

Why should we wash each other's feet as part of communion? In addition to being commanded to do it (Jn. 13:14, 15), the practice says something quite similar to the bread and cup, but without the sacramental overtones. This practice has not yet been overlaid with gold and silver ornaments, and it does not smack of otherworldliness, although the stole (derived from the Latin word for towel) priests wear is a symbol of foot washing.

Foot washing symbolizes our being broken for each other and the world while the bread is symbolic of Jesus' body which was broken for us. To wash the feet of our brothers and sisters is to reach out and make the covenant visible. It is a concrete sign of what it means to be the body of Christ. Here is an excellent symbol of cleansing and being freed from the bondage of sin. Here is a symbol of the surrender not only of our pride, but our whole life in service to others. How better can we symbolize and dramatize the reality of cleansing, humility, service, and covenant community? How better can we symbolize our response to the new covenant?

> When he had washed their feet, and taken his garments, and resumed his place, he said to them, "Do you know what I have done to you? You call me Teacher and Lord; and you are right, for so I am. If I then, your Lord and Teacher, have washed your feet, you also ought to wash one another's feet. For I have given you an example, that you also should do as I have done to you. Truly, truly, I say to you, a servant is not greater than his master; nor is he who is sent greater than he who sent him. If you know these things, blessed are you if you do them. John 13:12-17.

We have argued that foot washing and a common meal need to be part of communion because it is so important that we never separate our relation to God from our relation to others, that we see the relation between the vertical and horizontal, between faith and life. Communion is a mockery if not accompanied by love and service to one another. It seems incomprehensible that communion would not be connected to a community of deep sharing and lead to even more love and concern. If this is so, then why not incorporate this message into the ritual just as Jesus and the early Christians did?

*   *   *

If we have correctly discerned its meaning, communion is legitimate only within a committed fellowship of believers who are all committed to living in the new covenant. Communion is meant to be an expression of community. Without this, the meaning of communion is distorted beyond recognition. It is important that communion be only for those who are committed Christians who are in right relation with God and the community. When we break bread and eat it we are stating our willingness to share Christ's death and die with Him, to take up the cross. We had better not say that unless we mean it. All, without condition, cannot be invited to communion. It is only for those who have been bound together in Christ.

It is especially important that there be reconciliation and unity in a church before celebrating the Lord's Supper. 1 Corinthians 11:17-34 makes this quite clear.

It is not true that Jesus tolerated sin and brokenness at the Last Supper. Judas was present, but Jesus knew that he had defected and so offered him forgiveness and by offering him the sop invited him to change his mind. Jesus offered forgiveness and acceptance to Judas and in the context of loving concern Judas was confronted with making a decision. Would he change his mind or would he leave? Regrettably, Judas decided to leave. It is doubtful that Judas would again have been accepted as part of the community without repentance (1 Cor. 5).

The invitation to communion confronts us with the need

for self-examination. Each time we participate in the Lord's Supper without genuine commitment and faith, the more the meaning of that experience is weakened. Part of the meaning of self-examination before communion is to examine if we are at peace with our neighbors. If we break bread together but have not been reconciled to each other, we dishonor the body of Christ. In most congregations this will mean postponing communion until there is reconciliation.

I well remember as a boy in the Church of the Brethren congregation I grew up in, we still had the practice of the annual deacons' visit. Each year before communion the deacons would visit each member and in the course of the visit had three questions to ask: (1) Are you still in the faith as you were at baptism? (2) Are you at peace with God and your fellowmen? And (3) are you willing to continue to work with the community of faith? If any of the questions could not be answered affirmatively, it was expected that the problem would be solved before communion time. Sometimes communion would need to be postponed. It was expected that when communion was held it would be a sign of love, forgiveness, and unity. Sad to say, in a move to be more modern, most Brethren have discontinued the practice and now tolerate disunity, brokenness, and unfaithfulness as part of the feast of love. There is little wonder that communion no longer has the meaning for the Brethren that it once had.

In the believers' church, people are more concerned about the status of the ones who take communion than the status of sacraments, more concerned about the status of the community than the status of the person in charge. Before communion the community must discern whether they are prepared to have communion.

Communion is a symbol and expression of unity, but will not create unity. Rather than a means of forgiveness, communion symbolizes that we accept the forgiveness that is offered to us. If deep divisions or broken relationships plague the community, communion will not heal them.

To have communion without unity is not to discern the body of Christ, to fail to understand what it means to be the body of Christ (1 Cor. 11:29). This is serious. The bread which we break is the *koinonia* of the body of Christ (1 Cor. 10:16). It is a testimony to our common unity in Christ. This is why the body needs to be discerned. How can we participate in communion if we are not in right fellowship with God and the community?

Open communion, taking communion with anyone, in practice means we have no imperative to seek unity and work through our differences. But if communion has this deeper meaning and we really desire to be in communion with everyone, then there is a real impetus for us to seek this.

Communion can never be entered into lightly, but must be a serious concern of all. At various times in community, the feeling that we were not ready for communion has led to serious soul-searching on the part of all and coming to a deeper unity. After going through this all have felt grateful that we took each other and communion seriously enough to come to unity before we did it. Communion can provide the occasion for coming to deeper unity.

When we take communion with each other, we are binding ourselves to Christ and to each other. We are declaring again that we are in right relation to God and each other. We lay down everything that divided us in the past and leave it behind. We renew the covenant with each other and God. How that can be done with people with whom we are not in unity is difficult to understand.

There is the question of how children can participate in activities such as communion which are only for members. Maybe the example of the Old German Baptist Brethren can be instructive for us. For their love feast and communion the members (all adults) sit around long tables but have their small children with them. During the agape meal the parents share some of the food with their children, although the children do not partake of the bread and cup. The older children and youth sit in the back apart from the congregation, but as the elders pass around the communion bread they quietly give some to the children as a sign of their love for them, telling them that they are also included. In this way they are both part of the fellowship but also not fully included. Somehow we need to give both of these messages to our children in community. Although communion may be only for believers, the elements of communion are not so sacred that no one may touch them. After communion the Old Order Brethren distribute what is left to the children, something the children look forward to.

How often to have communion can never be decided as a theoretical question. Communion can come only when and as often as the community is ready and feels prepared for it (which should be every day). At times that may be every day or every week or there may be a whole year without it. My own bias is that it is a special event and if done too often there is a danger of its becoming another ordinary ritual. Better to see every meal as an agape meal and occasionally specifically celebrate it as such. Every aspect of our lives can be an act of breaking bread and worshiping together.

Chapter 9

THE NONCONFORMING COMMUNITY

> If a man does not keep pace with his companions, perhaps it is because he hears a different drummer. Let him step to the music he hears, however measured or far away.—Thoreau.

Ethics of Redemption

The people of God are those who have left all to follow Jesus. Because they have a different Lord their whole existence stands in contrast to the world around them. Their relation to the world is one of the marks of their new life in Christ.

After two world wars (largely fought by "Christians") and the horrible atrocities of the United States in South East Asia, it is difficult to believe in the Christian character of Western civilization. The reality of our world is much closer to that of the pre-Constantinian church. Now as much as ever there is a real need to see that Christian faith cannot be identified with Western culture.

The essence of nonconformity of the church to the world lies not in rejecting the larger society or even in being a minority group living in contradiction to the rest of society, but rather in being a community which is given the power to live the style and quality of life seen in Jesus, a community which begins to live the new life of the kingdom God offers to us. The foundation of our nonconformity is conformity to Jesus.

Since we have died with Christ to the world (Gal. 6:14; 2:19, 20), we cannot be conformed to it. Jesus came to rescue us from "this present age" (Gal. 1:4). Because of the deep transformation that comes in the new birth there cannot help but be a great difference between those who have been changed and those who have not. To be born again is to be delivered out of the power of darkness and transferred into the kingdom of God (Col. 1:13). We are called to be sojourners and pilgrims (Heb. 11).

In Romans 12:2 Paul tells us to not be con*form*ed to this world but to be trans*form*ed. The word "form" in con*form*ed means outward form, fashion, style, while the "form" in trans*form*ed *(metamorphosis)* refers to essential nature and implies a radical moral change. Thus we could translate this verse to read, "Do not take on the outward form of this age but be changed on the inside." The point here is to be nonconformed not only on the outside, but to be transformed on the inside and allow that to be expressed in outward nonconformity. This transformation is to be as radical as the *metamorphosis* of a catepillar into a butterfly. Those committed to perpetuating the old age tell us to adjust ourselves to the old reality, but those who have been transformed by a different reality live in relation to that new reality.

The context for Christian ethics is a believing community that is already living in the new age, a community clearly distinct from the world. We are defined by the people we are a part of. Our identity is shaped by the people who define who we are. Some may laugh at groups like the Amish who take identity seriously, but those who do not take it seriously follow the crowd like ignorant sheep. Those who have no identity apart from the world have nothing solid in their lives.

The shift from a believing community to an individualistic understanding of the gospel has been an important factor in nonconformed groups accepting the values of the larger culture. Many Anabaptist-type churches in the nineteenth century moved from a strong concept of the church as a people of God, separated from the world, to an individualistic understanding of the faith and almost exclusive concern with personal salvation and personal ethics. The great doctrines of the church were individualized. With this came acculturation into American culture religion and increasing compromise with the world.[1] Christian ethics must always be an expression of Christian community. Christian responsibility is defined in relation to the Christian community rather than some other group.

Christian ethics are not a new law, a set of expectations for us to obey except for certain exceptions when they will not be most practical, but a call to enter a whole new order, a kingdom we can never leave to accomplish any worldly good. The teachings of Jesus are descriptions of what this new life in the kingdom will look like. Among the various groups and forces competing for our loyalty, we will be clear that Jesus and the Christian community have first and primary loyalty. Whenever we obey any voice that contradicts that of Jesus, for whatever reasons, we lose the power of the new life in the kingdom.

We are not to live in two different realms of church and world with two different standards. Our horizontal relationships belong just as much to the kingdom of God as our inner spiritual life. Faith is not something that involves only some higher or deeper aspect of our being, but our whole being. Not one fiber of our being may escape the transforming power of the Holy Spirit. All decisions are to be made in the context of living in the kingdom of God. Our faith is not acceptance of a few peculiar doctrines, but involves our whole identity.

The evidence in the New Testament that the church stands in contrast to the world is overwhelming and there is nothing to suggest that her radical stance toward the world was to be only temporary. In fact, it is explicitly stated that this antagonism would exist until the end of this age. Consider just two texts.

> What partnership have righteousness and iniquity? Or what fellowship has light with darkness? What accord has Christ with Belial? Or what has a believer in common with an unbeliever? 2 Corinthians 6:14, 15.
> Do you not know that friendship with the world is enmity with God? Therefore whoever wishes to be a friend of the world makes himself an enemy of God. James 4:4.

The reason for this antagonism is that the world has rejected the light which has come into the world. There is no hint in the Bible that the world is inherently evil but rather the message is that "The earth is the Lord's and the fulness thereof" (Ps.24:1) and, though fallen, it anticipates its final restoration (Rom. 8; Rev. 21). The point is not that the world is evil, but that it is living in rebellion against God.

The basis for Christian nonconformity to the world is not any distinction between spirit/matter, sacred/secular, invisible/visible, but between regenerate/unregenerate, faithful/unfaithful, church/world. It is an understanding that fallen creation and redemption are not identical. It is the difference between those who seek the light and those who are repelled by it.

This changes the whole issue. We need not reject anything on the basis of its being secular. In fact, we are to be deeply concerned about every aspect of life, for we have one unified life under the lordship of Christ. It makes little difference whether one is discussing the price of eggs, a current political issue, or a point of theology, for we are talking about life in the kingdom of God. We seek the regeneration of every sphere of life.

The distinction comes in the difference between church and world, between life lived in God's kingdom and life lived outside that kingdom. There is a separation between those who live by the hope of the coming kingdom and those who are captives to the spirit of the old age. The distinction is between those who are shaped by the world to come and those who cling to, justify, and defend the old order which is passing away. To not be captives of the old order allows us to be free to be servants and witnesses in the midst of the old order.

Our understanding of the relation of church to world is rooted in our understanding of baptism, in the free decision everyone must make for or against Christ's kingdom. Because everyone must make this decision, there is bound to be a parting of the ways.

This is not to claim that any of us are perfect or to deny that the old age is still with us. Indeed the struggle between good and evil is part of our daily lives. We may not self-righteously look in judgment on the world, for the judgment of God is on each of us. Neither may we have any scorn or hatred for the world's people. We can, however, affirm the new life which has been given to us and know that is different from the old life.

We need a whole reorientation on what Christian ethics is. John Howard Yoder points out that if we could understand that Christian ethics is first of all for Christians we would solve many of the problems of Christian ethics.[2] Instead of trying to adjust the clear teachings of Jesus to meet the needs of those who control society, as almost all the establishment theologians have done, we need to see that Jesus' teachings are for those who have forsaken all to follow Him.

Christian ethics are not based on what any reasonable person would do in a particular situation or station in life, but what the life, teachings, death, and resurrection of Jesus say to a person in that situation. All that we do is to be an authentic expression of what life in the kingdom is like.

Christian ethics demands behavior which is impossible

except through the power of God working among us. Many see faith as a force which can help in the realization of ideals and ultimate goals, but accept an unresolvable tension between what is and what should be. But God does not call us to do anything which He will not give us the power to do. A Christian may never say, "I know that's what God wants me to do, but I don't have the strength or courage to do it." It is a clear evidence of lack of faith in God's power to argue that we cannot live up to what God calls us to. God will give us the power to obey Him if we are willing. That our obedience is always incomplete in no way denies that it is possible.

The radical vision is accused of being a vision based on spiritual pride. But is it spiritual pride to suggest that Jesus actually meant what He said and that we will be given the power to do it? Maybe it is spiritual pride which prevents us from surrendering all and beginning to obey, that prevents us from being anywhere but in the middle of the road. The point is not that we are better or superior to the rest of the world, or wiser, or even more moral, but that we have a different vision of what God wants.

Those who water down the witness of the church in order to not offend are wrong not in going too slowly, but in their failure to give their sole loyalty to Jesus. Often the radical discipleship position is rejected not on the basis of biblical interpretation, but on pragmatic considerations. If the decisions were made only on the basis of the New Testament there would be no choice but to go the way of the cross and complete obedience rather than pragmatic judgment.

The Christian does not demand that everyone else accept the Christian ethic first or ask what would happen if everyone did it. We really do not expect that everyone will soon start following Jesus. But no situation of society, state, or religion can qualify the demands of the gospel, nor may they be modified to fit the needs of a smooth functioning society. The real question is not what everyone will do, but what God demands. The question is not, "What would happen if everyone would be a pacifist like you?" Christian ethics are derived from the order of redemption rather than the order of nature. Our cues come not from what is, but what will be.

We cannot construct a Christian ethic for unregenerate society. The state is pagan and will likely not live up to Christian standards. But Christians *can* be expected to. We will not be surprised when the state is violent, but that does not mean that we will accept violence. While we might not immediately expect the world to live up to Christian truth, we also know that God's will is the same for all people and that rejection of that truth and way will bring terrible consequences to the world. God does not have two wills—God wills all to be saints. Therefore we urgently call all the world to repentance, to the one straight and narrow way.

Relation to the Old Order

As Christians we are in the world but "not of the world" (Jn. 17:16, 18). We neither flee the world nor are absorbed by it. The new life we are called to is in the world and for the world. The Christian life is not otherworldly. It may not be *of* the world, but it is lived very much *in* the world. That the kingdom is not of the world (Jn. 18:36) in no way means that it is unrelated to life in the present world.

The theology which claims that the church is merely that part of the world which is aware of what God is doing in the world fails to recognize the radical nature of evil in the world and the radically transformed nature of the church. To identify the church with society denies the reality of the new humanity by blessing the old fallen order and losing sight of the new humanity God is creating. We need to see that our society is most unchristian precisely at the points where it is most religious, pious, and patriotic. C. Wright Mills described the central nerve of establishment religion when he wrote,

As a social and a personal force, religion has become a dependent variable. It does not originate; it reacts. It does not
denounce; it adapts. It does not set forth new models of
conduct and sensibility; it imitates. . . . In a quite direct sense,
religion has generally become part of the false consciousness of
the world and of itself.[3]

When it has come to this, when we no longer see the
contradiction between the gospel and the world systems we
have denied the lordship of Christ.

It is difficult to understand how on the basis of the Bible
one could find essential agreement between Christian faith
and human culture. We cannot simply accept the course of
history and identify it with God's will, for history teaches us
as much about the demonic as about God. The Enlighten-
ment view that the structures of society are good is not a biblical view. The structures are fallen. Although they of
themselves may not be evil, they are under the power of evil.
The problem is more than a few vices of society. Thus participation in the structures as a banker, policeman, or politician
raises the concern not only of avoiding those vices which are
contrary to personal ethics, but also questions of violence, injustice, and racism which are inherent in those structures.

The world is temporarily under the domination of the
forces of evil (2 Cor. 4:4; Eph. 2:2). It has gone mad with its
militarism, violence, sensuality, and greed. Unbelief and evil
also incarnate themselves and become flesh. The world is organized rebellion and unbelief, that which should be part of
Christ's kingdom but is not. The development of modern
democracy does not make irrelevant the New Testament
understanding of the relation of the church to the structures
(principalities and powers) of society. The world is still unregenerate, some still wield power over others, selfishness and
sin still abound. There is still a fundamental enmity to God.

The church perceives that the sickness of the world is not
due to a few flaws in the system that can be easily corrected

and reformed, but a problem which goes to the very roots and foundation of society. Any meaningful change must speak to that foundation, call for radical repentance, and provide an essentially new understanding and basis for life in all its relationships.

Rosemary Radford Ruether, the Roman Catholic scholar, states this view:

> The believers' church, then, is a separated people, not because of any inner sectarianism in its own life principle, but because it must exist in tension and conflict with a world formed along alien and hostile principles of existence, a world which instinctively recognizes the community of believers as a threat to the status quo, and to the foundations of its authority and power. The more clearly the believing community grasps its own principle of life, the more they will stand out against the system around them. The more they really live by those principles, the more they run the risk of being a dissident and even outlaw community *vis-a-vis* the "law and order"; that is to say, the systematized disorder of the system.[4]

Those who take history and the incarnation seriously, rather than seeing culture as autonomous and separate from faith, will see its need to be brought under the lordship of Christ. The point is not to see Christ as against culture or above culture, but as Lord and Judge over all, including culture. Rather than make any sweeping condemnation of culture, all cultural values and expressions are to be judged by what we know of Jesus. We begin not with some ideology of culture as proposed by H. Richard Niebuhr[5] and others, but with a believing community that seeks to follow Jesus in all things.

The church stands not against culture, but against degenerate forms of culture. It is not as simple as Niebuhr suggests. There has probably never been a group in history that has rejected all culture. The Amish, who Niebuhr would call being against culture, have a very rich culture. The question is not whether we are with or against culture (culture is not monolithic) but whether our primary loyalty is to Jesus and how that relates to every aspect of culture.

Rather than a sweeping rejection of everything, we reject any aspect of culture that is in rebellion against God. Some things we accept and some we reject. If we reject war, we do not necessarily need to reject schools. If we oppose Hitler, we do not need to reject Beethoven. Christ and culture are not necessarily in conflict. We are in conflict only with sin and all its cultural manifestations. There is no abstract formula of relation to culture. Sometimes we may do the same as the larger society, such as eating apple pie.

Although the Christian faith can never be identified with any one particular culture, it must always find expression in some cultural form. A counterculture is a culture. A sect which rejects the art of the prevailing culture soon develops her own art. In fact, one common feature of most sectarian art is simplicity, be it in architecture, music, dress, or decorations. They have style, but a different style.

We need to take a critical view of culture and be aware of how it reflects and communicates the values of the society around us. Art is to be appreciated, but must be rejected when it carries values that are in conflict with life in God's kingdom. Otherwise art becomes idolatrous. Likewise, Christians need not reject learning and scholarship, for there is no merit in being ignorant. We need not reject the world's knowledge, but it must be subjected to the test of the gospel.

Quite often throughout history when a community develops a distinctive life in relation to the larger culture this will be expressed in outer symbols of distinctiveness. Often this includes a distinctive dress like the Amish. A distinctive dress can be a powerful symbol of the unity and common commitment which exists in the community. When Christians put on a distinctive dress they do it not to put up walls between themselves and others, but as a means of communication to the world of who they are. It can be an authentic expression of a community's relation to the world.

Of course this can degenerate into an empty legalism and can even be an expression of pride and self-righteousness. But when the outer symbols are an expression of something real in our hearts and our lives together, they are a significant witness to each other and to the world of our unity. Maybe there is some truth to the Madison Avenue slogan that "clothes make the man." If our clothes say we belong to the world, maybe we do.

It is not possible to drop all outer symbols and still maintain the inner reality, for the inner and outer are not distinct realities, but related to each other. In case after case when nonconformed groups dropped their distinctive dress they also soon lost not only their nonconformity, but also their unity and community with each other. Actually they probably first lost the unity and only later lost the dress. We need to be suspicious of the idea that we do not want the church to tell us how to dress but are perfectly willing to let those who design the fashions to dictate to us how to dress.

Throughout church history various groups have stressed different aspects of biblical teaching in the area of culture, stressing separation from the world, identification, or transformation, ending up with an unbalanced view. It would seem better to see the Bible as a message to be taken as a whole, with all of it relevant to our lives, and then corporately discern what that says to our particular situation.

Our relation to culture is never static, for again and again we must bring the judgment of Jesus to bear on an ever-changing culture. Any conclusion we come to in this area is always open to new light and reconsideration. As the world changes and the Holy Spirit continues to work among us, our relation to the world will change. The Christian community will continually be in the process of discerning what is to be accepted or rejected in the world. The Christian community must not become frozen in any time period or one reaction to culture, although this is probably less serious than bowing before every passing fad.

It is essential that the Christian community always be in close contact with the world so that we can understand the world and be in dialogue with it. Jesus did not pray that we be taken out of the world, but only that we be kept from evil (Jn. 17:15). Our separation from the world is spiritual and cultural rather than geographic, a result of distinctive loyalties and values rather than spatial isolation. There is no evidence that the early Christians went the route of the Essenes and isolated themselves from the urban culture of their day. We are to be in the world just as Jesus was in the world—serving, healing, speaking the truth, and calling people to a new life.

At many points we may see God at work in the world, but even here we need to discern carefully. Not every moment that proclaims liberation actually brings liberation. Many social movements may point in the right direction but carry with them a whole load of philosophical baggage which is in direct conflict with the gospel. The church will relate to these movements if their goals are good, but will carefully discern the nature and limits of the relationship. We do not, out of either guilt or wanting to be with it, need to jump on every bandwagon that comes along. The Hebrew people were given the warning to

> Take heed to yourself, lest you make a covenant with the inhabitants of the land whither you go, lest it become a snare in the midst of you. Exodus 34:12.

It is important that we not be too strict in our relation to the world, for this may be a sign that we are not free from the world. Those who oppose pornography too vigorously may be dominated by a desire for it. We are to be liberated from sin, not only opposed to it.

Even though we may radically stand over against the old society, we also stand in solidarity with it, for we recognize that since all of our love and community has come to us only by the grace of God, we are not better than the world around us. There is no place for self-righteousness or pride. Never may we turn our backs to the world. In fact, the more evil a situation is, the more important it is that we relate redemptively to it. We are not afraid of sin. We go right to the sin that is the basis of any evil situation with the knowledge that the power of sin has already been broken.

While the Christian community recognizes the existence of two kingdoms and the divided state of humanity, she can never accept it or be happy with it. Although there is a separation between church and world, that is not what God wants. Ultimately God wants the whole world to become part of His kingdom. Although the kingdoms of this world are temporarily under Satan's control, they *shall become* the kingdom of our Lord and Christ (Rev. 11:15). God will be victorious in the world just as God is victorious in our community. God is at work in the world seeking to redeem the world.

Rather than reject society, we focus on the new society which is coming. Although we recognize the demonic powers at work in the world, we also recognize that these forces were defeated in the resurrection and that it is Jesus Christ who is ultimately in control of the world. This faith is not limited to the private dimensions of life, but directly related to the events of history and concern for social justice. Although we can never expect the unregenerate world to live by the Christian ethic, we do hope for the conversion of the world and actively work for social justice and call the world to accept the lordship of Christ. We always have the hope for the world to be regenerate. This hope gives us a new relationship to the world.

The Christian community is the beginning of that victory, those people "upon whom the end of the ages has come" (1 Cor. 10:11). The Christian community is primarily not a leavening force in the old society, but the beginning of a new society in the midst of the old. Our task is not to sew new pieces of cloth on an old garment (Mk. 2:21). Although hopefully the Christian community will have a good effect on society, *her primary task is not to better society but to be the beginning of a new society.*

Working Through the Structures

It is important that we be realistic about the degree to which we can participate in the system and change it. Usually it changes us more than we ever change it. It is not so much that it is wrong to work for the state, but that we are called to a new order which makes most of the old irrelevant. We might also remember the advice of 2 Timothy 2:4: "No soldier on service gets entangled in civilian pursuits, since his aim is to satisfy the one who enlisted him."

Maybe the most important teaching in the New Testament regarding our relation to the old order is Jesus' response to the question of who would be greatest in His kingdom. Jesus told His disciples that they were not to lord it over others, but rather be servants (Lk. 22:24-27). This is to be our relation to the world. It rules out many positions in society. John C. Wenger writes that the early Anabaptists refused any kind of government posts because they did not want to relate to people on any basis except the redemptive love of the gospel.[6]

There are some functions in society, such as policing, which are necessary only because of sin. Christians will not participate in functions of society which faith makes unnecessary. In many positions the use of coercion, violence, or compromise are essential parts of the work. We should be clear that we cannot use either the methods or the structures of the old age to bring about the goals of the new age.

As Christians we can participate in the structures of society to the extent that we are able to discern God's activity there, refuse to compromise ourselves, and are acting out of a disciplined community which will hold us accountable for our actions and help us to discern what is and is not of God.

The radical church is regularly accused of being irresponsible and withdrawing from the world. But before we naively accept the principle of responsibility we must define it. What is our responsibility and how do we discern it? Let us not accept any responsibility before we examine it and understand what it entails. Too often "responsibility" becomes self-justifying and idolatrous. We can never accept "responsibility" as an autonomous moral absolute.

We are repeatedly told that to be responsible we need to be involved in the social structures, but little is said about what this means. We are to vote, but usually this means church members voting on opposite sides, canceling each other out, and making a farce of Christian unity. On what basis shall we be responsible and responsible to whom? It is interesting to note that most of those who argue most vigorously for Christian involvement in the social structures reject a specifically Christian ethic, arguing that our ethics are based on the order of nature rather than redemption. Christians in the power structures are expected to do what any "reasonable" person in that position would do.

Both conservatives and liberals believe that Christians should be involved in the structures and that they will work by the rules of the system rather than an outside ethic. It is assumed that the Christian in business or politics will always do what is right, but it is seldom spelled out what right would mean. The Christian senator may be either a hawk or a dove, may vote for or against social programs. All too often all this means is learning to view problems from the perspective of those in power rather than of those who are at the bottom. Specifically how Christian commitment and the Bible are relevant to responsibility are never very clear. But if the Christian does not come to the structures with a unique perspective and ethic, what is the argument for Christian involvement?

Do we really mean to call the early church before Constantine an otherworldly withdrawal from responsibility and the medieval church the example of Christian involvement in the world? In the countries where there has been the closest identification of church and society, and church members are most deeply involved in the power structures, we do not find a higher standard of social morality or a more vital church.

After trying for around fifteen hundred years to Christianize the world by trying to control it, we have reluctantly given up because we know that it did not work. What we need to see is that the whole enterprise was wrong from the beginning. The Constantinian vision failed not because it was not given a wholehearted try, but because the vision itself was faulty.

Withdrawal from Christian responsibility occurs whenever we submit to the values and demands of the fallen world, when we do not have the power of resistance, witness, and victory demonstrated by the early church. To live responsibly means to stand over against the systems of oppression and domination. We do not need to accept the confusion and distortion of thinking that the two alternatives are "responsibility" and "withdrawal" and not realize that the real question is rather what it means to be the faithful and visible church that relates to the world on the basis of the new life we have in Christ.

Of more concern than Christians being in the world (how many are not) is *how* they are to be in the world and what they are to do while in the world. The problem is not that Christians are uninvolved in the problems of racism, materialism, and militarism, but that they are involved too much and in the wrong way. Maybe the emphasis needed today is to "come out from them, and be separate from them" (2 Cor. 6:17). The word "separate" here means not a casual separation, but a cutting off with no intention of returning.

The New Testament describes God's people as strangers, pilgrims, and aliens. We are strangers in that we do not feel at home here. We are pilgrims, for we are on our way to a new city. We are aliens, for our citizenship is in another kingdom. We are exiles who can accept no privileged position in society. We have different values from those who live a settled life. One of the central problems of the church has been the transformation from a minority perspective to an attitude of being the establishment and so needing to protect her interests.

As pilgrims we have no responsibility to defend, support, or maintain the structures of the old age which is passing away. Rather we are asked to come out of Babylon (Rev. 18:4). There is no hint in the New Testament that Christians are responsible for the moral structure of the non-Christian world or to maintain the old structures. Jesus avoided involvement in the structures and Paul pointed more toward separation than integration. Jesus did not attempt to demonstrate solidarity with society by cooperating with sin in order to make a "more positive witness." The call of the New Testament is not to lose our visible witness in order to leaven the whole lump, but to be the visible body of Christ. For a community to be totally faithful to Jesus who is the Lord over all history is the best way to be responsible to society.

The health and even survival of society does not depend on Christians compromising in order to work effectively within it. In fact, the more Christians compromise their vision to work within it the less there will be of an independent vision to give light to the government. But even more important, ultimately we know that God is in charge of history, not we, and it is He who will bring history to its conclusion.

Our task is, as a church, to live out God's purposes.

Our primary work in social change goes beyond changing the hearts of individuals or transforming power structures, for it comes from the understanding that the main social structure through which God's redeeming work is effected in the world is the Christian community. Our energies for world betterment are channeled through the church for our hope for a new social order is found more in the church than in the world. Our best efforts at "saving the world" are directed toward building up the body of Christ, the firstfruits of the new order.

The creation of Christian community is the most radical political action one can ever experience, especially if it involves breaking down social barriers, proclaiming liberty to the captives, and establishing justice. It is the coming to concrete reality of a new life that will not only show what is wrong with the old, but point so clearly to the new which is possible that the old can no longer command our loyalty and devotion.

Much more important than involvement in the old age that is passing away is the extent of our involvement in the new which God is creating. More important than defending any culture or power is calling together people from every nation and tribe to be the new people of God. Our responsibility to the world is always first to be the church, to embody what God wants to say to the whole world, to live and demonstrate what salvation means.

Rather than an escape from the world this is a creative way of standing in the world. The refusal to cooperate with certain aspects of society is not a withdrawal from society but a positive witness to and interference with the structures of evil. The living of a new alternative is highly visible. Sometimes our best contribution to the world will be found in standing over against the world, in pointing in a new direction. We are set apart in order that we may have something to contribute to the world. God called out Abraham to be a blessing to all nations. We must be close enough to society to be able to speak to it but removed enough to have something to say to it.

Rather than an irrelevant oddity in the midst of a progressive society, the radical churches have often been on the cutting edge of social change. They have been the innovators, the ones with a universal vision. They have initiated social action, prison reform, peace, antislavery, and civil rights movements. Note the contribution of Methodists to the development of trade unionism in England. Often they have made a deep contribution even when they never intended to, as for example the Jehovah's Witnesses' contribution to civil liberties which has come from their refusal in many ways to cooperate with the state.

The existence of a believers' church introduces, if not insures, the element of pluralism into the larger society, for by her very nature the believers' church is a community which lives by a different reality than does the larger society. This is one of the main reasons the establishment has often felt the need to repress free church movements.

By being liberated from dependence upon legal and established authority, the free churches have been able to develop a moral authority which has been more potent than any established authority which has to rely on coercion and threats to maintain itself.

Someone has suggested that one percent of the population refusing to go along with something is more influential than 30 percent working for change. Most of the major changes for good in history were the results of groups which refused to conform. The people who have been most effective witnesses for the kingdom of God have been those who tried only to be faithful. The point is not to change society, not to be effective or even different, but to be faithful to Jesus and His kingdom.

The Suffering Community

The symbol of our relation to the world is the cross. Our relation to the world is one of love, but often the reaction to that love will be separation and hostility. The New Testament repeatedly warns us that if we remain faithful we can expect persecution. To drink of the cup which Jesus drank will mean suffering and death, rejection and humiliation. The true church is a suffering church, hated and despised by the world, for those committed to the prince of darkness cannot bear to see the light.

There is only one point at which we are asked to imitate Jesus. We are not expected to dress like He did or imitate every aspect of His lifestyle. But we are asked to deny ourselves, and take up the cross (Mk. 8:34-37). At the point of contradiction between the call of Jesus and the demands of the world we are called to take up the cross.

The cross is more than learning to live with one's rheumatism or station in life or an inner struggle with guilt. It is the result of our struggle against the forces of evil in the world which inflict suffering on us because of our sole allegiance to Jesus. The cross comes at the point righteoueness and sin meet. It is the result of our nonconformity to the expectations of society.

Any attempt to live the gospel will lead to the cross. Suffering for the cause of righteousness is one of the marks of true discipleship. The cross comes as a rejection of the limitations of an imperfect world in favor of nonconformed obedience to Jesus. Persecution is based primarily on the intensity and the integrity of the Christian witness, rather than the moral level either of the Christians or persecutors. It is significant that the word "martyr" carries the meaning of both witness and unearned suffering. Witness and suffering go together.

Much of the persecution and probably the most dangerous kind is a very mild variety: pressures to make little accommodations here and there, to soften our witness, to adopt a more positive attitude toward the powers of the world.

In order to live the gospel of Jesus we must be willing to accept the suffering of Jesus and pay the price of rejection by society. Suffering is not something we seek, but comes as a result of our witness. Persecution, however, is not a proof that we are faithful. We are not to have a martyr complex or seek persecution. We never seek to cause offense although we know that the truth we live and speak may be offensive.

The cross we are called to bear is not just any kind of cross. It is not the cross of Constantine or the Crusades, but the cross of Isaiah 53, the way of redemptive love. The cross is not a gun, the lamb is not a wolf; the dove is not a hawk or an eagle, and neither is a servant a slave master. The way of the cross is to love our enemies and turn the other cheek. It implies a community which serves rather than rules, suffers rather than injures, crosses social barriers rather than builds them. We do not have a more important cause for which to manipulate and coerce people, but a cause which prevents us from manipulating anyone. As Paul puts it,

> We have renounced disgraceful, underhanded ways; we refuse to practice cunning or to tamper with God's word, but by the open statement of the truth we would commend ourselves to every man's conscience in the sight of God. 2 Corinthians 4:2.

When the church exchanged the way of the cross for the role of the persecuting church it was no longer a faithful church.

Although within the Christian community we experience mutual submission to each other, the New Testament understanding of submission is not dependent on the other person having a right attitude. We are called to submit ourselves not only to those who are "kind and gentle but also to the overbearing" (1 Pet. 2:18). In this Jesus is our example (1 Pet. 2:21-23). We need to recognize, however, that there is a big difference between relationships of mutual submission and relationships where we voluntarily submit ourselves to those outside the church who have no intention of being submitted to anyone. Often this will involve suffering. This is part of what it means to take up the cross, to drink of the cup which Jesus drank.

Although we are prepared to suffer at the hands of the world's system, we do not despair, for we live in the hope of the resurrection, we have the promise that God will never allow more than we are able to bear (1 Cor. 10:13), and we look forward to the day when the kingdom of God will be completely victorious over the world. Indeed, the way of the cross is the way of victory; unearned suffering is redemptive. It is a preparation for victory. One of our most powerful weapons against the powers of evil is suffering. Here is one of the great advantages of the oppressed. Through their suffering they will triumph.

It is the cross rather than the sword, suffering rather than might that make the most difference in history. The success of the church under Constantine was her undoing. Although the cross is foolishness to the Greeks and a scandal to the Jews, to them that believe it is the wisdom of God and the power of God (1 Cor. 1:18-25). The hope of the cross is the resurrection. "The blood of the martyrs is the seed of the church."[7] The church will be strongest when she gives up her desire for power and effectiveness and accepts the foolishness and weakness of the cross.

The Church and the State

Any discussion of our relation to the state must begin with our understanding of the church rather than any philosophy of government. The shape of our relation to the state will be an expression of our life in Christian community. Our first concern is neither cooperation nor separation, but obedience to Jesus and His kingdom. The Christian is first of all committed to the universal kingdom of God, second a member of the local expression of that kingdom, then a member of the international community, and only way down the list a member of a nation state.

As citizens of Christ's kingdom, we refuse to seek power and control over government not because we expect the end to come soon, because we want to remain pure, or because we think government is unnecessary, but because the mission of God's people is completely different from that. Christ's call to us is not to ensure that history will come out right or to subjugate God's enemies, but to be a new people who will begin to fulfill God's purposes for all humanity. The church is to be a moral force independent of the world, representing in the midst of the world the demands of God upon the whole world.

One of the most important elements in the fall of the church was her joining hands with the state. When the church and state became allies the church ceased to be an expression of Christ's kingdom. The real sectarianism in a negative sense is to identify the church with the causes of one's nation. The church's blessing of civil authority as Christian has meant little more than a cheap acceptance of anything civil government does.

With the acceptance of Christianity as the one official religion of the Roman Empire after Constantine, and later the growing unity of church and state, came one of the worst tragedies of Christian history. The church ceased to be what God called her to be. Within a short time a persecuted community became a presecuting institution, culminating in the Crusades and Inquisition, and then Hiroshima and Vietnam. The people of the cross became a people of the sword and supersonic bombers. A peculiar people became a privileged people. Soon the radical primitive communities were transformed into an institutional, worldly church with a growing accommodation to pagan culture, lowered standards of membership, sacramentalism, hierarchical control, clericalism, inequality and class distinctions, and accumulation of worldly power. As Harold S. Bender put it,

> She no longer resembled that little band of disciples who had responded to the invitation of Jesus to repent of their sins and come out from the world to follow him in simple obedience. Jesus was poor; the church was rich. Jesus was defenseless; the church was powerful. Jesus was despised and rejected by men; the church was sitting in the seats of the proud and mighty in the land.[8]

Peter Chelcický, the fifteenth-century Czech reformer, used the image of the net of the church being torn and ruined by catching two whales: the emperor and the pope.[9] Because of this catch soon there was little difference between church and world.

One of the reasons establishment churches have not been able to accept radical discipleship has been their alliance with the political establishment. Zwingli opposed infant baptism until he realized this would bring too much conflict with the authorities. There has been a clear understanding that to accept the radical position would lead to loss of the church's position of power and prestige and transform a respected institution into an exile church. Thus the establishment churches compromise the demands of Jesus so that they might be able "to have more influence on society."

The Methodists in the United States illustrate the position of most establishment churches. The first Methodist *Discipline* in America, written in 1784, stated that American Methodists would be obedient to Wesley during his lifetime. After his death they would continue in union with the English Methodists insofar as "consistent with the Cause of Religion in America and the political Interests of these States."[10] What blasphemy! It could hardly be stated more clearly. The interests of the state came ahead of the demands of the gospel and the unity of the church.

Although the neat integration of church and culture is frayed and there is a growing awareness that all is not well in Babylon, the radical distinction between church and world called for in the New Testament is not yet accepted by most people. The radical implications of living in a post-Constantinian era are not obvious to most. Christian ethics are still defined in terms of what would be best for society. The institutional church still sees her role as teaching and legislating morality for the whole society. Many still consider the church to be dependent on the powers of the world for her existence and support. It is still difficult for many to conceive of the Christian faith standing in contradiction to their society. That the message of judgment and repentance may be for us is difficult to accept. Scheiermacher spells out this view in a most frightening way:

> Every nationality is destined through its peculiar organization and its place in the world to represent a certain side of the divine image. . . . For it is God alone who directly assigns to each nationality its definite task on earth and inspires it with a definite spirit in order to glorify herself through each one in a peculiar manner.[11]

For too long the church has been as one of the pillars of society, helping hold up the structures. The mission of the church has been seen to provide the moral and spiritual resources to ensure the existence of society. The assumption is that if the church did not do this the world would fall apart or be turned over to the devil.

The role of church being chaplain to society has been understood in two ways. One has been the sacramental function of blessing whatever happens in society. The chaplain is loyal, depends upon the structure for support and authority, and can be expected to support what the structure does. Ethics are usually not seen as an important concern.

If the chaplain is strong enough, there may be the opportunity to influence the structures to do the right things. This is the classical puritan approach. Now the task is not primarily to bless, but to enforce the standards of the church on others. In either case, the purpose of the church is seen in the same way: to give support to society. The church is seen as a vital part of the power structure.

The purpose of the Christian faith and the church is not to bless the institutions and values of society but to bring judgment to bear upon them and call for repentance. It is not to justify and rationalize the traditions and sentiments that hold society together but to obey the God who holds the destinies of all societies.

Among both liberals and conservatives there is still the dream of the church having enough power and influence to induce the whole society to live out the Christian vision. Both are willing to impose their position on others. We find the same attitude among those Christians who give wholehearted support to revolutionary groups. They also see the purpose of the church being to support the structures of society, only in this case new structures. Those who want to see clergy plainly visible in progressive movements also see the church as a chaplain to society. Their argument with conservatives is that the church has been supporting the wrong social-political order, not that Christians should not see sanctifying social systems as part of their mission.

The tragedy of this way is illustrated by an example from United States history. While revivalism and the church gave important motivation for the Abolitionist movement which was especially strong in the Midwest, the identification of Christianity with the cause of the Union forces in the Civil War became the basis of a conservative Republicanism and American culture religion which was to dominate the United States for a hundred years and could easily justify imperialism, national expansion, and manifest destiny.[12] Whenever we identify the cause of the church with prevailing attitudes we are building the foundation for much trouble in the future. Our life and witness can be universal only to the extent we are free from sanctifying any given society or order. The church should not be identified with the political or social order of any territory or state.

Although in some ways there was no separation of church and state in the Old Testament, there was a clear separation of Israel from the other Near Eastern states. Throughout the Old Testament there is a recognition of this conflict between God's people and the kingdoms of this world. The New Testament is quite explicit about the state being part of the old order that is passing away.

Although the state is not part of the realm of redemption, this in no way implies that the gospel is not political. The Bible is intensely concerned with the issues of history and social justice. The kingdom of God is a political reality. It has to do with how we relate to each other in community, how we deal with power, how we order our economic lives. After all, we do have a King.

We must not simply accept that there are two kingdoms and thereby comfortably accept two different standards, thus shielding the state from God's judgment. We cannot refuse to deal with social issues for that would deny Christ's lordship over all. When the church refuses to deal with social issues, all too often this means an uncritical acceptance of pagan values. The true prophets in Israel were those who did not say what the king wanted to hear, but spoke the word of judgment and repentance. Too often it is seen as proper for the church to bless society but improper to call for repentance. It is considered proper for a preacher to support a war, but not to protest against it. Because we recognize that ultimately Christ is Lord over all the structures of society, we can speak to the world in Christ's name and call the world not only to ethical responsibility, but to the one who is ultimately in control.

We are political, but our politics is the politics of the kingdom rather than the politics of Caesar. Our platform is the gospel. It includes voluntarism, suffering love, and a new life of economic sharing with a rejection of violence and coercion. This new politics is expressed as a community. While Caesar's politics is based on law and coercion our politics operates by love and the rule of the Holy Spirit.

As representatives of the new politics, we let the state know whenever we see the actions of the state to be in opposition to God's commands. We will fight against oppression and injustice and remind the state that it is not God. Rather than harmonizing and blending of religion with the needs of society, the faithful Christian community will preach the true gospel which will include proclamation of judgment upon the idolatry of militarism, materialism, and power politics. The goals of the nation will be shown to be not those of Christ's kingdom. We will speak on moral issues before they become political issues. Where the state does what is right we will give praise to God.

*   *   *

Should the church encourage the state to legislate morality? This is a tricky one, for usually our answer depends on what we are talking about. Most everyone wants the state to outlaw murder but many would hesitate on outlawing adultery. In times of crisis the popular tendency among church people is to use state power to accomplish the goals of the church. The church still primarily turns to the state and use of tax money to deal with social problems.

There is nothing wrong with calling the state to stop doing what is evil, but it is important that any message of the church to the state be an expression of what the church believes and lives. A radically segregated church cannot rightly tell the state to integrate. It is interesting to note that the churches which lack discipline among their members are the most ready to rely on civil legislation to perpetuate their views. They ask the state to enforce what they cannot resolve in their own group.[13] Did you ever hear of the Amish trying to impose their morality on others?

The church has little right or authority to ask society to legislate what she cannot make a general discipline among her own members. If a church is living by a certain code or ideal, then it is proper for the church to call the larger society to accept this ethic also. Whether the larger society will accept this ethic is not for the church to decide, of course. That must be worked out in public discussion, taking into consideration any objections. It is important for the church to recognize that she is a minority and cannot speak for society, much less legislate for it.

John Woolman and the Quakers give us an example for social action. Woolman put his energies into "talking up" the matter of slavery among Quakers. After the Quakers saw that holding slaves was incompatible with the faith and they no longer held slaves, they were able in a convincing way to confront the larger society. Unless we first live it, how can the world take us seriously? The significant impact of the early church came not from social pronouncements but from her faithfulness to the new life of the kingdom in the midst of the marketplaces and the daily life of the world around her.

*   *   *

Any discussion of the Christian's relation to the state is incomplete without reference to Romans 13 and related texts. What do these texts mean for a community of aliens and exiles (1 Pet. 2:11) who live in nonconformity to the old order and all its sin (Rom. 12:1, 2)? The problem with these texts is not what they say, but what civil religion so often reads into them.

Rather than call for unconditional obedience to the state, Romans 13:1 boldly proclaims that the state is under

God and dependent upon God for its very existence. What a radical statement to make at a time when the state was considered divine and people were expected to worship the emperor. The word in Romans 13:1 often translated "ordained" can also be translated "given orders." Governments are not independent authorities but are under the orders of God. Sometimes, however, governments become rebellious against God's orders and make themselves the final authority. At that point we turn to Revelation 13 where an idolatrous state is portrayed as a beast to be resisted.

The state must be demythologized. Its purposes and goals are not ultimate as ideological states claim. The state is one of the last places to look for a source of renewal and community. *At best* the state has a function of keeping things from completely falling apart and helping to hold the evil powers in check. According to Romans 13, God's purpose for the state is to punish the evil and protect the innocent, although quite often the state fails to do this and instead protects the guilty and punishes the innocent.

People today have greatly exaggerated the importance of government. Little good is said about government in the Bible. For almost three hundred years Israel survived without a human king. God was their king. But Israel wanted to be like the other nations and have a king. Through the prophet Samuel, God warned them that this desire was an act of disobedience and that having a king would only bring trouble. God allowed Israel to have a king and in less than a hundred years the nation was divided. Throughout history governments have probably created more problems than they have solved.

Clearly we are not to be rebellious against the state. Rather we are called to be respectful to officials and to subject ourselves to the state. When we submit ourselves to non-Christians or to the state, we are not committing ourselves to doing what the state wants us to do, but rather allowing

others to decide what will happen to us. Jesus did not do what
Pilate wanted, Stephen did not give in to the mob, and Paul
did not cease from preaching just because he was told to, but
they did submit themselves and put themselves in the hands
of their captors. The early Christians even in their refusal to
obey Caesar remained subject to Caesar.

1 Peter 2:13 tells us to subject ourselves *for the Lord's
sake* which is quite different from doing it for the state's sake.
Maybe the clue to why we subject ourselves is found in 1
Corinthians 9:19: "For though I am free from all men, I have
made myself a slave to all, that I might win the more." The
concern of the New Testament is not "law and order" or
patriotism, but our witness to the gospel. For the same reason
1 Peter 3:1 tells Christian wives to be submissive to their
unchristian husbands. It is to win them for Christ. That
changes the issue. Our concern is to act in such a way that the
emperors and presidents will repent of their sin. We are to act
in a way that will "put to silence the ignorance of foolish
men" (1 Pet. 2:15). Rather than blind obedience, that calls for
prophetic witness.

1 Peter 2:17 first calls us to honor all people and then
goes on to command us to honor the emperor. Honor does
not exclude speaking the truth in love to the king. To honor is
to take seriously and will sometimes include speaking the
word of judgment. To call to repentance is not to show dis-
respect, but to take seriously God's demands on the state.

This means, of course, that we will cooperate with all of
the legitimate functions of the state such as traffic regula-
tions. As Christians we will obey the law and be generally
cooperative as long as this is not in conflict with the demands
of the gospel. We are willing to give to Caesar whatever
belongs to Caesar, but we will not give anything to Caesar
that belongs to God. Our lives and our loyalty belong to God
and not to Caesar. We do not owe two years of our lives to
our country. Our loyalty belongs only to Christ and His

kingdom. We can never pledge allegience to Caesar's king-dom or his flag.

Too often we read only the first seven verses of Romans 13 and fail to read them in context. The verses immediately before and after these seven call for the Christian to do noth-ing that would conflict with the command to love one's neighbor. All demands of the state must be subordinate to the great commandment to love neighbor and God. The com-mand to feed the enemy comes before any attempt of the state to forbid showing love to the neighbor. If the state tells us to kill our neighbor, we must refuse. This includes paying taxes to support war. We may not support or cooperate with any illegitimate functions of the state.

The New Testament makes clear that "we must obey God rather than men" (Acts 5:29). Whatever we do is to be based on obedience to God, not like or dislike for any state. The issue is holy obedience. Whether we obey any law or not has nothing to do with the goodness or badness of any government, but the demands of God on our lives. When an evil government asks us to do something good we will agree, and when a good government asks us to do what is evil, we will refuse. The claims of God come ahead of those of the state.

*   *   *

With the New Testament understanding of Christ's kingdom and the nature of Christian community it is not possible for us to support or cooperate with war. The new community has already beaten her swords into plowshares. To accept violence and war would be a denial of all we have said thus far about the essence of the church and the gospel.

The defenseless, reconciling love we know in community must be a part of a total lifestyle in relation to the whole world, not just to those in our community or our nation. Our relation to the world is an expression of our relation to each other in community. Our defenselessness *(Gelassenheit)* and readiness to die for each other is commanded in the New Testament not only in relation to our brothers and sisters in community, but especially toward the "enemy." What a contradiction it would be for us to engage in violence or war. We will also reject any employment inconsistent with defenseless love. As Christians, we cannot accept any relationships or occupation which rely on the use of coercion or defense.

It is not a coincidence that most Christian communities throughout history have been pacifist, including the Roman Catholic religious orders. The early church didn't permit any of her members to be in the military. Their understanding of the gospel could not permit it. Pacifism is a necessary ingredient of Christian community because it is the consistent expression of a deeper ethic that is essential to community. The attitudes, values, and lifestyle that support violence are destructive for community.

One of the keys to the whole problem of Christian faithfulness is the renunciation of violence. In the bloody history of the establishment church, what clearer sign of unfaithfulness and corruption do we have than the church's support for war? In modern war almost always there are "Christians" on each side killing each other. Most churches still refuse even to say that Christians should refuse to kill other Christians. For a Christian to kill other Christians on the basis of nationalist goals is a serious offense against the unity of the body of Christ. To put nationalist aims ahead of Christ's church is serious.

The way of the cross is unconditional and undiscriminating love. We love not only the lovable, the reliable, the honest. We do not prefer our neighbor's life over the life of the foreigner, the life of the innocent over the life of the guilty. Christian love reaches out even to those who would destroy us. Even as God loved us when we were still in rebellion against God, so we are called to an active love for our enemies. If we only reach out to our friends we are no better than anyone else, for even the publicans and Gentiles do that (Mt. 5:46, 47). How can we communicate this love to someone if we consider that person our enemy and violently resist that person?

If Jesus Christ is the Lord of history and not we, then we approach the problem of violence from a completely different viewpoint. We accept nonviolence not because it works, but because we understand the victory of Jesus over the powers of death and violence. A Christian pacifist position is rooted in the resurrection. We need not act desperately if we believe in the sovereignty of God. The way of the cross is foolishness to those who do not believe in the resurrection, but we see it as the way of salvation. As John Howard Yoder puts it,

> The triumph of the right is assured not by the might that comes to the aid of the right, which is of course the justification of the use of violence and other kinds of power in every human conflict; the triumph of the right, although it is assured, is sure because of the power of the resurrection and not because of any calculation of causes and effects, nor because of the inherently greater strength of the good guys. The relationship between the obedience of God's people and the triumph of God's cause is not a relationship of cause and effect but one of cross and resurrection.[14]

The Church and Economics

One of the most neglected areas of Christian discipleship is economics, in spite of all the biblical emphasis on this subject.[15] The Old Testament is quite explicit with long lists of laws regulating economic relationships, and Jesus is recorded in the four Gospels as having mentioned the subject of money and economics more often than any other subject. And how explicit He was! "Do not lay up for yourselves treasures on earth" (Mt. 6:19). "You cannot serve God and mammon" (Mt. 6:24).

Mammon is a hungry god who competes with Jesus for our loyalty. Where your treasure is there your heart will be also. There is probably no group in history that became affluent which did not lose its faith. Repeatedly this is the story of the Hebrews. When things went well, they forgot the Lord their God. Prosperity is an enemy of community. When they become prosperous, many communities lose their vitality.

The more vested interest we develop in the economic system, the more difficult it is to remain open to God and change. Although being poor does not make us Christians, as long as we are happy and secure in the corruption of the old society we will not likely be ready to leave it to follow another Lord. That is why it is usually the poor and oppressed who hear the gospel most gladly. Jesus said it is easier for a camel to go through the eye of a needle than for a rich person to enter the kingdom (Lk. 18:24, 25). The sin of *pleonexia* which is so condemned in the New Testament literally does not mean avarice, as it so often is translated, but *having much.*

When the church becomes a part of the economic establishment a vast difference exists between that church and the New Testament community. Gaining wealth, power, and prestige are not marks of the true church. The church that relates closely to the economic power structures has been a conservative protector of the vested interests rather than a sign of justice and liberation, catering more to the values of the powerful and wealthy than serving the poor. The significant periods of church history were when the church did not have wealth and privilege.

Any talk of solidarity with the world can only mean solidarity with the outcasts and the downtrodden. Our lives and lifestyle will be identified with the poor of the world rather than with the rich and oppressors. We will look at social issues more from their perspective than from the perspective of those in power. It is important that at all times we deeply feel the pain and needs of the oppressed and long for a way to be given to reach out to them. The Bible not only says that God has the greatest compassion for those who suffer the most, but that the poor and oppressed have a special place in His plan of redemption. In the Old Testament it was a group of slaves that He chose to be His people and in the New Testament it was the poor who heard the gospel gladly.

In her relation to the world the Christian community will demonstrate what economic relationships should look like. Like the early Christians, the church will recognize that private property is the result of sin.[16] She will begin to live on a level on which everyone in the world could live if there were justice. She will exist to serve rather than to gain.

Not only does this have many implications for our personal lifestyle, but also for the general shape of the church. The church also needs to be poor and totally dependent upon God for her survival. For too long we have been unable to conceive of the church surviving without property. Maybe she will not be able to survive spiritually with her huge holdings. The church today cannot say, "Silver and gold have I none," and she also does not have the power to say, "Rise up and walk." The two may be related.

Today the church is one of the richest institutions in the world. She has huge investments in the capitalist system and vast holdings of property. Many churches and religious institutions are dependent upon their extensive endowments and investments. What a reproach to the body of Christ. Not only should the church not be rich while others starve, and profit from the exploitation of her investments, but what does this say about her faith in God?

If we cannot trust God to supply the needed money for the work He has called us to, can we trust Him for anything else? Unless the church is continually utterly dependent upon God to supply every need, it is unlikely that our primary trust will be in God. God wants us to totally rely upon Him so that we will continually look to Him for strength and guidance.

The more dependent we are upon God to supply every need, the more careful we will be to look to Him for every direction. If this is true, then we will not undertake anything unless God has called us to it. The church must exist by faith in God alone. All the silver and gold in the world are God's anyway, so what do we have to worry about? Only that we are doing God's will. If God sends us, He will be responsible for us.

A problem for many churches is receiving gifts. People give gifts to the church which the church does not want but feels she cannot reject. In this way many things come into the church without the approval of the people. Then there is always some ugly picture which everyone wants to get rid of but feel they have to keep in order not to offend the dear soul who gave it fifty years ago.

The early church refused to receive gifts from impenitent sinners or to profit from sinful occupations. When Marcion left the church, the large gift he had earlier given to the church was returned to him. The important issue here is to refuse all gifts which have any strings attached. The church that compromises her stand to placate a large contributor is in serious trouble. These gifts are too costly for any church to afford. Any gifts with strings attached must be rejected. Once given to the church, the use of that gift is to be decided only by the Holy Spirit as discerned by the community.

The Sect Cycle

It has been the opinion of many sociologists that sects go through various stages of development leading to acculturation back into the establishment. A new group begins with vitality and creativity and rejects much of the status quo. But within a few generations that sect readapts to her environment and may continue an organizational structure, but with only a few insignificant distinctions from the larger society.

There is certainly much historical evidence to support this view, but it is not true that it always need be this way or always is. In spite of the sect-cycle theorists, many of the believers' churches have demonstrated amazing vitality hundreds of years after their founding. The power of renewal which brought them into being can continue to bring new birth and life among them. Note the continuing concern for peace witness among the Historic Peace Churches. No one pattern of development is inevitable. The tendency to acculturate and lose the vision is just part of the sinful nature of the old age which can be resisted.

One difference between those who acculturate rapidly and those who live longer is related to the nature of their commitment and protest. A sect will lose her distinctiveness more rapidly if her protest and concerns can easily be absorbed by the larger society. Sects whose emphasis is on personal anxiety and guilt are soon acculturated into the larger society and become established churches while those whose origin included demands for radical repentance and social justice are able to maintain their existence for a long time.[17] A quick comparison of the acculturation of the Methodists with that of the Quakers or Mennonites makes this quite evident. The Quaker-Mennonite witness was more difficult to absorb into the larger society. The growing pietism of some Christian communities should be a serious concern, for it may be an important step in the acculturation process.

It is important that our protest go so deep into the heart of society that it can never be absorbed without radical change in the society. Such issues would include refusal to accept war, coercion, swearing oaths, and financial success. The issue is not the degree of our fervor, but where our allegience is. The more a community is in conflict with the established order of the larger society, the stronger the commitment of each member needs to be. Those groups operating in harmony with the larger society and with its support require much less commitment.

The real issue is not, as some have claimed, the amount of contact with the world, with increased contact bringing acculturation. The real issue is the spiritual life of the community. The basic dynamic of change is not in external forces, but what is happening in the community. Increased contact with the world may be an evidence of vitality. Acculturation is basically the result of loss of vision and vitality or contradictions (such as between teaching and practice) in the community. The essential ingredient is to have the whole of our lives centered in Jesus.

Another important variable is the relation of the sect to missionary activity. If the missionary emphasis is lost, the community becomes isolated and hardened with a loss of voluntarism and the development into a mini-establishment separate from the larger establishment. If the primary goal of missionary activity is new members, the vision is soon watered down by the new members. However, if the missionary message is challenging and deep, the sect will continually have a first-generation membership.

In addition to this, if each generation needs to make their own voluntary decision regarding membership there then will be no second-generation members. If the community is constantly being given new birth by God's Spirit, there will always be a new community with all the freshness that implies. The real issue is not whether the sect is old or young, but whether she is kept alive and new by the power of the living Christ.

Chapter 10

THE WITNESSING COMMUNITY

I tell you, if these were silent, the very stones would cry out.
—Jesus in Luke 19:40.

Community and Mission

God's work of gathering together His people into communities is not only for the salvation of those included, but for the salvation of the whole world. Since the Christian community is a sign of God's intention for the whole world, the community exists for the world rather than for herself. Someone has said that the church exists primarily for those who never go near her. Failure to witness to the world is a failure to take seriously God's sovereignty over the world. A community with no sense of mission has lost sight of the meaning of the incarnation and her own salvation.

Witness to the world is more than something we do. It is part of what it means to be the people of God. As some have said, the church does not have a mission; she is mission. The mission of the church is not a separate aspect of the life of the church, but a reflection and working out of the church's nature. The nature and mission of the church are two sides of the same coin. Since we exist only because of God's purpose for us, it is not a matter of choice whether we will participate in God's work of reconciliation in the world. We become part of the Christian community not to escape from the world, but to join God's mission of offering a new life to the whole world.

Although at times community may have meant retreat and escapism (a charge which has also been leveled against the institutional church), this is certainly not an inherent characteristic of Christian community. A group turned in on itself does not experience love and community very deeply and is not guided by the Holy Spirit. Times for retreat, reflection, and drawing closer to each other, may be needed, but these result in a new power to reach out. It is significant that Jesus' high priestly prayer for unity (Jn. 17) includes the call to mission. Unity in community expresses itself in service to the world.

The more deeply we experience community and God's kingdom, the more we long for its fulfillment in the world, and the more we experience liberation and victory over sin, the more we will see the need to struggle against the forces of death and evil everywhere. The more we experience God's love the more eager we will be to reach out and care for others. Community can make us more sensitive to the needs of others in the world.

The argument that community and outreach are in fundamental contradiction with each other has some validity, but it is too shallow. It can be, but need not be, true that the more we reach out, the more we detract from community, and the deeper we go into community, the more we cut ourselves off from the world. Activity may detract from community, but the more deeply we participate in God's work (rather than our own) in the world, the more the depth of community can be opened to us. The distinction between God's work and our own work needs to be made quite carefully, however.

A brief look at church history will quickly reveal that community has been a great source of mission and renewal. During the Middle Ages the dominant voice of the church in the area of missionary work, education, culture, and service was the monasteries. One of the distinctive marks of the believers' church tradition has been a deep concern for witness and mission which is seen as binding on all believers in every age. The modern Protestant missionary movement has deep roots in the believers' church, beginning with the Waldenses and Anabaptists and carried on by the Pietists, Moravians, Methodists, and Baptists. Among the Roman Catholics, the communal orders had a central role in missionary outreach.

Seeing the people of God engaged in mission is a concept that fits much better with those who see themselves as a missionary minority than with those who are pillars of society. All of the leaders of the mainline Protestant Reformation were opposed to missionary activity, arguing that the Great Commission was fulfilled by the early church and no longer operative. Until the rise of Pietism almost two centuries later, mainline Protestantism was almost completely devoid of any missionary calling. Now that a Christian society cannot any longer be assumed, the church everywhere is in a missionary situation.

Not only is witness and outreach an essential part of our vision, but it would be impossible to have a voluntary community without it. Without making a voluntary decision available to others there can be no free community.

An even deeper issue is the nature of the gospel itself. The concern of the gospel is universal. Even without the Great Commission, we still would have no choice but to share the good news with everyone. Jesus came to call sinners to repentance (Lk. 5:32), to reconcile the whole world to Himself (2 Cor. 5:19), to bring abundant life and a new creation to a fallen world. That ministry has now been given to His people. "As the father has sent me, even so send I you."

Not only do we have a mandate for evangelism, but the condition of the world demands it. Even creation is groaning for its redemption. With the world going to hell and us knowing the way to salvation, it is unthinkable that we would not be sharing and proclaiming that good news to the whole world. Wherever there is sin, there evangelism is needed. There is a real urgency about spreading the Word.

It is essential that people come into right relation with God, for it is our broken and alienated relation to God that is the root of our human problems. Unless we get that straightened out there is little likelihood that much else will ever be straightened out either. We cannot save ourselves or get ourselves out of the mess we are in. We are lost and need salvation.

The fallen world is not only stumbling in darkness, but it is also the world upon which the light has already begun to shine. The lost world is the prospective kingdom of God. We need to make that known to the world and call attention to the redemption that is even now occuring in the world.

An Expression of What We are Living

Hopefully our concern for witness grows out of the reality of the gospel in our lives rather than any desire to increase our membership or feeling that we need to be engaged in some kind of activity. The first question is not action or program, but to be what we have been called to be. We can ask for commitment to God's kingdom only to the extent we are committed to it.

The essence of the church is not program or activity. These may have their place, but if we forget to live as Christians ourselves, we have little basis for mission and no Christian community in which to include others. We need to be disciples before we can be witnesses. Unless we personally know the Lord and are living accordingly, we cannot speak meaningfully to others about Him. The point is not that we think Christian teachings are the best, but that we have come to know the power of God in our life together. There should not need to be any push or great effort to go and witness. That should come naturally out of the life of the community and our relation to the world. Evangelism is not primarily a program, but an inevitable expression of the hope that lives within us.

Our major concern is not with methods and strategies, but with living and being a visible alternative to the sickness of the world system, to be a sign and evidence of what God is doing and will do. Significant witness grows out of committed communities that discover a vision. That we have something to communitcate should be of greater concern than having better means of communicating.

It makes little sense to talk of the church going out into the world if she has no idea of who she is or what her message is to the world. The result is an evangelism with little content or expectation. Why should anyone want to be part of a church if membership has little meaning? It has been shown that the churches that have the most appeal are those with a clear vision.[1]

Maybe we need to ask what it means to be genuinely involved in the world and history. Without an identity over against the world we can have little mission to the world. Simply being in the midst of what is happening has little significance. Our real contribution to history comes when we point in a new direction and stand in tension with history. The best contribution we can make is to live the vision we have, to begin to make concrete what is possible, to be a bridge between the present and the future.

Maybe we are involved in too much activity. If we are involved in the Lion's Club, Scouts, all kinds of action groups, discussion groups, and every other activity available to us, we simply will not have time for community. It may well be that we can do some good through these groups, but the crying need in our world today is not for more good deeds, but for a new people who will embody a whole new way of life. To be that we will need to withdraw from much of the frenzy and

concentrate our efforts on what God wants to do among His
people. We cannot reach out from the community until we
are first truly in community. Elizabeth O'Connor put it this
way:

> We are going to know little about the task of reconciliation in
> the world unless we are in touch with what goes on in that
> world within ourselves and know how difficult reconciliation is
> there. We cannot begin to cope with what it means to build a
> world community unless we understand how difficult it is to be
> in community even with a small group of people, presumably
> called by their Lord to the same mission. Nor will we know the
> full power of the Spirit while we cling to our upper rooms.[2]

Certainly there is a need for people to reach out and give
a witness in the areas of public schools, social issues, neighborhood concerns, but much more important is that our witness in those areas come out of a reality in our Christian community, a life that embodies the ideals we hope to witness to.

We do not need a new program of witness or more
activity. *We need a revival!* Until our congregations become
communities of love, until we begin again to practice Matthew 18:15-20 and experience unity, until our lives together
are centered on Christ's kingdom, there will be no evangelism
worth discussing. It makes no sense to call dead churches to
begin a program of evangelism. They first need to be called to
Jesus. The first need is a rebirth of our congregations.

When the Book of Acts records great works in the early
church it reminds us that the believers were "of one mind and
one accord." They were living the gospel. Their message was
an expression of who they were. Until we receive that unity
we will not be able to reach out in any very meaningful way.
If things are not right in the community it is even difficult to
get anyone excited about reaching out.

Jesus said we *are* (not should be) the salt of the earth, the
light of the world. By our very nature we *are*. What can light

do other than shine? Being light is its own witness to darkness. A healthy tree *will* produce fruit. If love exists in the community it cannot help but shine on those outside community.

Unless we are living the gospel, there will be little power in our message. The life we live is the loudest sermon we will ever preach. The gospel is believable only as it is expressed by a community which is demonstrating it. Our most important witness is in our being, in the lifestyle of our Christian community. It is in our life together that we prove or disprove the depth and reality of our faith. Do we love each other and our enemies; do we demonstrate a visible alternative way of life? Can the kingdom be seen breaking into our midst? Community comes before mission. The church must have integrity and discipline before she can witness with any authority.

Although we must not wait until we are perfect before we reach out beyond ourselves, and even though it is true that new life is given to us as we reach out, it is also true that before we can meaningfully love and serve the needs of people outside the community, we must first be able to love and serve each other's needs in community. First we need to learn what it means to lay down our lives for each other before we can minister to the world. As Larry Christenson put it,

> Paradoxically, the love which the church shows to her own will, in the long run, become a greater blessing to the world than the love which she may manifest directly to the world.[3]

Building up the body of Christ is the greatest service we can ever give to the world. It is not coincidental that the overriding concern of the New Testament is the building up of the Christian community, or that Jesus spent more time building community with his disciples than in preaching.

Neither evangelicals with their preoccupation with the

individual or liberals with their preoccupation with changing structures have given much serious thought to the importance of covenant community in the task of evangelism. Our witness includes calling people to leave the old life of isolation and alienation and enter into a new community of those who have been drawn together by Jesus into a new life of wholeness and peace. This cannot be ignored, since it is impossible to respond fully to God's grace without becoming a part of His new people. A new birth implies a new home.

God's primary work in the world is not in changing individuals or power structures, but in creating a new covenant community through which both can be transformed. Evangelism then is not saving individual souls or changing the structures of society (or some combination of the two), but calling people into a new social reality with all its implications for transformed persons and liberated social relationships. Jesus first gave His disciples in experience of a new life in community before He opened their eyes to the real meaning of His ministry. Before they could comprehend what this meant, they first had to experience it. Unless we have a new life to call people to, evangelism is reduced to calling people to a private relationship with God or to a set of ideals that have no social reality.

It is certainly important to reach out to the lost, but how can we do that if there is no faithful community to call them into and no example shown of what the new life in Christ might look like. How many people have come to the church seeking a new life but received nothing because the church had nothing to offer? There is little reason to reach out if we have nothing to call people to or share with them when they do come.

Unless we have communities which will be able to nurture the new Christians, we will bring into the church a group of spiritual children who will remain children the rest of their lives just as the rest of our members will be. People need a lot of help in growing into mature faith and discipleship. To introduce people to the faith and then provide neither teaching or support is to raise children for the forces of confusion and deception. It may be more irresponsible than not witnessing at all.

When we have a redemptive fellowship we can reach out and care for the sick, we can include the spiritual orphans, those who are without roots or direction, within our community. We can provide the alternative people are seeking.

A word should be said here about strategies for missions and church extension. Instead of a church agency hiring people to go to another area to preach and start churches, a small community of people could move to a new area and make that their home. Rather than beginning by just preaching a new way, or trying to start a church, they would simply be a church and let their witnessing flow from their lives. Rather than making a solitary witness, they would be a community living and demonstrating a new life to which people could be invited. Rather than representing some foriegn constituency, they would be committing their lives to the people they would serve.

Although in the past churches often have spread through people seeking better economic opportunities, this could involve moving to areas of less opportunity in order to serve. Instead of being supported by money from "back home," they could identify with the people in their new home by supporting themselves, possibly through providing needed services for people in the area.

This would need to be a group large enough to establish their own identity and be enough of a community to be visible and open to others. It would be important that this not be a cultural island perserving the cultural identity of their "mother country," but that it would be a colony of the kingdom taking root in a new culture. As much as possible, without compromising the faith by over-identifying with any culture, they would need to identify with the local people. It would be especially important that they not live on a much higher economic level then their neighbors.

This involves a serious commitment and would need to be discerned carefully. Preferably it would involve an established community sending out people who already were living in community and would not need to struggle through becoming a community in the new situation. They could go to the new area and immediately begin to be the church.

Our best witness is not our words, but our changed lives, the new creation in our midst, a community that people can taste and see. Our witness is in being a new humanity in which all our social relationships demonstrate to the world how life is to be lived. We are a "letter from Christ" to be read by the world (2 Cor. 3:2, 3). The community embodies in her life the solution to war, hunger, alienation, strife, oppression, and whatever other problems haunt our world. Our primary witness is not in what we do, but in who we are.

Waiting to Be Sent

Not only is it important that we live and be what we preach, but also that we be sent into mission by the Holy Spirit (Rom. 10:15). The Spirit who gathers us together is the same Spirit who sends us out. We may not go, however, before we are sent.

There is little value in beginning an active program of witness if we have not been first sent and empowered by the Holy Spirit to do it. The general command in the New Testament is not enough. The call must come directly to us concerning how and where to go. Without this our work will be of little consequence. This is one reason so many ambitious programs fall flat on their faces. If it is "our" mission, it is doomed to failure.

All outreach must both be initiated and continued in the power of the Holy Spirit as discerned by the community. Our discernment will go far beyond asking if something is good or necessary. Unless the action is initiated by God, we have no call to do it. The action may be good, conform to biblical standards, be much needed, and yet not be what God intends for us. Need does not constitute a call. We cannot begin to respond to all the needs around us. The important question is what God wants us to be doing.

It is important that our actions not be dictated to us by the world. Jesus did not allow the world to set His agenda. He looked to the Father for that. All too often any new thrust in the secular world is echoed within a few months in church publications and dutifully added to the agenda of the next denominational councils. If we were more in tune with what God wants, instead of following the world, we would be ten years ahead of the world on most issues.

Christian faith is not a religion of fulfilling our duties and responsibilities, or reacting to needs around us, but rather an openness to any task God may give to us. Our action then includes a great deal of humility, for it is not what we do, but what God has given to us.

It is important that God be the originator of our work, not we; otherwise it is our work rather than His. Witness needs to be a response to God's love rather than an expression of ego needs. We should not plan our mission and then pray for God's help to complete it. We do not decide what our mission should be or choose a mission, but need to be open for the Spirit to give us a mission. Mission is a gift which is given by God.

A desire to serve or a concern for the lost is not sufficient qualification to do God's work. One must be called and sent. The Holy Spirit did not allow Paul and Silas to go to Bithynia (Acts 16:6, 7), but sent them instead to Troas. Paul deliberately did not go certain places. Jesus sometimes asked people to tell no one about Him. Gideon's army needed to be reduced before it could accomplish its task.

Our call is not willy-nilly going around extinguishing bush fires on every corner, but going out as we are sent and given the power to go. Too often we are like an electric fan which does little more than circulate warm air. How different when the cool breeze begins to blow. Football players cannot run with the ball anytime they want. There is a time to run and a time not to run.

When Jesus expressed compassion for the needs of the multitudes, He noted that "the harvest is plentiful, but the laborers are few" (Mt. 9:36-38). He did not then organize a crash program of evangelism or urge His disciples to identify with the needs of the people, but rather prayed that God would "send out laborers into his harvest."

Before being sent we may need to wait and pray. All too often we are in too much of a hurry to wait for God to send directions. We forget that the power of the Holy Spirit is given after much prayer and expectant waiting. Down through the centuries the church has made a significant witness only when this was realized. Maybe the greatest task before us at this moment is to wait and pray, to ask earnestly that we be given power to go out.

To wait expectantly is not at all passive. No, there is to be an urgency in our waiting. It is an active waiting. It is like waiting for an important event, a waiting that involves lots of preparation, expectation, excitement, and readiness to go.

This prayer and waiting involves a community which together discerns God's call to send us into mission. Together we pray and together we wait. Then when the call comes we are sent by the community. We do not go out on our own, but are sent by a community which has discerned God's call. We are sent by the Spirit and by the community.

It is important that as we go into mission we receive the support and help we need. One of the results of being on the cutting edge is that one gets cut up and needs a community to help deal with those cuts in a healing and redemptive way. A moving testimony to the significance of community as a support for witness is the example of the early Hutterians, commonly recognized as the most energetic in their missionary outreach of any group in the sixteenth century. Even though 80 percent of their missionaries never returned alive, they continued to send out more. For that to happen, both a strong faith and community of support are needed.

The Shape of Our Mission

There is no one form that our mission will take. Since we live in a pagan world, evangelism and witness are involved in all of our relationships with society. Whatever we do that points to Jesus is evangelism, be it preaching, handing out tracts, social service, or social action. There is no one way to witness to the kingdom, except that our words and our deeds are to be one.

Neither is there one thing we should be doing. Evangelism will include proclaiming good news to pagans, calling for personal decision, calling an apostate church to repentance, calling sin by its name, proclaiming release to captives, giving cups of cold water, and enduring persecution. The shape of our mission is the same as the life of Jesus in His mission to the world in which He took the form of a servant. It is important that our witness be an authentic expression of our faith and not a borrowed method which is an expression of a theology foreign to our own.

Our mission is to all the world, to every area of life. Although some avenues were closed to them, the early Christians made known the witness in every area that was open to them. They broke down barriers between Jews and Gentiles, slave and free, male and female. They rejected participation in the military and other structures which contradicted the faith. Paul made an appeal to Caesar.

The witness of the Christian community is also to the established church, reminding her of her calling and how she has strayed from that. Not only does the world need a people who will be a conscience to it, but the established church does also. Apostasy needs to be named and false teachings identified. Before we can call the world to repentance we really ought to ask the church to repent.

Part of our mission is to repeatedly restate the gospel message. In both the church and world there is a vast ignorance of what the Christian faith is all about. Teaching by word and deed are sorely needed. Most people are biblical illiterates. In our proclamation we cannot assume a knowledge of the faith on the part of the hearers. Most of our witness is to those who know little or nothing about the faith, except for many misconceptions.

Our witness will be dialogue with the world. We cannot speak *ex cathedra,* for in the mind of the world our message carries little authority. We cannot simply proclaim, "the Bible says." For too long we have assumed that we live in a Christian society, and that evangelism simply calls lost people back to what they once accepted, but departed from. That simply is not the way it is. Our witness is primarily to pagans who are biblically illiterate.

Our dialogue with the world will need to begin with listening to the world and honestly hearing what is being said. We cannot answer questions which the world is not even asking. First we will hear the questions and then discern what the message of the gospel is to those questions. Shall we preach repentance, judgment, forgiveness, hope, or what? We will not know if we do not first listen.

Our witness should not become mechanical. We have no easy answers, no set list of Bible verses or four spiritual laws to give to people automatically. Some people seem to be ready to speak to a person's condition before they even know the individual's name. Our response to others should always be a genuine response to their needs. No doctor uses the same prescription on all patients and neither can we. We will have quite different answers depending on whether the problem is slavery, oppression, hopelessness, loss of meaning, or guilt.

The more we identify with people and understand their problems, the more able we will be to offer help to them. Before others are able to hear us we must communicate love and concern for them.

Dialogue is not based on a willingness to relativize one's convictions, but to accept the other as a person, to listen, share, and learn. Indeed, we have much to learn from those with whom we disagree. Christians should be more open to dialogue than anyone else. When we know who we are and who our Lord is, we are able to reach out in love to everyone and receive what good they have to offer.

We can learn from the pattern of Jesus' ministry as suggested in Luke 10:8, 9, where Jesus is telling His disciples how to witness. Jesus suggests that first they eat what is set before them (identify and fellowship with the people), second, that they heal the sick (deal with their needs and demonstrate God's love and power), and then that they tell people about God's kingdom. The verbal part of evangelism comes last.

In our concern for dialogue we will reach out to others before they come to us. We will go anywhere people are. Our mission begins at home, but does not stop there. It reaches out across the whole world, ignoring and breaking down national, ideological, and cultural barriers, reaching out in love and respect to all people. No place is too far, too hot, too cold, too evil, or too inconvenient for us to go and share and serve.

The Good News of the Kingdom

The primary mission of the church today is the same as it has always been: to point people to Jesus and His kingdom. Everything else that we do is to be an expression of this. Our work is to proclaim the gospel, the good news that God loves us and seeks to save us, that in Jesus the powers of sin and death have been defeated, that a new kingdom has come and is coming in which we can already participate. Our work is to make known that "When anyone is united to Christ, there is a new world; the old order has gone, and a new order has already begun" (2 Cor. 5:17, NEB). We will invite people to enter that new world.

In Jesus Christ we experience a foretaste of the reconciliation of the whole creation to God (Eph. 1:9, 10; 2:14; 4:1-5, 13, 16; Rev. 21:1-5). With the prophet Micah we look forward to the day when

> they shall beat their swords into plowshares,
>   and their spears into pruning hooks;
> nation shall not lift up sword against nation,
>   neither shall they learn war any more;
> but they shall sit every man under his vine
>   and under his fig tree,
> and none shall make them afraid. Micah 4:3, 4.

Even lions will lie down with lambs and all tears will be wiped away. God's purposes for all creation will be restored. Our mission is always both an expression of that hope and pointing to it.

Our mission is to call people to reorient their lives because of what God has done in Jesus Christ and is doing now in our midst, to reorient their whole lives to the coming of the kingdom. It is calling people to turn from (repent of) their old life of slavery in sin to a new life of liberation in Jesus, calling alienated and lost people into the fellowship of the new creation. Nothing less will do. This includes the reminder that the only way to enter the kingdom is to renounce all that one has, a complete commitment and surrender of all to Jesus.

The emphasis in conversion is not on feeling, but on making a radical turn, change, and commitment in one's life, a transfer of allegience and loyalties. This may well include feeling, but the emphasis is on the commitment and change.

So often where the emphasis is on feeling, there doesn't seem to be much change or turning.

Evangelism centers on the coming of God's kingdom rather than on our status or our efforts to do good. We are to seek first, not personal salvation or a place in heaven, but the kingdom of God and His righteousness. In the New Testament, evangelism concerns not primarily accepting forgiveness for sins (although that is part of it), but accepting the rule of God over all our relationships. How easy it is to become sidetracked with either a spiritualized Jesus and a totally otherworldly kingdom or with reducing of the gospel to social concerns.

Evangelism includes a call to discipleship, to live in Christ's kingdom rather than the kingdoms of this world. Discipleship is more than the result of the gospel; it is an essential aspect of the gospel. Jesus' evangelistic message included the call to "take up your cross and follow me." Jesus is not only a way *to* life, but also a way *of* life. When calling people to commit their lives to Jesus, they need to be reminded that it is their whole lives that need to come under His lordship. The gospel relates to people's lives, be that sex, economics, education, or politics. In every activity of life the liberating power of the gospel can have its impact.

The New Testament does not offer cheap grace. Justification is for the sinner, not for sin. Salvation is not free; it costs us our lives. The gospel is not only relational; it includes norms, values, and expectations. Evangelism is a call to discipleship, not an easy appeasing of people's consciences. More is expected than "only believe." A whole new life is offered. The gospel is not a message of free grace with some fine print concerning discipleship and sanctification. It is all one message and all of it is good news. So why not tell all of it?

Evangelism includes a call to repentance, without which there can be no salvation. And those calls to repent need to be specific and concrete. Conversion is more than "peace in my heart," but includes also a demand that my life be changed. We cannot ask if it is more important to be forgiven for stealing or to stop stealing. The two cannot be separated.

Personal conversion and commitment to the kingdom must be based on an encounter with the living Christ rather than on being convinced intellectually or responding to an emotionally stirring appeal. Personal evangelism is basically not an appeal to conscience, world conditions, opportunities for service, or the need for a Christian home. Neither is it an appeal to people's selfishness—what it can do for them and how good it will make them feel. It is not selling fire insurance policies or offering free tickets to heaven.

Evangelism then is not inviting people to join our nice church, projecting a good image in the neighborhood, or blessing society's values. It is more than getting someone to accept some new ideas or even to believe in Jesus. Neither is it social action or primarily inviting people to accept forgiveness for their sins. It is much more than calling people to authenticity or offering peace of mind.

The church needs to have the courage to reject shallow evangelistic programs. So often mass evangelism is an accommodation to the spirit and values of the present age. An evangelistic program sometimes results only in bringing more unregenerate people into the church, making the church even more apostate than before. Rather than watering down the demands of the gospel to the point where the largest number can be included, the demands of the cross need to be made clear, even if this means no one will accept the call. It is important not to preach what people want to hear or fit the message to suit human desires. In our attempts to make the gospel palatable and acceptable, we distort it. We cannot take the offense out of the gospel and still have the gospel.

The issue in evangelism is not the response, but whether the witness is faithfully made without compromises in the face of apathy and opposition on the one hand or eager acceptance on the other. Our witness is judged not by the subjective response of individuals or our effectiveness in social change, but by whether it is faithful to the character and message of the Lord Jesus to whom our witness should always point.

Evangelism is witnessing of Jesus Christ, but not any christ. It is not the christ who blesses wars, supports racism, and condones greed for money and power. It is not just an inner christ, not an Americanized, Protestantized christ. No, it is the living Christ of the New Testament who both calls us to a totally new life and gives us the power to live it.

The good news is good news wherever it is spoken or to whatever aspect of life it is addressed, be it personal decision, liberation of captives, or freedom for the oppressed. Since reconciliation with God includes becoming reconciled with the neighbor, both are significant concerns. When we preach the kingdom we preach peace, for the Messiah brings peace. In His kingdom

> Love and fidelity have come together;
> justice and peace join hands. Psalm 85:10, NEB

Those who do not preach this peace have missed an important part of Jesus' kingdom.

The nature of the gospel is such that we cannot help but relate it to the social issues. But it is important that we relate the gospel, rather than the latest findings of the social sciences, to the critical issues of today. Preaching on social issues without presenting the hope of the gospel is bad news. The church should be prepared to speak on any "secular" issue not as sociologist, economist, or political scientist, but from the perspective of the gospel as related to the vital spiritual and moral issues involved in the questions. The Christian community as a corporate body should not take a stand on social issues when the spiritual concern is not clear.

But we also cannot help but take a stand whenever the issues are clear.

The goal of transmitting a particular behavior pattern (love, nonconformity, mercy) is impossible and its attempt only leads to diminishing returns. What must be communicated is the faith which will lead to new behavior. We do not primarily teach pacifism. Instead we proclaim the faith of obedient following, a faith that will lead to pacifism. Otherwise our message will be a moral bondage with no power rather than a liberating message that includes the power to change.

It is most significant that people's lives can be changed, that new life is possible. If we neglect people's personal spiritual needs and fail to confront them with their relation to God and the kingdom, we both do them a disservice and miss a vital aspect of the gospel. We can tell people that God is and that He loves and cares, that He knows our sin and the guilt we feel, that He understands our despair, oppression, and lostness. We can tell people that their debt is already paid, that the bondage of sin has been broken and that there is hope. We can tell them that God is waiting to include them in His new community.

An important aspect of our mission is calling people to make a personal decision regarding Jesus and His kingdom, inviting them to break their loyalties and allegiances to all other kingdoms in order to participate in the new reality Jesus extends to us. The decision one makes concerning this is the most important decision one can ever make. It affects the course of the rest of one's life. Nothing can be the same anymore. This decision is really serious and should never be entered into lightly. It is not simply "receiving Jesus into our hearts" as some would have us believe. It means dying to oneself and living in the shadow of the cross.

Please, brothers and sisters, never ask persons to commit their lives to Jesus without informing them of what that involves. Ask them first to count the cost.

A young man who had an emotional conversion experience at a high-powered revival meeting came to a believers' church to be baptized. As soon as he was baptized he jumped up and shouted, "Praise God, it's finished." The Anabaptist elder who had baptized him replied, "No, brother, it has just begun."

If our emphasis is on discipleship, we will not call people to be saved, but rather preach that salvation is a gift of God which comes to us as we renounce sin and our loyalties to the old order and false gods. It is as we make that break and commit ourselves to God that we experience the new birth and salvation. Most of those who preach "getting saved" say that before we talk about discipleship we need to get the individual saved and then those things will take care of themselves. But seldom do these "saved" people ever get to the concerns of discipleship. Calling people to Jesus means calling them to *follow* Jesus.

We must go beyond the simplistic formula of many evangelicals who assert that we need not concern ourselves with social problems, for what is really needed is for people to learn to know Jesus and be born again. If this happens, we are told, then the solution to these problems will soon follow. Praise the Lord! But don't hold your breath. If a person is born again, what then does one do other than ignoring social problems and trying to get others "saved" so they can also ignore them? How does a born-again believer deal with war, racism, poverty, and injustice, with family breakups, broken relationships, and the deep inner needs of people?

Service

The way we reach out to others is in the form of a servant, to wash the feet of others just as Jesus washed the feet of His disciples, including Judas' feet. The commands in the Bible to care for the needy, to take care of the poor are perfectly clear (Ex. 22:22; 1 Tim. 5:16; Deut. 15:1-11). Isaiah said,

> Is not this the fast that I choose. . . .
> to let the oppressed go free,
>   and to break every yoke?
> Is it not to share your bread with the hungry,
>   and bring the homeless poor into your house;
> when you see the naked, to cover him,
>   and not to hide yourself from your own flesh?
>
> Isaiah 58:6, 7.

Today Jesus comes to us as "the least among us," the poor, the sick, the imprisoned, the naked, the hungry, the enemy. Whatever we do to the least of our brothers and sisters we do to Jesus (Mt. 25:31-46). If our communities are Christian, there is no question how we will respond to the needs in the world. We will be servant communities. The basin and the towel will be the sign of our relation to the world.

Someone has suggested that we are not called to be good Samaritans, but innkeepers. Jesus is the Good Samaritan who brings people to us. God then is seeking innkeepers.

The Christian community exists always as a servant, reaching out to serve the needs of others. Jesus' response to John the Baptist's question whether He was the Messiah was to state that "the blind receive their sight, the lame walk, lepers are cleansed, and the deaf hear, the dead are raised up, the poor have good news preached to them" (Lk. 7:22).

The nature of the gospel is to give and share. Those who have died to self are free to live for others. Paul tells us to

> Have this mind among yourselves, which is yours in Christ Jesus, who, though he was in the form of God, did not count equality with God a thing to be grasped, but emptied himself, taking the form of a servant, being born in the likeness of men. And being found in human form he humbled himself and be-

came obedient unto death, even death on a cross. Philippians
2:5-8.

Not only does the call to accept the lordship of Jesus include a commitment to serve the needs of others, but serving
the needs of others also is one of the primary ways we point
to the lordship of Jesus over our lives and the coming of His
kingdom. As we reach out in love to others (and especially to
our "enemies"), we are telling them about God's love for
them. Service, if it points to Jesus Christ, is evangelism. Our
servanthood explains to the world the very nature of God and
His unconditional love in Jesus.

It is often through Christian love and service that people
come to know Jesus and His community. Although they may
be able to gather large numbers, few have ever been
converted and brought to a deep Christian commitment by
fancy cathedrals, powerful institutions, or smooth organizations. Humble acts of service are a much better witness to the
gospel.

Little needs to be said about the needs around us. Since
we will always have the poor with us, we need not worry
about what there is for us to do. The development of the
welfare state does not in any way make the church's servant
role unneeded. There may be some areas where the state may
care for some needs, but at the deepest levels the state has
done little or nothing. If the state decides to take over
activities (like hospitals) pioneered by the church, then the
church will reach out in new areas of service the world has
not yet thought of or is not ready to do. There are always jobs
others consider too degrading, jobs we may be called to
perform.

Wherever people are lonely, sick, oppressed, or imprisoned the Christian community will respond. In disasters
like floods and earthquakes the Christian community will almost immediately be there to provide blankets, clear away

the debris, and start rebuilding. The Mennonites, Quakers and Brethren have been especially noted for this. The resources of the whole community are available for the needs of others.

This love and service extends even to our enemies. Dirk Willems, a Dutch Mennonite, understood the essence of the gospel when officers came to arrest him in 1569 for his Christian views. In order to escape arrest and death, he fled but was pursued by the police. After managing to escape across the ice of a frozen dike he noticed that the policeman who had pursued him had fallen through the ice and was struggling helplessly in the icy water. In compassion Dirk turned around and saved the life of the officer, whereupon he was arrested by that officer and later burned at the stake for being an Anabaptist heretic. Such is the fruit of Christian love.

In times of war we will be giving aid on both sides, including sending medical aid to those called our enemies. The New Testament directly commands us to give aid and comfort to our enemies (Rom. 12:20). In times of war, the reconciling role of the Christian community is especially important. Although we will not pick up a gun, we are ready to respond to need, and especially to that of "the enemy."

*   *   *

Engaging in service carries with it many dangers, six of which we will mention. *The first is do-goodism* which is often an expression of guilt feelings. It is trying to work our way into heaven, trying to prove how good we are. Do-goodism stinks. All our good deeds will never atone for our sin. If there is something wrong in our lives, we need to straighten it out before our service can be an authentic expression of liberated living. But if our good deeds come out of something real in our lives, they do not stink.

A second danger is paternalism. "Look at those pitiful people. I guess we ought to help them since they can't take care of themselves. Out of our graciousness we will help those below us." That also stinks and the poor do not want any more of it. As Christians we give because of what we have been given, as a glad response to what God has done for us. Before we can serve, we must see ourselves as beggers. As we give we must be prepared to receive, to allow others to share what they have with us. Sometimes we are too proud to receive.

For our service not to be paternalistic, we need to take on a whole lifestyle of servanthood which will mean being available to others, being more concerned about others than ourselves, subordinating our futures to those of others. Subordinating ourselves means a renunciation of status, power, and privilege. A servant is a subordinate. A privileged church is not a servant church. We seek to serve rather than dominate. As Paul put it. "I am a free man and own no master; but I have made myself every man's servant, to win over as many as possible" (1 Cor. 9:19 NEB).

There is a big difference between helping someone and being someone's servant. Helping others comes from the position of superiority. We help others by giving of our surplus. But God did more than that for us. God went so far as to share Himself, to make Himself vulnerable to humanity. He identified Himself with the plight of humanity and took our sin upon Himself. The cross is the supreme symbol of servanthood. In the same way we are asked to give ourselves as a living sacrifice. That servanthood begins as we become servants of each other in community, as we submit our lives to Jesus and His body. To be a servant in a Christian sense is not to be inferior or to be forced into slavery, but to be a person who out of love has freely given up one's own independence in order to fulfill the purpose of someone else.

Rather than giving handouts to the poor, we are called to closer relationship with them and to identify ourselves with them. Instead of starting with one's base and community among the rich and comfortable, and from there reaching out to serve the poor (charity), there is the possibility of identifying with the poor, the widows, the orphans, the lepers, the powerless, the outcasts, and from that community reaching out to the rich and comfortable, inviting them to repent, to become part of the new kingdom God is creating. Then instead of charity there can be the possibility of justice and shalom. Isn't this just the approach described in the Bible?

The best we have to give is ourselves. We become part of the poor because among them we find Jesus who is hungry, naked, imprisoned, and oppressed. We love them because God loves them. We reach out to them to commune with them. Our sharing is an expression of a relationship of brotherhood and sisterhood which is possible with them. That is not paternalism.

A third danger is that there may be strings attached to our service. Worldly institutions like governments act out of self-interest. They are concerned about economic partners and political allies. They know that those we help today may be our friends tomorrow. As Christians we give and serve only because we love and care and for no other reason. Ultimately, we are serving God, not the world. We act not out of any ulterior motives, not to gain favors, not to change structures, not to further any cause, but because we have to, because that is who we are. Servanthood is a gift to those who have died to self. We simply do it with no thoughts of any return.

In our service, need and being sent are the only criteria. Who we serve cannot be based on race, religion, political ideology, geography, or their likelihood of becoming converts. We have no hidden agenda. Rather than trying to predict or control the results of our service, we give ourselves with abandon and trust the results to God's work.

A fourth danger is that our service can be a Band-Aid approach, a rationalization for not getting to the real problem. When children are cutting their feet on glass in the street, we need not only bandages, but also to get a broom and sweep the glass off the street. This is not to criticize the use of bandages, for they are necessary and many times we will not see the real need before we do the secondary things. But this must not prevent us from moving beyond social service, to working for social justice, to calling for repentance in the structures of society. It is also important that our service help people to help themselves and not make them dependent on us.

A fifth danger is that we try to do more than we are able to do, that we be smothered by an avalanche of need. If a church has life, she will attract the drunks, the destitute, the lost. Sick people are attracted to healthy groups. And they all will be welcome. It is important, however, that we not allow ourselves to be overwhelmed by these people. In that case we would have nothing to offer. We should never allow needs outside the community to exhaust us to the extent that we will not be able to meet the needs of anybody. If we do not have ourselves together, we cannot be of much help to anyone. At times we may need to limit how much we do. We may even at times need to say no to requests for help. Even Jesus at times felt the need to remove Himself from the crowds and their needs.

It is important not to be idealistic about service. It is only those who have illusions that are ever disillusioned. We are not going to go out and save the world. Service is not easy, nor is it glamorous. Service is emptying bedpans, changing diapers, cleaning toilets. It is not always very nice and often it gets boring. Besides that, most of the time we will never receive any credit or thanks for what we do. If we are serious about service we had better have a tough enough faith to back it up.

A sixth danger is that we see service as all that is needed and fail to see the relation of service to the Word. So often we think that if we live our faith we do not need to talk about it and so we separate word and deed. We need to go beyond the narrow view of being concerned only about people's spiritual condition to being concerned with the whole person. But many are just as narrow and will relate to people's physical needs but be unwilling to relate to their deeper spiritual needs.

We will have a deep respect for humanitarian deeds, but will also recognize the differnce between good deeds and Christian service. Service is not full if it does not point people to God, the One who can speak to their condition far better than we ever can.

One of the best times to articulate our faith is when people ask us about why we live a life of service. If we are doing anything worthwhile, they will ask. When they ask we need to be ready to share our faith with them.

We can learn much from groups like the Salvation Army who give much of their time and energy to service, but undergird this with prayer and demonstrate a real concern for the whole person, including their relationship with God.

The Lamb's War

In the Book of Acts the gospel was proclaimed in such a way that people heard a message that convicted them and called them to a new life. There was transforming power in that message. Do we have a message that can speak to people's condition? Do we have a message that can cut to the heart of the world's sin? Do we have any sure word from the Lord?

Our witness is not designed to please or appease, but to convict and convert. We are called to preach the uncompromising gospel. We cannot accept the concern that preaching not "rock the boat." The revolutionary aspects of the gospel may not be toned down, nor may we avoid everything controversial. When the gospel is forthrightly preached it brings response, both positive and negative. If the church truly preached the gospel, the world would shake and tremble. But that gospel is not being preached. Personal salvation is being preached, the social gospel is talked about, there is talk of going back to the Bible and an outpouring of the Spirit, but seldom is the gospel preached with power.

Evangelism relates to the reality of sin. The early Christians saw themselves engaged in a cosmic, mortal struggle with the forces of evil. They knew they were wrestling not "against flesh and blood, but against the principalities, against the powers, against the world rulers of this present darkness, against the spiritual hosts of wickedness in the heavenly places" (Eph. 6:12). Jesus was crucified because He confronted and struggled with those powers. But in that struggle, Jesus was Victor. If we understand Jesus' defeat of those powers, that will greatly affect our response to them. We then can face them unafraid, knowing that our resistance will also lead to victory.

Our evangelism must come to grips with the power of sin in the world and confront those same powers with the atoning work of Jesus Christ. The false doctrine that we cannot do anything about evil and injustice needs to be rejected. Evil can be conquered. Eberhard Arnold has seen clearly that the attack upon evil is very much a part of our mission. As he says it,

Where there was no peace, peace must be made; where everything was in chains, freedom must dawn; where injustice ruled, justice must take its place; where love and joy had grown cold, the joy of love breaks through; and where each one lived for himself, community comes into being. An all-out campaign against evil is launched: no area of life can escape being attacked. Resistance breaks down. The conscience of the world wakes up. The conscience of the Church is on the march.[4]

The early Quakers conceived of this aspect of evangelism as "the Lamb's war," a unique combination of the Christian hope with social action, the lordship with the servanthood of Christ. This concept is based in the Book of Revelation where Jesus is majestically described as a Lamb, one who is worthy to open the scroll (Rev. 5:9-14) and as a conquering King who makes war on all the nations and kings who resist His rule (Rev. 19:11-21). This is the nonviolent Lamb who laid down His life for the sins of the world. In Revelation we read of the war of the Lamb and the victory of the followers of the Lamb over the forces of evil.

> They will make war on the Lamb, and the Lamb will conquer them, for he is Lord of lords and King of kings, and those with him are called and chosen and faithful. Revelation 17:14.
> Now the salvation and the power and the kingdom of our God and the authority of his Christ have come, for the accuser of our brethren has been thrown down, who accuses them day and night before our God. And they have conquered him by the blood of the Lamb and by the word of their testimony, for they loved not their lives even unto death. Rejoice then, O heaven and you that dwell therein! But woe to you, O earth and sea, for the devil has come down to you in great wrath, because he knows that his time is short! Revelation 12:10-12.

The Lamb's war is the struggle against all that is not what God intends for His world, be it pride, lust, materialism, abortion, militarism, injustice, or oppression. We struggle against evil on every level, both in the human heart and the structures of society. Christ is now in the process of overthrowing Satan and his kingdom of evil and establishing His reign of peace. We are engaged in an all-out war, a fight to the death against evil, both in our own hearts and in the world. This call to battle is also found in the book of Daniel.

> . . . the God of heaven will set up a kingdom which shall never be destroyed, nor shall its sovereignty be left to another people. It shall break in pieces all these kingdoms and bring them to an end, and it shall stand forever.   Daniel 2:44.

The Lamb's war begins in the community as we learn to hear and obey the living Lamb in our midst. It presupposes an obedient, gathered community. The moment we respond to Christ's kingdom we are enlisted in the army of the Lamb and join the battle for people's hearts and loyalties and work for truth and justice.

The Lamb is a conquering Lamb, but He conquers by suffering love and the sword of the Spirit rather than any carnal weapons which are the tools of the demonic forces of the old age. Many metaphors in the New Testament refer to fighting, but since we are not fighting against flesh and blood, our weapons cannot be physical. Since the weapon is love, we cannot injure anyone in this war. Our only weapons can be "the armor of God" (Eph. 6:13-18), truth, righteousness, the gospel of peace, faith, salvation, the sword of the Spirit, and prayer, none of which include violence. Violence and coercion cannot be among our weapons. In describing the Lamb's war, James Nayler, the early Quaker, wrote,

> He [Christ] puts spiritual weapons into their hearts and hands
> ... to make war with his enemies, conquering and to conquer,
> not as the prince of this world ... with whips and prisons, tor-
> tures and torments on the bodies of creatures, to kill and
> destroy men's lives ... but with the word of truth ... returning
> love for hatred, wrestling with God against the enmity, with
> prayers and tears night and day, with fasting, mourning and lam-
> entation, in patience, in faithfulness, in truth, in love un-
> feigned, in long-suffering, and in all the fruits of the spirit, that
> if by any means he may overcome evil with good.[5]

The church in the New Testament is pictured as a militant people radically confronting the forces of evil and continually finding themselves in conflict with the old world. Jesus routing the money changers from the temple is an example for us. We are in constant struggle with the evil powers, but the church keeps advancing and even the gates of hell will not stop God's people. When Peter made his famous confession of faith, Jesus responded that upon that rock He would build the church and that even the gates of hell would not prevail against her (Mt. 16:18). God's people are pictured as storming the forces of evil and nothing, not even the gates of hell itself, will be able to stop God's people. We are militantly attacking the forces of evil. Our militancy includes no force or coercion, however. We go armed only with truth, love, and the sword of the Spirit. Eberhard Arnold compares this noncoercive power with light.

> Light does not work like dynamite, yet it is stronger. The weapons of light fight without any murderous force against the works of darkness. Love does no evil to its neighbor. And nevertheless at the eleventh hour before the coming Day, it puts an end to the waxing powers of night and their violent works. Anyone who wants to put a dark cover over his hostile actions can pile up as many mountains of dark, hateful thoughts and deeds as he likes: we know that there are rays that in all quietness penetrate even the thickest walls of the strongest fortresses. When the working of the Spirit's light is perfect, it has latent in it a power to remove and overcome that is stronger than all the forces of destruction.[6]

There is nothing passive about the New Testament ethic. Too often we confuse Stoicism with Christianity. Epictetus said that if someone beats you, grit your teeth and bear it, and continue to love that person as a brother or sister. The Christian ethic is not to grin and bear it, not to tolerate evil, but to fight back aggressively with prayer, love, and kindness, and work to overcome evil with good. Where hostility exists we do not seek to repress it, but actively break it down through positive actions. If our enemy is hungry, we offer food. We fight back, but we do not fight back with evil or vengeance.

We are the salt of the earth and we ought to rub it in. This does not imply any arrogance or lack of compassion, however. In the lions' den Daniel fearlessly faced the lions, but he did not pull their tails. All acts of witness must be expressions of love. Without this, the witness is not an expression of the kingdom. Even judgment is proclaimed with compassion and regret. The true prophet always includes him/herself in the judgment that is proclaimed. As we criticize, it is important that we be aware of how we also are part of the problem. The problem is not only those bad people out there, but also us.

The preaching of the gospel will include condemnation of sin. Those who are obedient can never be silent in the face of massive evil. Our message will include the note of judgment, especially as it applies to the hearers. We will not preach against sin in general, but will be specific. Nor will we vaguely claim that Jesus is the answer, but will say *how* He is the answer *to what*.

Every evangelist has a list of sins. Paul had his list (Gal. 5:19-21). Today evangelists are well-known for their preaching against the sins of adultery, drinking, and stealing. Developing conviction regarding sin is considered one important aspect of evangelism. Is it not strange that in a century of world wars and the threat of nuclear holocaust so few preachers have been willing to include war in their list of sins, to say nothing of racism, exploitation, and greed? Why does their list not also include militarism, imperialism, and nationalism?

When a businessman complained to John Henry Newman (1801-1890) that his preaching was interfering with his business, Newman replied, "Sir, it is the business of the church to interfere with people."[7] Our evangelism must come to grips with the powers of sin in the world and confront those powers with the atoning work of Jesus. While sin is rooted in the human heart, its influence is deeply imbedded in every institution. In fact, demonic powers are especially active and destructive where they posses social structures. None of those powers can escape the power of Jesus Christ, however. The work of God in the world in addition to coming to needy hearts also deals with fallen structures. Our evangelism cannot help but be related to those structures. Witnessing to the planners of war is evangelism. In fact, we can even call it personal evangelism. The Bible never makes any distinction between personal salvation and social concern. God wishes to extend His salvation to the whole creation and rescue all that is under the domination of sin.

The early revivalism in the nineteeth century was not afraid to deal with social issues and proclaimed the lordship of Christ over all of life. Later revivalism with its smooth evangelists, however, was careful not to offend the rich and powerful from whom they received their money. Instead they concentrated on personal piety and the sins of the working class and supported the status quo. Any meaningful call for repentance was gone.

The New Testament says when the gospel was preached, the poor heard it gladly. Although the poor also need to be confronted with their greed and materialism, today we seem to have a message that the rich hear more gladly than the poor. Maybe we need to take another look at our message. What is it saying to the poor, the downtrodden, the despised? All too often it comes across as oppression, rationalization for exploitation, justification of the status quo, as bad news rather than good news, as slavery rather than liberation. Why should the masses of the world not reject the faith if they see Jesus as the symbol of those who exploit, enslave, and destroy? How can they listen to those of us who have blood on our hands? Our failure to agonize over injustice is a sign of a deep spiritual problem.

In the war of the Lamb we will plead the cause of the poor and downtrodden before the powerful. We will act as advocate for them. In doing this we will act as more than mediator. We will confront the powerful and often be a thorn in their flesh. They will not be able any longer to use Christianity to justify their wickedness. We exist not as a power group to put pressure on society, however. The power is not in us or what we control, but in the truth which we both live and proclaim.

The Lamb's war is a work of reconciliation. Even as "God was in Christ reconciling the world to Himself," so we have been given the ministry of reconciliation (2 Cor. 5:18-20). Love of the enemy is more than a result of the gospel, it is at the heart of what the atonement (at-one-ment) is. Reconciliation is what happened on the cross and is an essential part of our witness. We ignore, jump over, and break down the barriers of class, race, and nation that divide people. We are to be a healing presence in the world.

The church is called to be a reconciler, but that does not mean that the role of the church is primarily to be a mediator. We will speak the truth and often that will bring to the surface great amounts of hostility, hatred, and sometimes even violence. Attacking the demons is a serious matter. The gospel does cause offense. A sinful world does not want to hear about a righteous God. Sometimes the church will be a polarizing force in the world. Jesus came not to bring peace but a sword. Without repentance and the cross there can be no reconciliation.

At times our witness may need to be in areas where we are unwanted. Because we are rejected is no sufficient reason to quit, although we need to discern when to shake the dust off our shoes and not throw pearls to swine.

Voluntarism

This raises again the concern for voluntarism. In all our witnessing we dare not lose sight of our commitment to voluntarism. Our methods must always be consistent with the way of the cross. This means a rejection of all manipulation, gimmicks, and enticements. Evangelism is sharing the gospel, not trying to manipulate people into being Christian.

There are no shortcuts to the conversion of the whole world, be it coercion, psychological manipulation, or watering down the gospel to the point where it will offend no one, or resorting to Madison Avenue organizational and technological expertise to blitz the nation for God. To the extent we believe in God, we will reject all gimmicks and not bait people with either guilt or the promise of extraordinary rewards.

Our witness is not intended to make people in our image, nor is it to be so simple that the only response that is needed is to raise one's hand while no one else is looking. We intend our message to be taken seriously and for it to involve a profound struggle in which the person is free to make his/her own decision. The goal of evangelism is helping others to comprehend, not to induce others to yield themselves. That is between them and God. It is not for us to figure out what techniques will bring the desired response, for if we are successful, it is likely that the results will be our own work, rather than God's action, and thus will be hollow and short-lived. Paul understood, as does any social scientist today, that the power of persuasion is not necessarily dependent on the work of the Holy Spirit (1 Cor. 2:1-5).

We are not called to save souls. That is the work of the Holy Spirit. Our only task is to witness. Evangelism is sowing seed. After the seed is planted, we can only humbly and hopefully wait for God to quicken the seed. We know that we cannot convict or convert, but that the Spirit through the Word can. So often our witness reveals a lack of faith in God. Since we are not sure God can do His work, we try to do His work for Him. The more we believe in the greatness of God, the less we will feel the need to try to convert people ourselves.

We will, however, aggressively seek those who are lost and sometimes confront them when they would rather not be confronted. People are more often running from God than seeking for Him; rather than hungering for the truth, most seek to avoid it. We do not just ignore these people. We seek them out.

Evangelism need not be a violation of others' dignity and freedom. Rather than being coercive or manipulative, Christian evangelism is helping give others the opportunity and freedom to decide for or against Jesus. Many times we become so tolerant with others that they interpret it as rejection. If we care for others, we will want to share and call them to what we know is so important. Evangelism is a service to others. It is making Christian commitment a genuine option for others. To not give them this choice is to limit their freedom.

Chapter 11

THE REBIRTH OF COMMUNITY

God always wants to have a place, a community, which belongs to Him really and truly, so that God's being can dwell there. God needs such a place from where He can work for the rest of the world. There must be a place on the earth from where the sun of God's kingdom shines forth.[1]

—Christoph Blumhardt.

If you at least to some extent agree with the direction we have been pointing, what do you do if you are a member of an established congregation in which there is little community? How do we relate to the institutional church and how do we find community? How can a group which is not a community become a community?

The first answer is to deal with ourselves, to surrender our whole lives to Jesus. No program or structure, be it small groups, task forces, or even prayer groups, will bring new life to the church. The rebirth of community must begin in our hearts as we open our lives to God's love.

Second, it is God who will recreate His community among us, not we. Where people turn to Jesus and His kingdom, they are brought together into a deep fellowship. The most important element in the rebirth of the church is a rebirth of faith, a new commitment to the living Lord.

What is needed is not to build new enthusiasm for the church, but to find a new vision and a deeper faith. The rebirth of the church is the result not of changing structures but a rediscovery and new appropriation of Christian faith. Creating new forms or models is not the answer. Rather a new reality must break into our midst out of which new forms may come.

The answer must begin with you. Begin by straightening out those things in your life which are holding you back. Community can be given only as we let go of our commitment to what is and like Abraham begin a journey to a new land promised by God. Allow yourself to be open to the leading of the Holy Spirit in your life. Share honestly with others who are also seeking.

It is not enough to be committed to the idea of community. We need to be committed to a particular, real community. Otherwise, we actually are committed to an invisible church rather than a visible believers' community. We need to reject the modern spiritualist option of advocating a view which is not embodied in any community or movement of which we are a part. The New Testament vision of the church is the same as its view of the new creation, faith, and love. These are not Platonic ideals, but realities based on what God is doing among us. Even though incomplete and imperfect, the church is a reality, not an ideal. What has now begun is a sign of what is coming. Our commitment should be not to an ideal *out there* for which we are striving, but to a reality that we are already living.

There is always the danger of our commitment to some abstract ideal community which does not exist becoming an excuse for never committing ourselves to any real community. It is easy for us to be more committed to some ideal than to the community God wants to give to us, for whenever things are difficult we retreat into our dream world rather than face the struggles before us. We then set up our own demands and standards and are unable to submit ourselves to what God wants to give to us. Using our ideal as an excuse, we cut ourselves off from community and God. We become proud, judgmental, and demanding. We forget that no ideal or dream can bring people together the way God can.

If you earnestly desire community, there are at least three possible ways in which God may be leading you. You may be led to become a part of an existing community, to help your congregation become a community, or to participate in forming a new community.

Seriously consider whether you are being called to an existing community. There are many existing communities who are already trying to live this vision.[2] Why wait? By serious interaction with one of these groups you can test concretely whether God is leading you to full community.

At the very least, you should visit some of the existing communities to gain more than an intellectual image of what community can be. This experience can be of tremendous significance in helping you decide what you should do. Even if you do not join an existing community this experience will be of great help in working with another group.

Another possibility is for a whole congregation to be reborn and transformed into a Christian community. There are examples of where this has happened, but they are few. Remember that what is called for is a completely new understanding of the church, a drastic turning around, rather than some minor reforms. Minor reforms may only be a diversion from the real task. A reborn congregation would not leave the essential features of the institutional church intact.

For this to be a possibility there must at least be a real openness, if not commitment, from the leadership of the congregation. Unless they are open, little can happen as a total congregation. If those who control the congregation are set and closed, there is no point in trying to force them to change. If they want to stay as they are, then one's energy might best be put some place else. It is only frustrating to begin with people who are satisfied with the status quo. For renewal to come in a congregation there needs to be an awareness of need, a real hunger for something deeper, a willingness to trust God, and the cooperation of the leadership. If there is little likelihood of your congregation going in this direction, the most gracious and loving thing for you may be to leave and unite with those who are ready to move ahead. Rather than creating a lot of frustration for the congregation and yourself, maybe the best approach would be for you to begin living a life of community and let that be your witness to them.

Another question is whether you are in basic agreement with the heritage and stated beliefs of the congregation. It is not fair to work against the identity of a particular group. If you are in basic disagreement with it, it could be better to find a group with whom you are in unity.

If there seems to be a real openness in the congregation, you might begin by prayerfully sharing your concerns with them. It would be better if others could do this with you. Maybe you could begin by taking an important decision to the congregation and asking them to discern the answer with you. Maybe there could be a month or a year of Bible study centering around the biblical understanding of the church and how this relates to the congregation. Maybe the sermons could focus on this question. But always remember that the central question is whether the congregation is willing to give complete loyalty to Jesus and follow Him the whole way. If not, there is no point in continuing. Unfortunately, most people have found this approach to be a frustrating one. Most people are more open to discussion than to taking any concrete steps.

One approach is to work toward strengthening the requirements of membership. Some congregations have initiated a renewal-of-membership covenant with some meaningful commitment to accompany this. This is moving in the right direction, but usually it does not go nearly far enough, for the congregation is still a secondary group with little discernment or mutual support for each other. Neither is this the new beginning that is needed.

At some point some crucial decisions will have to be made. Will there be a true turning, will the people make a new commitment, will they decide to start anew? Can there be agreement to make a new covenant with each other, a covenant which will be binding on all who accept it? If your congregation lacks the elements of true Christian community, it needs to experience real repentance, a radical turning around, and a new birth. Rather than having any hope in reforming the congregation, our only hope can be in its rebirth with a new structure on a proper foundation.

If a large congregation wants to be fully the church, it may be helpful to divide the congregation into smaller groups for sharing, confession, discernment, and discipline. One suggestion is for the primary functions of the church to take place in these smaller communities, including possibly even membership and baptism. These groups would be the heart of the church. Note, we are not simply talking about small groups, but communities which would be fully the church. The larger congregation then would be a gathering of the smaller communities for mass meetings for worship, guest speakers, and mission work. Reba Place Fellowship has some of these characteristics. This is the structure of some Pentecostal groups in South America. They function as house churches and regularly have mass meetings at one place for the whole city. A large congregation could be a community of communities.

It is important that a small group be seen as more than a small group, more than a study, prayer, or task group, but as a church, as a full Christian community. One of the problems with the Pietist cells was that they did not see themselves as fully the church. We are talking about more than a small cell which meets regularly to share their spiritual and devotional pilgrimage, but a corporate body with a new style of life. We mean not small groups in the church, but small groups being the church and doing the functions of church.

One of the weaknesses of the small-group movement has been that the groups have not had much permanence. They are a good experience for those involved, but after they are gone everything reverts to where it was, except for possibly some new vision and dedication on the part of some of the participants. For the most part small groups have not led to the rebirth of the church. If the group is only a task group, when the task ends the group ends.

If a group is a church, there will be an interest in a broad spectrum of concerns, not only interpersonal relations, Bible study, prayer, or action. Activities will encompass many areas of life and will include eating together, singing, prayer, interpersonal relations, Bible study, and sharing of concerns. All aspects of life will be of concern to the group.

Rather than being part of many interest groups, it is better to be intensively part of one which will have broader concerns. Most of us already have too many meetings to attend. Hopefully this community will not be just another activity to drain more of our energy, but rather be the life-blood of our energy and vision. This can replace many of the other meaningless activities.

There is also the possibility of seeing one's community as being simply a small group within a congregation. Although this is frequently suggested as the answer, it seems to have more serious problems than are usually recognized. Seldom are these small groups communities with much commitment, depth, stability, and permanence. The relationship to the old congregation brings many pressures to compromise and water down the radical demands of discipleship. Unless the whole congregation is reborn, there will continually be inherent conflict between the direction of the community and that of the congregation. In this conflict there will continually be the question of where one's loyalty really is, and which group really comes first, plus all the dangers of appearing self-righteous, exclusive, elitist, and judgmental.

Being a full member of two churches hardly seems possible. Rather than have any forced relationships due to a community's membership in a congregation, it seems better to be part of a community which is free to be the church and free to call others to join as they are led to the community. Also, for a small group within an established congregation really to be the church would probably soon be seen as putting it in competition with the congregation.

Another possibility is that God is calling you to be part of the formation of a new community. Before trying to start a new community, test carefully whether you are actually being led of God to do this rather than to join an existing community. Could it be that your desire to start your own community is based on something else, such as ego needs, pride, or unwillingness to submit to anyone else?

Another important question to ask is why you should put all the energy and time into the struggle to get started when there are already communities who have gone through this and are moving ahead with more important concerns? The process of starting a community is a slow and painful one, with lots of discouragement and frustration. Add to that the fact that few new beginnings ever last very long. We must seriously ask whether it is good stewardship of our lives to go through all this effort when there are existing communities. But it may also be that God is calling new communities into existence.

If you have a carefully tested call to be part of a new group, remember that communities usually do not spring up over night, but are the result of a long, slow process of being drawn together. Remember, it is not we, but God who must build the community. Be careful not to have too high expectations or become pushy. Organisms grow naturally. Community cannot be forced or legislated. Be careful not to impose community on others. When you begin, many unexpected things will happen. You can never neatly plan out any strategy.

There is the danger of structure moving ahead of the Spirit. A group can come to a common commitment to operate by consensus, for example, but not have the common commitment to Jesus who is the only One who can make consensus work. The commitment must come before the structure.

Spend more time talking about the meaning of your commitment to Jesus and each other than the specifics of how you will share your money. Be open and clear about what it is that you are doing. Never lose sight of your purpose. If you have a group of friends who are not willing to make a commitment at this time but are searching, get together and search together. But do not waste your time trying to get a group together that is not seriously interested in being together. Always be honest with each other about where you are.

Another danger in the formation of a new community is that people will be drawn into something that they do not understand and become caught in relationships and commitments that they never voluntarily made, because they did not realize what they were getting themselves into. This often happens in the formation of new groups and causes a lot of hurt. When relating to an existing community one can see and test more clearly whether one wants to make the commitments called for by that group. But when the community does not yet actually exist, that is very difficult to test.

It is best for a new community to have some mature people in it, and it would be helpful if some have had some experience with Christian community. As soon as possible name those with leadership gifts and support them. Also, if a group remains too small, there may not be enough spiritual gifts for the group to function properly. If there are only several of you, pray and seek together for God either to send others to you or for you to be led to some other community. At first it may be necessary to have all closed meetings in order to get yourselves together before you become open to new people. After all, you will not be able to include others if it is not clear what it is they are being included in. As soon as possible make a covenant with each other. At the very least this would include a commitment to follow Jesus together.

A new community should seek relationships with and help from more experienced Christian communities. New groups in the New Testament received help from the more mature groups. This is important whether one is working with a congregation or a new beginning. We need to associate with some other groups beyond ourselves and see ourselves as part of a larger history.

New communities may want to associate in some way with the established church. The early Christians continued to relate to the temple and synagogues as long as that was possible. In the Old Testament the true prophets uttered harsh judgments, but they did not turn their backs on their people. It is good to keep in relationship with old structures, but important not to be defined or confined by them. We should have no desire to be separate from God's apostate people, but neither may we compromise our calling for the sake of maintaining relationships. It is important that we have a burning love for the established church and that we be grateful for whatever relationships are possible, but never may we let the old church hold us back. We need not worry about being dismissed for being too radical. If we continue to live out our calling in a consistent way and demonstrate love, we will not be dismissed forever.

We need to be careful in relating to established churches that we do not lend support to presenting the gospel in a way that helps to immunize people against the claims of the gospel. Each of us should be painfully aware of how so much preaching and talking without the life to back it up is a real hindrance to people hearing and responding to the Word. Our full participation in the established church could actually be a stumbling block for others if it is not clear that we represent something different.

The answer is not easy, but it is simple. As God leads you, do it. And the best way to do it is to begin doing it. Begin to really seek God's will for your life, begin to lay down everything that holds you back from following Jesus, and open your life to receiving the gift of community.

And remember to wait on the Lord. Anything you try to do on your own is doomed from the start. "Unless the Lord builds the house, those who build it labor in vain" (Ps. 127:1).

POSTSCRIPT

God's message to the world through Jesus Christ is that God desires reconciliation and a life of communion with all people. God wants His children to return to Him and to be reconciled to Himself and to each other. We believe true reconciliation leads to brotherhood and sisterhood.

Those who are being reconciled are called to lay down their lives to Christ and the church so that God can truly mold them and use them as His ambassadors of reconciliation.

We believe this book can be helpful in pointing the way to find what you are seeking—a life of love and community with God and His people. We share this book with you, the reader, in the hope that you will find it of service to you in your search for a meaningful and joyful life as a disciple of Jesus Christ and as a member of His body on earth—the church.

New Covenant Fellowship

NOTES

Author's Preface

1. Eberhard Arnold, *History of the Baptizers Movement* (Rifton, N.Y.: Plough Publishing House, 1970), pp. 219-221. First published in *Mennonite Quarterly Review* (July 1969).

2. We will be using the term "believers' church" throughout this study, since it seems to be the best term. The apostrophe after the "s" indicates the collective nature of the church. The term "believers' church" in no way implies that there are no believers in other traditions, but that being a fully committed believer is the basis for membership in this tradition. Other terms like Reformed, Catholic, or Orthodox, could be considered equally presumptuous. For a good discussion of these terms see Donald F. Durnbaugh, *The Believers' Church* (New York: Macmillan, 1968), pp. ix-8. This whole book is an excellent introduction to the history and beliefs of the believers' churches.

3. Franklin H. Littell, "The Contribution of the Free Churches," *The Chicago Seminary Register*, LX (September 1970), p. 49.

4. A weakness of this book is the absence of much description of Christian communities and how they are actually living out this vision. It may be helpful to read this book in connection with Dave and Neta Jackson's excellent book on contemporary Christian communities; *Living Together in a World Falling Apart* (Carol Stream, Ill.: Creation House, 1974).

Chapter 1. The Church as Community

1. T. S. Eliot, "Choruses from 'The Rock' " in *Collected Poems, 1909-35.* Quoted in J. Robert Nelson, *The Realm of Redemption* (Chicago: Cloister Press, 1951), p. 64.

2. Paul S. Minear, *Images of the Church in the New Testament* (Philadelphia: Westminster Press, 1960).

3. Galatians 6:15, 16; Ephesians 2:12; Hebrews 8:8-10.

4. John Howard Yoder, "A People in the World," *The Concept of the*

Believers' Church, ed. James Leo Garrett, Jr. (Scottdale, Pa.: Herald Press, 1969), p. 258.

5. C. Norman Kraus, *The Community of the Spirit* (Grand Rapids: Eerdmans, 1974), p. 23.

6. *Ibid.,* pp. 24-25.

7. Lewis Benson, *Catholic Quakerism* (Philadelphia: Friends Book Store, 1968), p. 74.

8. The distinction between visible and invisible was first made by Augustine and has been seen as a means of rationalizing what had happened since Constantine and Theodosius. Augustine understood the radical difference between the New Testament understanding of the church and the inclusive establishment to which he was committed. See Emil Brunner, *The Christian Doctrine of the Church, Faith and the Consummation,* tr. David Cairns (Philadelphia: Westminster Press, 1962), pp. 27-33.

The mainline Reformers (Zwingli, Luther, and Calvin) in their struggle against the Roman Catholic view of the church in some cases pushed this thinking to the extreme and maintained that the only true church is invisible. Although they believed in justification by faith alone, they still wanted to maintain the mass medieval church with all its power and coercion. The doctrine of the invisible church was a convenient way of handling the contradiction. It is also related to their limited view of the extent to which regeneration and victory over sin can be known in the lives of believers.

At the same time the 16th-century Anabaptists saw the New Testament calling for visible communities openly committed to living out the gospel. This vision of the church and rejection of compromised institutional religion was too much of a threat for those committed to the medieval structures and is an important reason for the persecution of the Anabaptists. If the Anabaptists had simply given up any attempt to form visible congregations they might have avoided much of their suffering.

9. *Ibid.,* pp. 28-29.

Chapter 2. The Faithful Community

1. *The Complete Writings of Menno Simons,* ed. J. C. Wenger (Scottdale, Pa.: Herald Press, 1956), p. 225.

2. Dietrich Bonhoeffer, *The Cost of Discipleship,* tr. R. H. Fuller (New York: Macmillan, 1959), p. 36.

3. For an extensive sociological analysis of commitment see Rosabeth Kanter, *Commitment and Community: Communes and Utopias in Sociological Perspective* (Cambridge: Harvard University Press, 1972), pp. 64 ff. I find a sociological analysis to be quite inadequate, however.

4. The meaning of being broken by the Spirit is discussed by Watchman Nee, *The Release of the Spirit* (Indianapolis: Sure Foundation, 1965).

5. Robert Friedman, "An Epistle Concerning Communal Life: A Hutterite Manifesto of 1650 and its Modern Paraphrase," *Mennonite Quarterly Review*, XXXIV (October 1960), pp. 249-274. This whole manifesto is a moving statement of the importance and meaning of living in full community.It has recently been republished in a new translation along with the confession of Claus Felbinger. Andreas Ehrenpreis and Claus Felbinger, *Brotherly Community: The Highest Command of Love* (Rifton, NY.: Plough Publishing House, 1978).

6. Judy Alexander, "Servanthood and Submission," *The Other Side*, IX (July-August, 1973), p. 42.

Chapter 3. The Sharing Community

1. Quoted by Leroy Judson Day, *Dynamic Christian Fellowship* (Valley Forge, Pa.: Judson Press, 1960), p. 30.

2. Eberhard Arnold, *The Early Christians* (Rifton, N.Y.: Plough Publishing House, 1970), p. 17.

3. *Ibid.*, p. 18.

4. Gerhard Uhlhorn, *Christian Charity in the Ancient Church* (New York: Charles Scribner's Sons, 1883), pp. 6-9.

5. For further comparison of Christian compassion with Plato, Aristotle, and the Stoics see *Ibid.*, pp. 32-40.

6. Minear, *op. cit.*, pp. 163, 164.

7. Quoted by Robert Friedmann, *The Theology of Anabaptism* (Scottdale, Pa.: Herald Press, 1973), pp. 71, 72.

8. Eberhard Arnold, *Inner Land* (Rifton, N.Y.: Plough Publishing House, 1976), pp. 402, 403.

9. Max Delespesse, *The Church Community: Leaven and Lifestyle* (Ottawa: The Catholic Centre of Saint Paul University, 1969), argues convincingly that Jesus was clearly a communitarian and that this was the standard practice of the early church. Thus the whole New Testament needs to be read with this understanding. See especially pp. 14-19, 40-44.

10. Arnold, *The Early Christians*, p. 183.

11. *Ibid.*, p. 100.

12. *The Ante-Nicene Fathers*, Vol. I, ed. Alexander Roberts and James Donaldson (Grand Rapids: Eerdmans, 1967), p. 148.

13. Delespesse, *op. cit.*, p. 41.

14. *Ibid.*, p. 42.

15. Eberhard Arnold, *Foundation and Orders of Sannerz and the Rhön Bruderhof, Section I* (Rifton, N.Y.: Plough Publishing House, 1976), p. 5.

16. See John Howard Yoder, *The Politics of Jesus* (Grand Rapids, Mich.: Eerdmans, 1972), pp. 34-40, 64-77.

17. Peter Walpot, "True Surrender and Christian Community of Goods," *Mennonite Quarterly Review*, XXXI (January 1957), p. 60. Reprinted by Plough Publishing House, Rifton, N.Y., p. 43.

18. Quoted by Harold S. Bender, "The Anabaptist Vision," *Recovery of the Anabaptist Vision,* ed. Guy S. Hershberger (Scottdale, Pa.: Herald Press, 1957), p. 50

19. Michall Frantz, "Simple Doctrinal Considerations . . ." in Donald F. Durnbaugh, ed., *The Brethren in Colonial America* (Elgin, Illinois: Brethren Press, 1967), p. 453.

20. Quoted by Kanter, *op. cit.,* p. 106.

21. Ante-Nicene Fathers, Vol. III, *op. cit.,* p. 46.

Chapter 4. The Discerning Community

1. John Howard Yoder, "Binding and Loosing," *Concern 14* (Scottdale, Pa.: Concern, 1967), p. 9.

2. R. W. Tucker, "Revolutionary Faithfulness," *Quaker Religious Thought,* IX (Winter, 1967-68), p. 8.

3. Edward Schweitzer, *Church Order in the New Testament* (Naperville, Ill.: Alec R. Allenson, 1961), pp. 211, 212.

Chapter 5. The Discipling Community

1. Frederick Norwood, *Church Membership in the Methodist Tradition* (Nashville: The Methodist Publishing House, 1958), p. 11.

2. Clarence Jordan, *Sermon on the Mount* (Valley Forge, Pa.: Judson Press, 1970), p. 99.

3. Quoted by Donald G. Bloesch, *The Reform of the Church* (Grand Rapids, Mich.: Eerdmans, 1970), p. 79.

4. Another whole chapter dealing with the healing ministry of the church should have been written for this book, but I did not feel able to write it. A significant aspect of the life of Christian community is ministering in the area of broken relationships and the inner needs of people, helping people to struggle with all the hurts, fears, and sins that keep them from seeking first God's kingdom. This includes both personal and social concerns.

5. Norwood, *op. cit.,* p. 88.

6. Marlin Jeschke, *Discipling the Brother* (Scottdale, Pa.: Herald Press, 1972), p. 47.

7. *Ibid.,* p. 50.

8. Words spoken by Eberhard Arnold on July 17, 1933, *To Experience the Person of Jesus Is a Great Grace* (Rifton, N.Y.: Plough Publishing House, 1975), pp. 3, 4.

9. Also see Matthew 6:14, 15; 18:35; Mark 11:25; Ephesians 4:32; Colossians 3:13.

10. John Howard Yoder (*The Politics of Jesus, op. cit.,* pp. 215-232) points to a deeper meaning of justification than the traditional Protestant interpretation of it referring to the status of our guilt before God, showing

that Paul's writings on justification refer more to being set in right relationship, to breaking down the dividing walls of hostility (Eph. 2).

11. Hobart Mowrer, *The Crisis in Psychiatry and Religion* (New York: D. Van Nostrand, 1961).

12. Yoder, "Binding and Loosing," *op. cit.*, p. 30.

13. Heini Arnold, *Freedom from Sinful Thoughts* (Rifton, N.Y.: Plough Publishing House, 1973). This little book makes the point so clear that we need to *confess* rather than *repress* or *express* our negative feelings.

14. Jeschke, *op. cit.*, p. 129.

15. Yoder, "Binding and Loosing," *op. cit.*, p. 2.

Chapter 6. The Voluntary Community

1. Jeschke, *Discipling the Brother, op. cit.*, p. 30.

2. *Ibid.*, p. 34.

3. John T. McNeill, *The History and Character of Calvinism* (New York: Oxford University Press, 1967), p. 176.

4. Quoted by Henry Townsend, *The Claims of the Free Churches* (London: Hodder & Stoughton, 1949), p. 258. Actually, although Luther made some good statements on religious freedom, in practice he supported the repression of movements he considered a threat. See Rolland Bainton, *Studies on the Reformation* (Boston: Beacon Press, 1963), pp. 20-45.

5. Quoted by Franklin H. Littell, *The Free Church* (Boston: Star King Press, 1957), p. 92.

6. Quoted by William R. Estep, *The Anabaptist Story* (Nashville: Broadman Press, 1963), p. 192.

7. John Howard Yoder, *The Politics of Jesus,* op. cit., p. 45.

8. *Ibid.*, p. 174.

9. This can be seen in the recommitments made when there was a change of leadership (Deut. 31; Josh. 1, 23, 24; 1 Sam. 12). Also the covenant was renewed at special times of revival (2 Chron. 34:29-33; Neh. 9, 10) and possibly every seventh year (Deut. 31:9-13).

10. For a fuller discussion of this issue, see Dave and Neta Jackson, *op. cit.,* pp. 75-79.

11. Elizabeth O'Conner, *Call to Commitment* (New York: Harper & Row, 1963), p. 25.

12. George H. Williams, ed., *Spiritual and Anabaptist Writers* (Philadelphia: Westminster Press, 1957), p. 77.

13. Eberhard Arnold, *Foundation and Orders, op. cit.*, p. 36.

14. D. T. Niles, "The Work of the Holy Spirit in the World," *Christian Mission in Theological Perspective,* Gerald H. Anderson, ed. (Nashville: Abingdon, 1967), p. 100.

15. This is argued quite thoroughly by Kurt Aland, *Did the Early Church Baptize Infants?* (London: SCM Press, 1963).

16. Thieleman J. Van Braght, *Martyrs Mirror,* tr. from the original

Dutch from the Edition of 1660 by Joseph F. Sohm (Scottdale, Pa.: Herald Press, 1972; ninth edition), pp. 153-171.

17. Vernard Eller, *In Place of Sacraments* (Grand Rapids, Mich.: Eerdmans, 1972), p. 45. This is one of the best books on both baptism and the Lord's Supper and I am indebted to brother Eller for his contribution.

18. Van Braght, *op. cit.*, p. 119.

19. *Ibid.*, pp. 153-171.

20. Eller, *op. cit.*, pp. 71, 72. For a fuller discussion not only of this question, but the broader relationship between theologies of baptism and their implications for education and evangelism, see Gideon G. Yoder, *The Nurture and Evangelism of Children* (Scottdale, Pa.: Herald Press, 1959).

21. An important part of the Anabaptist understanding of baptism is that it is a seal of the covenant made with God and the church. See Robert Friedman, *The Theology of Anabaptism* (Scottdale, Pa.: Herald Press, 1973), pp. 134-138. Just as circumcision was a sign or seal of the old covenant (Rom. 4:11), so baptism is a seal of the new covenant. For an excellent scholarly study of the Anabaptist understanding of baptism see Rollin Stely Armour, *Anabaptist Baptism: A Representative Study* (Scottdale, Pa.: Herald Press, 1966).

Chapter 7. The Organized Community

1. Quoted by Howard H. Brinton, *Reaching Decisions*, Pamphlet #65 (Wallingford, Pa.: Pendle Hill Pamphlets, 1952), p. 5.

2. For a more detailed argument of this position see John Howard Yoder, "The Fullness of Christ," *Concern 17* (Scottdale, Pa.: Concern, 1967), pp. 57-60. This whole article is one of the best studies of leadership in the New Testament.

3. Emil Brunner, *The Christian Doctrine of the Church, Faith, and the Consumation, op. cit.*, p. 35.

4. Calvin Redekop, *The Free Church and Seductive Culture* (Scottdale, Pa.: Herald Press, 1970), pp. 100-103.

5. Quoted by Henrick Kraemer, *A Theology of the Laity* (Philadelphia: Westminster Press, 1958), p. 61.

6. Paul M. Harrison, *Authority and Power in the Free Church Tradition; A Social Case History of the American Baptist Convention* (Princeton: Princeton University Press, 1959), pp. 217, 218.

7. John Howard Yoder, *The Ecumenical Movement and the Faithful Church* (Scottdale, Pa.: Mennonite Publishing House, 1958), pp. 28-35. A sad fact among contemporary Anabaptist groups is a tendency to allow feelings of disunity with other groups to be an excuse for not actively seeking unity. If these groups were true to their heritage they would be more actively seeking dialogue and fellowship with other groups.

8. *Ibid.*, p. 21.

9. Durnbaugh, *The Believers' Church, op. cit.*, pp. 289-295.

Chapter 8. The Worshiping Community

1. From the hymn, "O Brother Man."

2. Vernard Eller, *op. cit.,* p. 31.

3. We are using the Quaker term "meeting for worship" rather than "worship service" because we cannot assume that in every meeting for worship there will be worship. The terms "going to church" or "having church" should be completely dropped from our vocabulary, for the church is to be a body of people, not something we do on Sunday.

4. Quoted in Gerald H. Anderson, *Christian Mission in Theological Perspective* (Nashville: Abingdon, 1967), p. 149.

5. Evelyn Underhill, *Worship* (New York: Harper & Brothers, 1957), p. 313.

6. Millard C. Lind, *Biblical Foundations for Christian Worship* (Scottdale, Pa.: Herald Press, 1973). Lind shows that both Old and New Testament worship was related to God's covenant community and concerned with the kingdom of God.

7. Eberhard Arnold, *The Early Christians, op. cit.,* p. 188.

8. Quoted in *Agenda,* (Elgin, Illinois: Church of the Brethren, February 21, 1972), Section 2.

9. Max I. Reich, "Congregational Silence," reprinted in *Quaker Witness,* XXX (Fall, 1976), p. 8.

10. Harold S. Bender, *These Are My People* (Scottdale, Pa.: Herald Press, 1962), pp. 43-45.

11. William Stringfellow, *A Private and Public Faith* (Grand Rapids, Mich.: Eerdmans, 1962), p. 48.

12. Eller, *op. cit.,* p. 86.

13. Peter Rideman, *Confession of Faith,* tr. Society of Brothers (Rifton, N.Y.: Plough Publishing House, 1970), pp. 192, 193.

14. Eller, *op. cit.,* pp. 106-118.

15. *Ibid.,* p. 109.

Chapter 9. The Nonconforming Community

1. Martin Schrag in a significant study has detailed how this happened in the Brethren in Christ Church, a classic example of this process. *The Brethren in Christ Attitudes Toward the World* (unpublished PhD dissertation, Temple University, May 1, 1967).

2. John Howard Yoder, *The Original Revolution* (Scottdale, Pa.: Herald Press, 1971), pp. 118-130. This whole book is a good introduction to Anabaptist understanding of ethics and relationship of church and world.

3. C. Wright Mills, "A Pagan Sermon to the Christian Clergy," *The Nation,* CLXXXVI (March 8, 1958), p. 200.

4. Rosemary Ruether, "The Believer's Church and Catholicity in the World Today," *The Chicago Theological Seminary Register,* LX (September 1970) pp. 6, 7.

5. H. Richard Niebuhr, *Christ and Culture* (New York: Harper Torchbooks, 1951).

6. John C. Wenger, *Even unto Death* (Richmond, Va.: John Knox Press, 1961), p. 87.

7. For a detailed account of the suffering of martyrs down through the ages see Van Braght, *Martyrs Mirror, op. cit.*

8. Bender, *These Are My People, op. cit.*, p. 80.

9. Donald F. Durnbaugh, *The Believers' Church, op. cit.*, p. 55.

10. Quoted by Frederick Norwood, *Church Membership in the Methodist Tradition, op. cit.*, p. 18.

11. Quoted by Franklin H. Littell, *The Free Church, op. cit.*, p. 82.

12. Franklin H. Littell, *From State Church to Pluralism* (New York: Anchor Books, 1962), pp. 61-73.

13. *Ibid.*, p. 62. Littell shows how this was true in regard to slavery in the United States before the Civil War.

14. John Howard Yoder, *The Politics of Jesus, op. cit.*, p. 238.

15. For a more detailed examination of the biblical teaching on economics and the contradiction to capitalism, see my *Beyond the Rat Race* (Scottdale, Pa.: Herald Press, 1973).

16. Eberhard Arnold, *The Early Christians, op. cit.*, p. 17.

17. See J. Milton Yinger, *Religion, Society and the Individual* (New York: Macmillan, 1957), pp. 150-152.

Chapter 10. The Witnessing Community

1. Dean Kelly, *Why Conservative Churches Are Growing* (New York: Harper and Row, 1972).

2. Elizabeth O'Connor, *Journey Inward, Journey Outward* (New York: Harper and Row, 1968), pp. ix-x.

3. Larry Christenson, *A Charismatic Approach to Social Action* (Minneapolis: Bethany Fellowship, 1974), p. 105.

4. Eberhard Arnold, *Inner Land, op. cit.*, p. 171.

5. Quoted by Richard J. Foster, *Quaker Concern in Race Relations Then and Now* (Privately published manuscript in possession of author, 1973), pp. 152-153.

6. Arnold, *loc. cit.*, pp. 371-372.

7. Quoted by Franklin H. Littell, *The Free Church, op. cit.*, p. 72.

Chapter 11. The Rebirth of Community

1. R. Lejeune, *Christoph Blumhardt and His Message*, tr. Hela Ehrlich and Nicoline Maas (Rifton, N.Y.: Plough Publishing House, 1963), p. 81.

2. For a list of communities, see Dave Jackson, *Coming Together* (Minneapolis: Bethany Fellowship, 1978), pp. 167—199. Not all these communities represent the same direction as described in this book, however.

FOR FURTHER READING

Arnold, Eberhard. *The Early Christians.* Tr. Society of Brothers.
————— *Inner Land.* Tr. Hutterian Society of Brothers.
Rifton, N.Y.: Plough Publishing House, 1975.
————— *Salt and Light.* Tr. Society of Brothers. Rifton, N.Y.:
Plough Publishing House, 1967.
Arnold, Emmy. *Torches Together.* Tr. Society of Brothers. Rifton,
N.Y.: Plough Publishing House, 1971.
Bender, Harold S. *These Are My People.* Scottdale, Pa.: Herald
Press, 1962.
Bender, Ross Thomas. *The People of God.* Scottdale, Pa.: Herald
Press, 1971.
Benson, Lewis. *Catholic Quakerism: A Vision for All Men.*
Philadelphia: Friends Book Store, 1968.
Bonhoeffer, Dietrich. *The Cost of Discipleship.* Tr. R. H. Fuller.
New York: Macmillan, 1959.
————— *Life Together.* Tr. John W. Doberstein. New York:
Harper & Row, 1954.
Brunner, Emil. *The Christian Doctrine of the Church, Faith, and the
Consummation.* Tr. David Cairns. Philadelphia: Westminster
Press, 1962.
Delespesse, Max. *The Church Community: Leaven and Life-Style.*
Tr. Kenneth Russell. Ottawa: The Catholic Centre of Saint
Paul University, 1969.
Driver, John. *Community and Commitment.* Scottdale, Pa.: Herald
Press, 1976.
Durnbaugh, Donald F. *The Believers' Church: The History and
Character of Radical Protestantism.* New York: Macmillan,
1968.

Durnbaugh, Donald F., ed. *Every Need Supplied: Mutual Aid and Christian Community in the Free Churches, 1525-1675.* Philadelphia: Temple University Press, 1974.

Ehrenpreis, Andreas, and Claus Felbinger. *Brotherly Community: The Highest Command of Love.* Rifton, N.Y.: Plough Publishing House, 1978.

Eller, Vernard. *In Place of Sacraments.* Grand Rapids, Mich.: Eerdmands, 1972.

Estep, William R. *The Anabaptist Story.* Nashville: Broadman Press, 1963.

Friedmann, Robert. *The Theology of Anabaptism.* Scottdale, Pa.: Herald Press, 1973.

Garrett, James Leo, ed. *The Concept of the Believers' Church: Addresses from the 1967 Louisville Conference.* Scottdale, Pa.: Herald Press, 1969.

Hershberger, Guy F., ed. *The Recovery of the Anabaptist Vision.* Scottdale, Pa.: Herald Press, 1957.

Hostetler, John A. *Hutterite Society.* Baltimore: The John Hopkins University Press, 1974.

Jackson, Dave and Neta. *Living Together in a World Falling Apart.* Carol Stream, Ill.: Creation House, 1974.

Jackson, Dave. *Coming Together.* Minneapolis: Bethany Fellowship, 1978.

Jeschke, Marlin. *Discipling the Brother.* Scottdale, Pa.: Herald Press, 1972.

Klaassen, Walter. *Anabaptism: Neither Catholic nor Protestant.* Waterloo, Ontario: Conrad Press, 1973.

Kraus, C. Norman. *The Community of the Spirit.* Grand Rapids, Mich.: Eerdmans, 1974.

Lejeune, R. *Christoph Blumhardt and His Message.* Tr. Hela Ehrlich and Nicoline Maas. Rifton, N.Y.: Plough Publishing House, 1963.

Littell, Franklin H. *The Free Church.* Boston: Starr King Press, 1957.

——————— *From State Church to Pluralism.* Garden City: Doubleday & Co., 1962.

Littell, Franklin H. *The Origins of Sectarian Protestantism.* New York: Macmillan, 1964.

Miller, John W. *The Christian Way.* Scottdale, Pa.: Herald Press, 1969.

Minear, Paul S. *Images of the Church in the New Testament.*

Philadelphia: Westminster Press, 1960.

Nee, Watchman. *The Normal Christian Church Life.* Washington, D.C.: International Students Press, 1969.

O'Connor, Elizabeth. *The Call to Commitment.* New York: Harper & Row, 1963.

Redekop, Calvin. *The Free Church and Seductive Culture.* Scottdale, Pa.: Herald Press, 1970.

Rideman, Peter. *Confession of Faith.* Tr. Society of Brothers. Rifton, N.Y.: Plough Publishing House, 1970.

Ruether, Rosemary Radford. *The Church Against Itself.* New York: Herder and Herder, 1967.

Snyder, Howard A. *The Community of the King.* Downers Grove, Ill.: Inter-Varsity Press, 1977.

Wallis, Jim. *Agenda for Biblical People.* New York: Harper & Row, 1976.

Webber, George W. *God's Colony in Man's World.* New York: Abingdon Press, 1960.

Wenger, John C. *Separated unto God.* Scottdale, Pa.: Mennonite Publishing House, 1951.

Westin, Gunnar. *The Free Church Through the Ages.* Tr. Virgil A. Olson. Nashville: Broadman Press, 1958.

Yoder, John Howard. "Binding and Loosing," *Concern #14,* a pamphlet series for questions of Christian renewal. Scottdale, Pa.: Concern, 1967, pp. 2-32.

——————— *The Ecumenical Movement and the Faithful Church.* Scottdale, Pa.: Mennonite Publishing House, 1958.

——————— *The Original Revolution.* Scottdale, Pa.: Herald Press, 1972.

——————— *The Politics of Jesus.* Grand Rapids, Mich.: Eerdmans, 1972.

SUGGESTIONS FOR BIBLE STUDY

The People of God
Gen. 12:1-3
Ex. 19:4-8
Lev. 26:11-13
Deut. 7:6-11
Eph. 2:11-22
1 Pet. 2:9, 10

The New Humanity
Lk. 12:32-40
Jn. 3:1-21
Rom. 8:18-25
2 Cor. 5:17
Eph. 2
4:17-32
Col. 1:13-22
Jas. 1:18

*The Fellowship of
Believers, Covenant*
Gen. 12:1-3
Jer. 31:31-34
Jn. 15:1-15
1 Cor. 1:4-10
Heb. 8:6-13
1 Jn. 1:7
4:7-21

The Body of Christ
Rom. 12
1 Cor. 10:16, 17
12
Eph. 4

Discipleship
Mt. 7:21
Mk. 8:34—9:1
10:28-31
Lk. 14:33
Rom. 6
Gal. 2:20
Phil. 3:7-11
Jas. 2:14-26

Sharing
Lev. 25
Mt. 6:19-21
23:8-10
Jn. 13:34, 35
Acts 2:44-47
4:32-35
1 Cor. 12:25, 26
2 Cor. 8:1-15
Jas. 2:1-9

Discernment
Is. 42:1-9
Mt. 18:15-20
Jn. 14:12-28
Acts 6:1-6
13:1-3
15
1 Cor. 1:10
2 Cor. 6:14—7:1
1 Jn. 3:19—4:6

Discipline
Mt. 5:23, 24
7:1-5
18:15-35
Lk. 17:1-4
Jn. 20:21-23
1 Cor. 5:1—6:8
Gal. 6:1-10
Eph. 4:25-32
Col. 3:12-15
2 Thess. 3:1-15
1 Tim. 1:19, 20
2 Tim. 3:2-5
Jas. 5:19, 20
Tit. 3:10, 11

Baptism
- Mt. 3
- Mk. 1:1-8
- 10:38
- Acts 1:5
- 2:38
- 10:47, 48
- 19:1-7
- Rom. 4:11, 12
- 6
- 1 Cor. 10:1, 2
- 12:13
- Col. 2:11, 12
- 1 Pet. 3:20, 21

Worship
- Ex. 3:1-12
- Ps. 33
- Is. 1:10-17
- 6:1-8
- 55
- Mt. 5:21-24
- 6:7-15
- Jn. 4:19-24
- 9:31
- Acts 1:1-14
- 2:42-47
- 1 Cor. 11:17-34
- 14:26-40

Witness
- Mt. 10
- 16:13-28
- 20:20-27
- 25:31-46
- 28:16-20
- Lk. 10:1-37
- Jn. 21:15-17
- Acts 1:1-8
- Eph. 6:10-20
- Phil. 2:1-16
- Rev. 12:10-12
- 17:14
- 19:11-21

Leadership
- Mt. 18:1-4
- 20:20-28
- 23:1-12
- Mk. 9:33-37
- Lk. 4:31-37
- Jn. 13:1-17
- 1 Cor. 12
- Phil. 2:1-11
- 1 Thess. 5:12-15
- 1 Tim. 3, 4, 5
- 1 Pet. 5:1-11
- Tit. 1:5-11

Nonconformity
- Ex. 34:12
- Mt. 5, 6, 7
- Jn. 17:6-26
- Rom. 6, 12
- 2 Cor. 6:14—7:1
- Gal. 1:3-5
- Eph. 4:25-32
- Heb. 11:13-16
- Jas. 4:1-4
- 1 Pet. 2:19-25
- 1 Jn. 2:15-17

INDEX

Art Gish was born and raised on a farm in Lancaster County, Pa. He is a graduate of Manchester College and Bethany Theological Seminary and has served as a pastor in the Church of the Brethren.

He did alternative service as a conscientious objector in Europe, working in a home for crippled teenagers and international work camps. He participated in the civil rights movement in Chicago and the Poor People's Campaign in Resurrection City. He has also been active in the peace movement.

He is the author of *The New Left and Christian Radicalism* (Eerdmans, 1970) and *Beyond the Rat Race* (Herald Press, 1972).

Art and his wife, Peggy Faw Gish, are members of New Covenant Fellowship near Athens, Ohio. They are the parents of Dale, Danny, and Joel.

People interested in Christian community are welcome to visit New Covenant Fellowship.